Rethinking Gender and Youth Sport

Much writing on gender and sport is focused upon the negative impact of girls' exclusion from the arena, suggesting by inference that current practice in sport and physical education offers an uncomplicatedly positive sport experience for boys, and that gender, in and of itself, offers a simple starting point for research into young people's experience of sport.

Rethinking Gender and Youth Sport seeks to articulate certain themes which, it is suggested, might contribute to broadening and furthering discussion in the area of gender, youth sport and physical activity. This collection considers a number of themes relating to gender in sport, including:

- the body;
- competence, ability and school physical education;
- cultural change and diversity;
- gendered spaces;
- human rights and well-being.

Authoritative writers have contributed thought-provoking chapters which will prompt the reader to rethink the ways in which gender is understood within the context of youth sport.

Ian Wellard is Head of the Centre for Physical Education Research at Canterbury Christ Church University, UK.

International studies in physical education and youth sport
Series Editor: Richard Bailey
Roehampton University, London, UK

Routledge's *International Studies in Physical Education and Youth Sport* series aims to stimulate discussion on the theory and practice of school physical education, youth sport, childhood physical activity and well-being. By drawing on international perspectives, in terms of both the background of the contributors and the selection of the subject matter, the series seeks to make a distinctive contribution to our understanding of issues that continue to attract attention from policymakers, academics and practitioners.

Also available in this series:

Children, Obesity and Exercise
Prevention, treatment and management of childhood and adolescent obesity
Edited by Andrew P. Hills, Neil A. King and Nuala M. Byrne

Disability and Youth Sport
Edited by Hayley Fitzgerald

The Pedagogy of Human Movement
Richard Tinning

Positive Youth Development Through Sport
Edited by Nicholas L. Holt

Rethinking Gender and Youth Sport

Edited by Ian Wellard

Routledge
Taylor & Francis Group

LONDON AND NEW YORK

First published 2007
by Routledge
2 Park Square, Milton Park, Abingdon, Oxon OX14 4RN

Simultaneously published in the USA and Canada
by Routledge
270 Madison Ave, New York, NY 10016

*Routledge is an imprint of the Taylor & Francis Group, an informa
business*

Typeset in Sabon by Prepress Projects Ltd, Perth, UK
Printed and bound in Great Britain by TJ International Ltd, Padstow,
Cornwall

British Library Cataloguing in Publication Data
A catalogue record for this book is available from the British Library

Library of Congress Cataloging in Publication Data
Rethinking gender and youth sport / edited by Ian Wellard.
p. cm.
Includes bibliographical references and index.
ISBN 978-0-415-41093-9 (softcover) – ISBN 978-0-415-41092-2
(hardcover) 1. Sports – Social aspects. 2. Physical education and
training – Social aspects. 3. Sex discrimination in sports. 4. Sports –
Sex differences. 5. Sex role. I. Wellard, Ian.
GV706.5.R47 2007
306.483–dc22
2007017232

ISBN10: 0–415–41092–4 (hbk)
ISBN10: 0–415–41093–2 (pbk)
ISBN10: 0–203–93361–3 (ebk)

ISBN13: 978–0–415–41092–2 (hbk)
ISBN13: 978–0–415–41093–9 (pbk)
ISBN13: 978–0–203–93361–9 (ebk)

Contents

Figures

Tables

Contributors

Rachel Allwood is based in the School of Sport and Exercise Sciences at Loughborough University, UK.

Richard Bailey is Professor of Pedagogy in the Faculty of Education at Roehampton University, London.

Andrew Bloodworth is based in the Centre for Philosophy, Humanities and Law in Health Care at the University of Wales Swansea, UK.

Brian Davies is Professor of Sociology of Education in the School of Social Sciences at Cardiff University, Wales, UK.

John Evans is Professor of Sociology of Education and Physical Education in the School of Sport and Exercise Sciences at Loughborough University, UK.

Ken Green is Professor of Applied Sociology of Sport in the Department of Sport and Exercise Sciences at the University of Chester, UK.

Kevin Lamb is Reader in Sport and Exercise Sciences in the Department of Sport and Exercise Sciences at the University of Chester, UK.

Mike McNamee is Reader in the Centre for Philosophy, Humanities and Law in Health Care at the University of Wales Swansea, UK.

Dawn Penney is Senior Lecturer in the Faculty of Education, University of Tasmania, Australia.

Angela Pickard is Senior Lecturer in English Education and Dance in the Faculty of Education at Canterbury Christ Church University, UK.

Emma Rich is Lecturer in the School of Sport and Exercise Sciences at Loughborough University, UK.

Andy Smith is Lecturer in the Sociology of Sport in the Department of Sport and Exercise Sciences and the Chester Centre for Research into Sport and Society at the University of Chester, UK.

Miranda Thurston is Professor of Public Health in the Centre for Public Health Research at the University of Chester, UK.

Gordon Waitt is Associate Professor in the School of Earth and Environmental Sciences at the University of Wollongong, New South Wales, Australia.

Ian Wellard is Head of the Centre for Physical Education Research at Canterbury Christ Church University, UK.

Kath Woodward is Senior Lecturer in the Sociology Department at the Open University, Milton Keynes, UK.

Foreword

Within discussion of young people's sports and physical education, gender has often been presented as a 'problem' to be solved. This is hardly surprising as there is plenty of evidence of unequally distributed provision for boys and girls, as well as the subtle yet powerful influences of gendered attitudes and expectations linked to bodies and behaviours in sport. However as Ian Wellard's collection of chapters ably demonstrates, there are few aspects of sport that are not touched in some way by gender.

The range of topics and the diversity of conceptual and ideological perspectives represented here mark the book out as challenging and important. The articles contained within this exciting book are bound to prompt debate; they may well stimulate ideas that challenge orthodoxies and broaden the discussion further.

This is an important title within the *International Studies in Physical Education and Youth Sport* series. I hope readers find it as thought-provoking as I do.

Richard Bailey

1 Introduction

Young people, gender, physical activity and sport

Ian Wellard

If sexual discrimination is objectionable in most other areas of our lives, why should it be acceptable within sports?

(Tännsjo and Tanburrini 2000: 101)

This book has been prompted by my involvement in research exploring a range of physical activities young people engage in. Much of this research had been conducted with the general presumption that physical activity in the form of sports, play and recreation, whether in or out of school, is an essential and enjoyable aspect of every young person's everyday life (or should be). However, although the benefits of physical activity and sport for childhood development are well documented (Bailey *et al*. 2004), it is still the case that a significantly large number of young people, particularly girls, either are not engaging as much as they would like or are not provided with the opportunities to do so.

Previous research exploring masculinities in the context of amateur and social sports participation (Wellard 2003, 2006a) has suggested that 'gender' is still a factor in many young people's ability to take part and plays a significant part in their experiences once engaging. However, gender on its own is sometimes not sufficient in explaining the underlying difficulties. As a report to the World Health Organization (Bailey *et al*. 2004) suggested, much of the writing on girls and physical activity has tended to explore the negative aspects of exclusion from what is considered a male arena of sport (Scraton 1992; Birrell and Cole 1994). Although important and relevant, this position has resulted in descriptive accounts of women's exclusion which could be seen as surreptitiously consolidating existing gender divisions or binaries (Butler 1993) without taking into consideration other social factors such as age, the body, geography, economics and race (Bale 1993; Shilling 1993; Lavoie 2000; MacDonald 2003). Consequently, many investigations into gender in sport have, albeit with original good intentions, reinforced the assumption that all boys benefit from sport whereas all girls are excluded.

The social interpretation of biological sex does continue to influence the way sport, physical activity and physical education are constructed for girls and women (Scraton 1992) and it is still difficult to displace historically formed assumptions that physical exertion and assertion are less beneficial to girls' overall development. In addition, the social understandings of concepts such as 'motherhood' dictate that girls are seen as passive carers rather than as active providers (Woodward 1997). Evidence tends to suggest that many of these values are still supported. Consequently, such presumptions are limiting and, ultimately, harmful, since they construct social and cultural barriers to participation and engagement in personally beneficial and socially prestigious activities (Bailey 2005). Concern is greatest during childhood, as girls' early experiences often provide the foundation for future participation (Birrell and Cole 1994; Hall 1996; Oliver and Lalik 2001; Cockburn and Clarke 2002).

Early experiences of physical activity

For many young people the only experiences of regular physical activity are within the context of school physical education lessons (Sallis *et al.* 1997). Scraton (1992) identified how the early experiences of school sport were important in terms of girls' future participation. Aspects of physical education lessons which were initially regarded as lesser concerns for school governing bodies, such as specific uniforms for physical education lessons or the standards of showering facilities, were found to be significant in girls' lived experience of school sports. Recognition of individual experience of the body has often been overlooked in favour of broader policy-driven issues relating to health and educational provision. Particularly in sports, there are many occasions where the body is literally on display and this has the potential for the individual to be exposed to negative emotional experiences of shame and bodily embarrassment (Probyn 2000). In consequence, sport has the potential to be a source of embarrassment by way of being an activity where the body is foregrounded. In the school setting, physical education 'uniforms' can often be revealing and communal showers can be the source of unwanted displays of the naked body, particularly at a time when girls are becoming more acutely aware of the social female body. The recognition of the body as a contributory factor in shame is equally significant for boys and highlights the importance of incorporating this aspect within any study of youth sports.

Studies have also highlighted a greater emphasis upon discipline in physical education compared with other aspects of the curriculum. Post-structuralist theory has been influential in these accounts of the disciplined body, especially in the way power is located in knowledge structures (Foucault 1977). Additional emphasis on discipline in the context of physical education lessons suggests that distinctions are being made between the supposedly cerebral pursuits of academic study and corporeal activities, and that differing forms of regulation are required.

By the time students enter secondary school, they have developed clear activity preferences. Bedward and Williams (2000) found that dance and gymnastics are either loved or hated by most students by the time they reach secondary school. They also found that enjoyment in gymnastics was closely related to personal ability whereas those who disliked it found the experience humiliating. Similarly, opportunities for creativity and expression in dance were understood positively. What becomes apparent is that bodily performances play an important role in the experience of physical education, not only in terms of bio-mechanical dexterity but more in the way that social bodily performances become central to whether a sport is enjoyed or not. Lack of ability is a contributory factor, but there are many other social situations which emerge that have the potential to cause humiliation. Elements considered essential to the performance of a sport, such as competition, demonstrations of technique and winning or losing, are not sufficiently explored in terms of the impact this has upon the individual, especially if the context is in a school lesson rather than a professional, elite sport.

Some ways to combat the negative experience of sport which many school children face include the provision of a broader curriculum, more practical applications of uniform policy and teaching strategies which enhance rather than diminish self-esteem (Butler 2006). However, one solution often proposed is to focus upon ways in which girls can have access to the same range of activities as boys. This can be problematic, as it does not take into consideration one of the main causes of negative experience, chiefly, the elements within the practices involved in school sports which contribute to the experience of them in terms of shame and humiliation. These are not areas which are the sole reserve of girls, but are equally experienced by boys who do not conform to those same expectations which restrict the girls. Thus, work which incorporates the acknowledgement of a range of subordinated masculinities within the context of sport needs to be applied (Mac an Ghaill 1994, 1996; Redman 2000; Frosh *et al.* 2002; Wellard 2002, 2006a).

Gender and physical education

Physical education lessons present an important arena for the construction and consolidation of dominant and subordinate masculinities and femininities (Paechter 2003a). The sites where physical education is located, such as the gym, sports hall or playing field, function as the context for displays of hegemonic forms of heterosexual masculinities and the subordination of others or alternatives. Moreover, the ideal types of bodily usage expected within physical education can be regarded as generally located in traditional understandings of male and female sports. Therefore, the different bodily usages encouraged by secondary school physical education both permit and support the development of particular masculinities and femininities. In Paechter's (2003a: 47) words, 'In secondary schools in particular, physical education lessons are an important arena for the displaying and acting out of masculinity and femininity, particularly those forms which could be described as hypermasculine and hyperfeminine.'

According to this argument, much of physical education remains gender-segregated and a place where specific gendered performances are expected and encouraged. This is particularly the case for young men and women when there is more uncertainty about what constitutes correct or appropriate performances. For some theorists (Connell 1995; Theberge 2003), sport (school sports in particular) operates as a means of presenting broader social constructions of gender and identity. Physical education, therefore, provides an important arena for boys to act out 'hypermasculinity' (Paechter 2003a). Consequently, the relationship of girls and femininity to physical education is more complex, partly because the agenda is set by the boys and interest in sports is excluded for girls by their male peer group.

Expressions of femininity are often demonstrated by resistance to physical education and sports in a similar way that expressions of masculinity are demonstrated through sporting prowess and resistance to 'passive' academic work in the classroom (Frosh *et al.* 2002). School sports continue to reinforce gender binaries which position the activities of girls as subordinate to boys (Scraton 1992; Paechter 2003a):

> The dominance of competitive sport in popular culture, though less than heretofore in the official PE curriculum . . . and monadic, surface-focused fitness practices discourage the development and use of open, communicative bodily practices and forms.
>
> (Paechter 2003a: 57)

Theoretical debates surrounding the gendered practices evident within physical education and school sports are informative as they offer support to claims that studies within this area need to include consideration of the body and broader academic approaches. However, many theoretically focused studies do not always provide any concrete solutions or ways forward and, ultimately, maintain a theory/practice binary (MacDonald 2003). What is clear is that methods are required which can cut through and break the stranglehold that gender stereotypes have on traditional forms of physical education and sports. An essential part of this is awareness in the range of ways in which gender is acted upon. Consequently, particular issues emerge which need to be considered in any future investigations of young people, gender and youth sports, such as:

1 a recognition/awareness of the gendered constructions and binary divisions which operate within (and external to) current physical education practices;
2 reflection on the influence of hegemonic masculine constructions of bodily performances which may restrict girls' and boys' participation in physical education and school sports and wider physical activities.

Drawing upon a broader theoretical base is important and it is by incorporating theories from other disciplines that further investigations into the experiences of young people in sport and physical activity can be made. Consequently, it is suggested that the following need to be considered *with* gender in any further research into gender and youth sport:

- the body;
- competence, ability and school physical education;
- diversity;
- cultural change;
- gendered spaces;
- human rights and well-being.

Rethinking gender and youth sport

The collection of writing contained in this book was drawn together bearing in mind the above themes. It was initially intended to divide the book into sections and include contributions which drew upon a specific theme. However, as the book developed, it became clear that the writers were engaging with many of these themes rather than just one. For the sake of clarity, the chapter layout has been kept in the original format, but without formally distinct sub-headings.

In Chapter 2, Dawn Penney provides an initial overview of young people and sport. There have been many developments in recent years, not only in academic thinking, but also in state interventions. Australia has appeared to take the lead in many policy-related issues within the area of school sports and in particular girls' participation. The Australian Sports Commission produced one such document (1999) detailing strategies devised to encourage women and girls to take a more active part in sport. Part of that provision was the recognition of the role of schools within this process as the only organisations that can ensure the provision of sport for the majority of young people. In this document they listed a series of strategies to help achieve this principle within the school setting. Although these strategies cover a broad range of issues and may be difficult to accommodate in all cases, putting down on paper a series of objectives provides the opportunity to move towards particular goals and, ideally, these goals can be adapted and revised as need be. The formulation of a series of strategies also helps identify further issues of potential conflict. For instance, one of the problems highlighted within their list is the apparent assumption that all boys experience sports in the same way. Thus the point about single-sex competition providing a better way for all to have a 'fair go' does not sufficiently address the differing versions of masculinities and femininities. Equally, the strategy to provide private changing facilities for girls assumes that boys are less conscious about their bodies during adolescence than girls. Dawn Penney, as someone who has experienced school sports within both Australia and the UK, provides an account of the complex and interconnected debates which impact upon contemporary youth sport. The chapter highlights the competing and sometimes conflicting agendas of a range of organisations (governmental, public and private sector, educational) which all claim to have a vested 'interest' in the lives of young people.

The full significance of the body as a central theoretical concern was really acknowledged only at the latter stages of the last century (Turner 1984; Frank 1990; Shilling 1993). More recently, however, accounts of the body have attempted to incorporate a broadly post-structural position in which the focus has been on the heterogeneous techniques, practices and forms of training which are constructed through discourse and regulate the individual. Too often, however, post-structural arguments have been generated through secondary readings of historical texts which have contributed to a boom in other sociological studies adopting similar research methods. Turner (2002) has described a consequent problem in contemporary social theory as being related to the proliferation of text-based 'descriptive' sociology. Turner suggests that mainstream sociology has failed to develop concepts which relate to the individual. Instead, it has focused on the structures governing individual bodies, leaving little room to explore the potential of individual agency.

Recognising the social and physical factors which are apparent within the arena of sport provides a way in which we can evaluate current practices and mount a challenge to those which exclude particular bodies. For example, a cold, muddy pitch or a hot, dusty field can be experienced physically by the body in many different ways, regardless of gender, whilst, at the same time, culturally derived expectations of 'how to behave' in such conditions contribute as well.

Other disciplines have already set out to challenge many taken-for-granted assumptions relating to gender. Particularly within feminist theory (Butler 1990; Segal 1997; Paechter 2003a), and more recently in Queer Theory (Jagose 1996; Caudwell 2003, 2006), there have been attempts to subvert some of the traditional practices found in broader society, but these, too, can equally be applied to sports, especially in terms of social factors such as gender, age and ability.

In Chapters 3 and 4, Kath Woodward and Angela Pickard, respectively, explore the extent to which embodiment is constituted both through and beyond gender. Woodward describes how the presentation of the body is a key factor in the construction of social identities and, within the arena of sport, body performances present an even greater significance. The chapter explores the relationship of embodiment to social identity within the context of young male boxers. These boxing bodies, as Woodward describes, are 'heroic' bodies, ones which defend as well as inflict damage. Boxing, literally, foregrounds the body in terms of both representations of heroic masculinity as well as shaping a particular way of contemplating a particular form of masculine identity. As a contrast, but at the same time highlighting the importance of the body as a central factor in the construction of identities, Pickard explores young girls' experiences of their bodies within the context of ballet. The body is again the focus, but in a binary opposition to the boxers' bodies. However, like the men that Woodward describes, negotiating pain increasingly becomes a central focus in the dancers' everyday lives, although the ways the young dancers do this provides sharp contrast to the male boxers. Both chapters provide the opportunity to critically assess general assumptions about gender and active participation in physical activities.

Taking into account the importance of recognising the body as mentioned above, the concept of 'abilities' within sports, and especially in school-based physical education (PE), becomes particularly significant, as it is here that forms of consciousness are embodied through the practices and rituals associated with it (Evans 2004). However, the way that ability is recognised and conceptualised through the practices of school PE often neglects the individual body. As Evans suggests, 'PE has become strangely disembodied' (2004: 96). The relationship of competence as a factor in taking part in many forms of organised sports is often overlooked. This applies to sporting participation on a number of levels, whether within the context of a school physical education lesson or as an initial entry requirement for joining an amateur sports club.

Critical thinking about ability has been a notable absence, particularly within education settings and organised sports practice. Often the focus is upon acquiring sporting competence and derived health benefits rather than the specific bodily practices which are required for participation (Evans 2004). The school sports field also remains a prime site for displays of hegemonic masculinity (Connell 1995; Mac an Ghaill 1996; Frosh *et al.* 2002) as well as a place to learn the dynamics of the hidden curriculum of physical education (Fernandez-Balboa 1993, 1997). Consequently, in schools, more support is given to those who display talent in the form of physical ability and expertise in the sports played. This can often lead to many sports ultimately favouring boys in mixed schools.

In Chapter 5, John Evans, Emma Rich, Rachel Allwood and Brian Davies explore an increasingly government 'performance'-based culture, in which the implications of Policy (with a capital 'P')-driven directives ultimately shape the way in which young people understand and act upon their bodies. Evans *et al.* demonstrate how young people are regarding their bodies as 'performance indicators' of successful (or not) membership of an image-based society.

Recognising the shifts in social patterns of leisure consumption is important. The emergence of an array of 'alternative' sports (Rinehart and Sydnor 2003) highlights the contrasting range of expectations by those entering into sports and physical activities. It is debatable whether many of the traditional sports which dominate school-based physical education lessons are able to meet the needs of a more demanding and consumer-literate younger generation. As Green (2002) suggests, a pronounced feature of adolescence is a flight from sports when they complete full-time education. Consequently, it could be claimed that much physical education rhetoric fails to acknowledge the actual participatory trends in sports and physical activity (such as swimming and cycling). It also fails to view young people's lives 'in the round' or take into consideration the broader dimensions of young people's lives for their participation rates and styles.

Recent research has highlighted increased levels of participation in sports and physical activity among young people, particularly in non-competitive, recreationally oriented sports. This is particularly evident in the participation rates for swimming and cycling, which may, in turn, provide another reason for the apparent lack of relevance of many traditional school-based sports for young people (Green 2002).

In Chapter 6, Ken Green, Andy Smith, Miranda Thurston and Kevin Lamb continue this debate by exploring sport provision for young people within UK schools. Their empirical research highlights that, whilst the national curriculum for physical education has adapted in many ways to provide a broader range of activities, there has been little significant change in gender stereotyping. Much of this relates to the continued practice of PE teachers of providing 'gender-appropriate' activities within the range of sports offered. Consequently, although participation patterns for young people in physical activities can be seen to be broadening and increasing, there is less evidence to suggest that the more deep-seated gendered stereotyping is being redressed.

Looking at alternative forms of physical activity can provide a means of challenging so-called 'traditional' forms of physical education (Kirk *et al.* 2000), characterised by:

- A reliance on command style teaching that is strong on group management and short on meeting the individual needs;
- The dominance of competitive sports, particularly team sports;
- A concern with the detail of technique development; and
- Biological and mechanical functionalism that objectifies the body and in so doing often loses sight of the whole person.

(Kirk *et al.* 2000: 58)

Identifying the components of traditional sporting activities, which invariably constitute much of school-based sports provision, highlights the need to look at the practices rather than attempting to make young people adapt. The practices inherent in traditional forms of physical education often operate at the expense of many 'other' forms. This is not to say that all aspects of traditional physical education are negative, but it does appear that for many young people there is an element of attempting to fit square pegs into a round hole.

In Chapter 7, Ian Wellard explores the gendered limits in contemporary sport, physical education and dance. The chapter explores the way in which established practices found in mainstream sports in effect 'restrict' alternative ways of being. Specific masculine performances create rigid boundaries which are difficult to extend. The chapter draws upon theory as well as research conducted with male physical education teacher trainees who, as part of their course, take part in a dance group. What was initially considered an opportunity to extend the limits of the young men's gendered perceptions ultimately highlights the restrictive practices inherent in mainstream sports and physical education. The men demonstrate how physical education can become a 'community of practice' (Lave and Wenger 1992) which continues to reinforce gender-based binary distinctions relating to who is 'able' to take part or not.

In Chapter 8, this theme of occupation or ownership of social space is continued by Gordon Waitt when he explores gendered spaces 'outside' the school or organised sport. He uses the example of surfing spaces in Australia, which originally emerged as significant cultural spaces for young people away from regulated, structured sports. However, within these physical and social spaces, specific gendered identities are established and performed. This chapter highlights the ways in which gendered identities are shaped through and by local spaces as well as the physical activity.

Although there are many important issues relating to the principles of human rights, it is considered that they should be a central concern within any legitimate study of sport and physical activity. However, as Kidd and Donnelly (2000) suggest:

> Despite the familiar moral claims of sports – the rhetoric of universality, fair play, character and a 'level playing field' – few of the initial proponents of modern sports ever intended to be universal and inclusive.
> (Kidd and Donnelly 2000: 135)

Consequently, the practices which are still evident within contemporary sports, and which influence the behaviours of the young people entering into it, need to be assessed within the context of the social, political and historical processes which have ultimately shaped them (Elias and Dunning 1986; Hargreaves 1986). An outcome of these historical processes has been a continuation of gender inequalities within sports (Hargreaves 1994; Hall 1996; McKay *et al.* 2000).

At the same time, recognition of human rights has developed to include the experiences of specific sections within the community whose voices have not always been heard, for instance children, the disabled, ethnic minorities and women. In the case of women, the Beijing Declaration (United Nations 1995) states that it is important to:

> Recognize that the status of women has advanced in some important respects in the past decade but that progress has been uneven, inequalities

between men and women have persisted and major obstacles remain, with serious consequences for all people.

Within the context of sport and physical activity, initiatives to counter inequalities in sports, such as those associated with calls for 'Sports for All', become meaningless if they do not take into account the rights of all human beings. Consequently, all the above themes directly feed into the central premise that every individual should have the right to enjoy their bodies through physical activities. Philosophical and ethical questions can, therefore, help us reflect upon the role of physical activity in the lives of not only women but all individuals, regardless of body type.

In Chapter 9, Richard Bailey, Andrew Bloodworth and Mike McNamee apply philosophical approaches to the concept of well-being as a basic right of young people within the organised setting of the school. The chapter considers gender as a specific factor in the achievement (or not) of meaningful participation in physical activities. Importantly, within the context of the overarching aims of this book, it prompts the reader to consider what the 'purpose' of sport is for young people. As much of youth sport is experienced within school settings or regulated by adults, there are many conflicting expectations about what sport or physical education should provide. Outcomes of taking part such as fun, enjoyment, learning, citizenship, health or competitiveness are considered important to varying degrees by a range of stakeholders. If these are considered within the context of gender, and taking into account all the other contributions in this book, then there are still, clearly, many questions relating to whether all young people's rights are being taken into account.

What next?

It is apparent that there is still scope for much more informed research within the area of gender and sports. This collection makes an initial exploration of some of the many factors which need to be considered when theorising about gender in relation to young people and physical activity. It is, however, important to make clear that the chapters included in this book are only a small part of a much wider debate. My role as an editor in this collection is shaped by my access to, and my position within, a community of scholars. Consequently, although I consider that I have been able to collect together contributions from a group of extremely eminent scholars, the works included here are not presented as a definitive guide to gender and youth sport. The 'Western' focus of this discussion is a clear indication that further research needs to be generated from other areas of the world. The absence of women's voices within research in this area from South America, Africa and Asia is evident and noteworthy (Bailey *et al.* 2004). Research from these areas would provide a valuable contribution to the increasing amount of material already being generated within the 'West'. At the same time, it is important to adopt methodological strategies which enable researchers to 'listen' effectively to children's voices. Incorporating interdisciplinary approaches to research enables further analysis of the issues highlighted throughout this book.

Young people (regardless of gender) do enjoy taking part in physical activities, but too frequently many current sporting practices ultimately deter or exclude participation. The continued emphasis upon who is 'able' or not to take part within current sports affects a disproportionate number of young people, who in different circumstances may relish the opportunity to engage in physical activities. The chapters that follow provide an attempt to 'rethink' gender in relation to young people and physical activity.

2 Physical education, physical activity, sport and gender

Contemporary connections and debates

Dawn Penney

This chapter starts from the premise that physical education needs to be seen as a cultural and political practice with the capacity to impact powerfully on the lives, lifestyles and well-being of young people. The impact with which I am concerned relates to participation patterns in physical activity and sport. More specifically, my focus is upon issues that underpin, but are often obscured in analyses and debates about, young people's current and prospective future involvement in physical activity and sport. My emphasis is that although 'impact' may be widely recognised as undeniable and, furthermore, a lived reality for many young people, its subtleties remain inadequately acknowledged in arenas of policy and practice.

The ways in which young people are able to express gender identities in and through physical activity and sport, and the pressures and expectations to express *particular* gender identities, are, I suggest, subtle yet highly significant aspects of the impact of physical education on lives, lifestyles and well-being. As a political and policy arena and as professional practice, physical education sees gender vividly intersecting with culture and politics. Literature and research has long reaffirmed that physical education has never merely been a matter of 'schooling the body' but, rather, about respectively schooling girls' and boys' bodies along culturally, historically and politically defined acceptable and desirable lines (see, for example, Evans and Penney 2002; Flintoff and Scraton 2001; Green and Scraton 1998; Kirk 1992; Scraton 1993). Perhaps most notably, that body of literature continues to grow and, furthermore, repeatedly highlight that whatever the rhetoric of political and policy pronouncements, physical education has been and remains very much about what is deemed to be an appropriate education, in bodily terms, not 'just' for young people, but most certainly for girls and for boys as distinctly positioned (and conceptualised) groups of young people. From that backdrop, this chapter focuses on longstanding and still dominant conceptualisations of gender, of participation, of sport and of healthy lifestyles that are embedded in contemporary physical education. It specifically pursues the limitations of particular conceptualisations from the perspective of the young people in whose interests politicians and physical educationalists variously claim to act.

Physical education: gender is necessarily a part of the agenda

Contemporary commentaries variously exploring gender and equity issues in physical education have clearly signalled the need for physical educators to make two fundamental shifts in thinking about gender within their 'classrooms' and in their curricula and pedagogical practices: (i) to move beyond dualistic approaches to gender and (ii) to similarly move beyond a sole focus on gender, to explore gender as complex and relational; that is, as always in dynamic relation with age, class, ethnicity, sexuality, cultural and national identity (Evans and Penney 2002; Azzarito and Solomon 2005). Yet, before considering either point, there is a need to acknowledge that inherent in contemporary debates around gender and physical education is a realisation that gender, conceptualised in essentially dualistic and simplistic ways, is inescapably embedded and expressed in our professional practice and integral to students' experiences within and beyond school. Children come to physical education with experiences, attitudes and expectations that mean that emerging and desired physical identities are invariably framed in gender-differentiated terms. Experiences in physical education will serve to either reaffirm or challenge boundaries in terms of the physical and simultaneously gender identities (masculinit*ies* and femininit*ies*) that are recognised as attainable, legitimate and desirable for girls or boys. Physical education is an arena in which, whether intentionally or not, the curriculum and teachers' professional practices enable and constrain students' exploration of gender identities – and particularly of identities that may be regarded as deviating from stereotypical social and cultural norms.

As a young person in physical education, whether I am a girl or a boy most certainly does matter. *Amongst other things*, that aspect of my identity can be expected to frame (in a boundary-setting sense):

- what it is envisaged that my interests in physical activity and sport will (and will not) be;
- how well I will be able to engage in physical activity and sport and in what ways;
- what sort of body and bodily competences I am/should be seeking (or not);
- how others will relate to me in participation situations;
- the extent to which and ways in which participation in physical education, physical activity and/or sport will prove to be personally fulfilling and/or empowering.

In some respects, assumptions relating to these points will be made irrespective and seemingly without acknowledgement that I am not only/merely a boy or a girl. Dualistic thinking is hard to escape or move beyond. As Paechter (2006) has identified, masculinity and femininity are still invariably conceived in singular terms, with both fundamentally tied to hegemonic masculinity. This limits our thinking not only about gender but also about young people and their prospective learning needs, interests in physical activity and sport, and current and prospective future lifestyles. Many young people involved in physical education and/or sport will be acutely aware that, although gender certainly matters, so too do other factors, and sometimes in very profound ways. My contention is that particularly at a time of such attention being directed towards body shape and size (see Chapter 5), (limited) understandings of gender need to be acknowledged as tied to (limited) understandings of ability and narrow perceptions about well-being, in physical education, physical activity and sporting contexts. As Evans and colleagues highlight in this collection, being accorded the label of 'fat' and/or clumsy may well be far more significant and potentially damaging in the current climate than my identity as a girl or boy in physical education. Inevitably then, the question can be posed, are we justified in retaining gender as a focus for attention in debates about physical education, physical activity and sport? This chapter reflects my view that such attention is justified *in the context of critical reflection and debate that focuses, first and foremost, on how we conceptualise and construct physical education in contemporary times.*

Physical education, physical activity and sport: rethinking relationships and reframing curricula

Physical education has long been recognised as associated with a range of policy/political objectives that position the subject as having a 'foundational' role to play in young people's lives, nurturing interests and potential as sportspeople, instilling 'good character', providing the skills, knowledge and understanding that will enable and encourage them to lead healthy and active lives (see, for example, Green 1998; Penney and Evans 1999; Penney and Chandler 2000). Further, the physical education curriculum has also long been thought about as, in essence, a collection of activities or sports, such that talk about physical education (in public and political arenas and within schools) will invariably be dominated by talk of doing and/or learning particular activities or sports. Such talk plays a part in continuing to shape what is regarded as legitimate curriculum content and what it is to be 'able' in physical education.

As I have stressed previously, none of this is neutral (Penney and Evans 1999, 2005; Penney 2006). Policy pronouncements, spoken and unspoken aspects of pedagogy, and staff room conversations all reflect and legitimise the expression of particular, inherently gendered, culturally laden and classed perceptions about curriculum and achievement (Evans and Penney 2002). Thus, the engrained 'logic' of 'the multi-activity model' (Siedentop and Tannehill 2000; see also Crum 1983; Locke 1992; Penney and Chandler 2000; Cothran 2001) has complexities that have remained largely obscured amidst the identification of varied curricula and pedagogic practices with this particular model. Reference to '*the*' model implies a false uniformity in curriculum offerings and experiences that has deflected attention from the reality that what are deemed to be the 'obvious', 'natural' activities to be included in physical education will be differently conceived on the basis of gender, culture and class dynamics. Further, perceptions and judgements about 'ability' will be framed in relation to those varying conceptions.

The above points are perhaps best illustrated by the particular physical education curricula that are still deemed to characterise elite public girls' and boys' schools in England respectively and, furthermore, firmly distinguish them from government-funded comprehensive schools. The physical education curriculum that will come to mind is simultaneously culturally laden, firmly classed and gendered along stereotypical lines. It will epitomise the multi-activity model, yet will be very different from the multi-activity curriculum that may be seen in schools set in other social and cultural contexts. As developed across schools, the multi-activity model thus simultaneously defines ability in physical education in sports performance terms *and* distinguishes various physical activity and sporting pathways as appropriate for particular girls and particular boys to pursue.

Viewed in these terms, the dominant curriculum model is revealed as inherently divisive, setting students apart from one another not merely within physical education lessons and between schools, but in terms of the life chances and life choices that they are enabled and inspired to pursue. The 'physically active and healthy lifestyle' that will be conceived as achievable, legitimate and/or desirable by particular girls and boys will be acutely different from that conceived as such by others. My contention is that physical education, and the multi-activity model in particular, continues to contribute to that fundamental educational and social inequity.

Yet, the 'logic' of the multi-activity model is *so* embedded and accepted in public, political and many professional settings that talk of 'alternative' ways of thinking about physical education can be guaranteed to attract puzzled, questioning expressions. The label of 'alternative' or 'other' itself speaks volumes about the continued resistance to curriculum debates and development that dare to step beyond long-established normalised boundaries. The boundaries are the means and basis for retention of a particular curriculum form and content. Importantly, they simultaneously serve to define legitimate and valued professional identities in line with that curriculum. Dominant professional identities also serve to express and reproduce stereotypically gendered images and understandings 'around' physical activity and sport. The pedagogic practices which we may see as the means and/or vehicle via which gender inequities continue to be reproduced within and by physical education arise from a curriculum and professional identity that is aligned, first and foremost, with the pursuit and celebration of elite sport performance (see, for example, Armour and Jones 1998).

The discussion that follows reflects a belief that if 'we' are serious about physical education as a foundation for participation in physical activity and sport throughout life, for *all* young people, there is a need to think critically about the conceptual underpinnings of the curriculum and pedagogic practices that are seen to characterise physical education and that are at the core of many physical education teachers' professional identities. The caution that I signal in referring to 'us' is in recognition that my discussion is no more neutral than the policies and practices that I address, and that others may hold very different views about desirable directions for curriculum development in physical education.

From sports performance to lifelong learning and participation in learning communities

In recent years physical education in England has come to occupy a highly profitable, yet at the same time seemingly precarious, policy and curriculum space. Variously, this might be described as a situation of straddling, sitting or falling between education and sport, while always also seeking to retain an arguably tenuous connection with health. The positioning has been characterised in (and simultaneously reaffirmed by) a host of policy initiatives and accompanying publications. It is certainly not my intention here to recount the detail of specific developments. Suffice to say that the past decade in England has been one of high-profile political and strategic alliances at a national level that have been the reference point and source of funding for the development of *physical education and sport* within and beyond schools. Whether 'learning' or 'high quality' has been the focus, the accepted, openly promoted and, prospectively, *sole legitimate* contemporary discourse is 'PE and sport' (see DfES/DCMS 2003, 2004).

From one perspective the situation can be regarded as one of unprecedented financial and resource gains arising from the explicit consolidation of an 'obvious' linkage. From a rather different viewpoint, the new (and now clearly dominant) discourse can be seen to powerfully express and reaffirm dominant assumptions about physical education, such that it now seems even harder to conceive of physical education as 'other than' sport; as orientated towards anything other than participation and performance in sport; and, finally, as distinct from sport in a 'delivery' sense. 'Getting children into sport – and keeping them involved' (Richard Caborn, then Minister of State for Sport and Tourism, cited in DfES/DCMS 2004) is presented as the means of achievement of a familiar host of educational and social outcomes. Simultaneously, the desired participation in 'PE and sport' is now explicitly conceived of as *'within and beyond'* the curriculum, in school and/ or in community-based sports clubs (DfES/DCMS 2004), with initiatives and accompanying investment firmly directed towards the strengthening of PE–sport/school–club linkages in provision.

In a context of unprecedented government interest and investment, stepping into the arena of critical debate is by no means easy. Yet it may be the very time at which such debate is most needed. My starting point is to return to the outcomes that the interest and investment is purportedly directed towards. As Richard Caborn articulated things, 'regular participation' (in sport) is the stepping stone to 'reduce obesity, improve fitness levels and, by improving concentration and self-esteem, can help attendance, behaviour and attainment' (cited in DfES/DCMS 2004). Amidst the conflation of 'PE and sport', what is arguably most telling here is not the outcomes identified but, rather, the perceived means via which they will be achieved. Participation in sport is presented as, in essence, what learning in physical education is fundamentally about, and, at the same time, is effectively reduced to. The portrayal of physical education so overtly 'as' participation in sport reflects and seems destined to further reaffirm the multi-activity curriculum model with its inherent inequities.

What then are the alternatives? What discourses can be recognised as notably absent and, simultaneously, offer a sound basis for curriculum development and, furthermore, government investment in education and, specifically, physical education (and sport)? I choose my words, their position and their representation carefully. This is about more than mere semantics. It is about defining and positioning physical education as educational practice and creating a premise from which contemporary educational discourses are the reference point for curriculum debate in physical education and, more specifically, the consideration of equity in physical education. In the discussion that follows I therefore turn attention to the prospective utilisation of discourses of 'lifelong learning', 'learning communities' and 'personalised learning' as a basis from which to challenge engrained inequities (particularly but never exclusively conceived in relation to gender) within and beyond physical education.

Lifelong learning and *learning communities* are discourses likely to have popular appeal in policy and professional arenas concerned with physical education. Longstanding claims/aims of physical education in relation to participation in physical activity and/or sport, lifestyles and values 'for life', can readily (conveniently and strategically) be aligned with the new discourse of 'lifelong learning'. The point may also be made that adopting the terminology 'physical education and sport' is an explicit acknowledgement that this learning occurs and is supported across a learning community that spans schools, community organisations and family and friendship groups. At a superficial level alignment with new discourses is thus relatively easy. Whether or not there is a sound basis to such alignment is an entirely different matter.

Lifelong learning may well be 'the flavour of the times, beloved of governments, policy makers and corporations' (West 2004: 138), a discourse that it is attractive to adopt. But to what extent is 'lifelong learning' embedded and expressed in physical education, particularly when conceived as 'physical education and sport'? The answer will most certainly depend upon how we define lifelong learning. In the European Lifelong Learning Initiative it was identified as:

> a continuously supportive process which stimulates and empowers individuals to acquire all the knowledge, values, skills and understanding they will require throughout their lifetimes and to apply them with confidence, creativity and enjoyment in all roles, circumstances, and environments.
>
> (European Lifelong Learning Initiative, cited in Watson 2003: 3)

West's emphasis that learning needs to be seen as 'lifewide as well as lifelong' (2004: 141) aligns with the notion of a support and development process that is a learning community commitment and activity.

Thus, these contemporary education discourses, and particularly their representation in the European Lifelong Learning Initiative, generate pointed questions to pose of 'physical education and sport':

- Which young people would liken their experiences to a stimulating, empowering, continuously supportive process that has enabled them to acquire knowledge, values, skills and understanding that are key to accessing and enjoying an active and healthy lifestyle?
- Which young people are consequently able and inspired to apply the knowledge, values, skills and understanding that they have gained in and through physical education and sport, 'with confidence, creativity and enjoyment' in a wide variety of roles, circumstances and environments?

The questions are posed with full recognition that straightforward answers are neither possible nor appropriate. As others adopting a critical perspective have similarly highlighted, the questions themselves are important (see Burrows and Wright 2004; Evans and Davies 2004). Their significance lies in the capacity to prompt acknowledgement that the lived realities of physical education and sport remain inherently and powerfully inequitable along lines that can never be exclusively attributed to gender or social class or culture or ethnicity or sexuality or physical ability. *Some* girls and *some* boys will be fortunate enough to enjoy stimulation and feel empowerment in and through experiences of physical education and sport within and beyond school. Individual participation patterns, the opportunities that they are able to access and the application of learning that they can pursue and demonstrate in their lives will all be testimony to the support (social, emotional and financial) that young people variously have from teachers, coaches, family and friends. *Some* girls and *some* boys will, in contrast, feel that opportunities to develop and/or apply *certain* skills, knowledge and understandings are denied to them, for potentially a host of reasons.

Choices and chances in terms of one's current and prospective participation in physical activity and sport will be shaped within and, undoubtedly, beyond schools. Influences on opportunities will be at times very obvious and in other instances subtle to the extent that they go unnoticed. In 2003, the Ministry of Education in New Zealand commented that:

> Learners are more motivated and self-directed when they can see the system works for them. A good system needs to be flexible enough, both in content and approach, to meet the varied needs of diverse learners.
>
> (Ministry of Education 2003: 18)

Such a statement seems acutely fitting in relation to the provision of opportunities for 'physical education and sport' within and beyond schools. The 'bottom line' appears very clear. Who feels that 'the system works for them'? Somewhat more problematically, who recognises that the system is embedded with assumptions about their needs and interests that have simplistic stereotypical underpinnings, such that the system is destined to fail to provide for their individuality?

A genuine commitment to the notion of physical education having lifelong relevance not merely for some but for *all* young people demands recognition of individuals, of their multiple identities and, most of all, the impact of those identities in relation to how young people feel in physical activity settings, about their physicality and about participation in physical activity and sport.

- What involvement in physical activity can I identify with . . . or not?
- When am I likely to feel marginalised, inadequate or, in contrast, confident and able?
- How do I feel about my body?
- What do I see as my potential as a participant in physical activity and sport?
- Do I feel (cap)able in 'physical education and sport' within, and beyond, schools? Do others see me as such?
- What do people see – or not?
- Do I feel welcome, accepted, valued amongst peers?
- Can I explain *why* I feel as I do?

Questions such as those above all too rarely feature in curriculum development in physical education or as an integral, valued element of pedagogic practice (see Hay and lisahunter 2006). They serve to highlight two key challenges of curriculum development framed in relation to the linked discourses of lifelong learning and learning communities:

- Collectively, can the members of the learning community provide the skills, knowledge, understandings and experiences that will mean that I 'feel able' in physical activity and sport settings?

- Can they ensure that 'the system' is in place to support and encourage me as an individual (who will be seen and acknowledged as such)?

In contemporary times characterised by a notable lack of acceptance of diversity in the most public aspect of my individuality, my physicality (see Chapter 5 below; Burrows and Wright 2004; Evans and Davies 2004; Garrett 2004), we need honest reflection. Can curriculum developers, physical education teachers and other professionals involved in the provision of physical education and sport say with confidence that they understand the skills, knowledge, understandings and experiences that will indeed mean that more young people will feel able, included and valued in physical activity and sport settings now and in the future? Clearer insights and critical thinking in those respects are a prerequisite to curriculum development targeted towards lifelong agendas and intended to be inclusive of all young people.

Further, if it is to be inclusive, physical education and sport needs to be a space and place within which young people will feel able and encouraged to openly express and celebrate their (gender, class, ethnic, cultural, sexual, embodied) identities. Crucially, the look, feel and form of that space and place will be different for different children. Curriculum planning, then, cannot be based on a vision of uniformity. It needs to acknowledge difference, recognise the value of difference and its significance for young people's current, potential and preferred future lives and lifestyles. Following Paechter (2006) I suggest that such an understanding of difference needs to encompass a recognition of 'masculinities' and 'femininities' 'as actual ways that real people [*variously*] construct and understand themselves in terms of how they "do" boy/man or girl/woman' (Paechter 2006: 262).

Third, 'curriculum' can no longer be conceived of in a traditional 'school-bounded' sense. Rather, the conception needs to align with the discourse of 'learning community' and the lived reality from the young person's perspective. School is one, by no means the only, site of current and/or prospective future learning and participation. Similarly, physical education teachers are not the only people playing a pedagogic role and framing pedagogic and power relations that position particular young people in particular ways. 'Connections' emerge as crucial if we are to avoid situations of perceived discontinuity and/or contradiction between learning and participation in schools and beyond it and, furthermore, if meaningful advances towards equity and inclusivity in education, physical activity, sport and society are to be made. Physical education teachers and teacher educators are positioned to either disrupt or reaffirm established understandings of health, fitness, physical activity and physical abilities that typically fail to embrace the complexities of gender, ethnicity, class and culture. They face the challenges of revealing the lack of neutrality in dominant discourses of physical activity, sport and health, and of prompting students to recognise their own tendencies to accept and seek to conform to dominant and inherently gendered, racialised and classed images, often without question. We then arguably come full circle, needing to reconsider whether contemporary policies and curricula relating to and impacting upon 'physical education and sport' are likely to support or impede such action.

Hargreaves (2004) identified the discourse of 'personalisation' as 'promising' in terms of its ability to act as a foundation for lifelong learning. The discourse has since been positioned at the fore of education policy in England and is integral to the 'Every Child Matters: Change for Children' programme (DfES 2007). 'A personalised approach to supporting children' is identified with

- Tailoring learning to the needs, interests and aspirations of each individual
- Tackling barriers to learning and allowing each child to achieve their potential.

(DfES 2007)

A discourse of 'personalised learning' has been 'visible', albeit not named as such, in education policy statements in Australia and New Zealand (see, for example, Ministry of Education 2003; Nelson 2005). It is another discourse, then, with evident political appeal but perhaps as yet a lack of clear meaning in either curricula or pedagogical terms, particularly in 'physical education and sport', within and beyond schools. The above bullet points leave us notably unclear about the extent to which any broader thinking about a physical education and sport curriculum can be expected. It is also important to recognise that discourses do not exist in isolation and always need to be considered in relation to existing and surrounding discourses (Ball 1990; Penney and Evans 1999). Thus, the discourse of personalised learning needs to be seen and located amidst little let-up in emphasis on the 'three Ts' (targets, tests and (league) tables) (Hargreaves 2004) as government foci. When viewed as a discourse instigated by a government recognised for its impatience to raise standards (Hargreaves 2004), personalised learning holds no inherent guarantee that a more socially just vision of learning and/ or health and well-being will inform developments in physical education and sport within or beyond schools.

Gender, physical education and sport: embedded, embodied, enacted

In conclusion and in the context of considering prospective responses to contemporary policy initiatives, it is appropriate to restate the centrality (not forgetting the complexity) of gender in physical education and sport. Gender discourses are embedded, embodied and enacted in the everyday lives of everyone involved in learning and participation communities; physical education teachers, teacher educators, coaches, parents, young people. Finding ways in which 'physical education and sport' can reconstruct itself so as to transcend inequities that are ingrained in curriculum and pedagogical relations within schools and in the external practices and discourses (of sport, physical activity, fitness and health), upon which the subject has traditionally drawn and to which it continues to relate, is no easy task. It remains, however, a key and inescapable professional responsibility for physical education teachers and teacher educators internationally.

3 Embodied identities

Boxing masculinities

Kath Woodward

Introduction

> Basically I were just a skinny kid at school and I used to get bashed around a bit and pushed about and I wanted to . . . you know, at the same time Tyson were on his way up and I used to get up at three o'clock at morning and watch Tyson. So I thought I'd give it a go. My mum weren't wanting me to box, but when I got to fifteen then I decided to give it a go and I came down and gave it a shot. I came down here because basically Bomber Graham were always in newspapers and Johnny Nelson, so I thought I'd give it a go.
>
> (Dave, 27)

In the twenty-first century, when boxing might seem to be an anomaly and even a throwback to earlier times when masculinity was defined in terms of physical aggression and courage, this is how Dave, a boxer in his late twenties, training at a gym in a northern UK city, looks back on his decision to take up the sport in his early teens. This is a story that is repeated frequently in gyms in many parts of the world and illustrates the continued popularity of boxing. Boxing still attracts young people, as participants as well as spectators, including women, although many of the sport's traditions are heavily weighted as masculine. Dave's account highlights two important aspects of the decision to 'have a go' at boxing. Firstly, he points to his own skinny body and what he attributes as the cause of his being 'bashed around' at school. Boxing is all about bodies and especially the transformation of skinny bodies that might get 'bashed about' into fit, powerful bodies that can take care of themselves and earn the respect of others. Secondly, this brief account highlights the importance of heroic role models of masculinity as illustrated by the reference to Mike Tyson in the media. This was before his conviction and imprisonment, although Tyson retained heroic status among young men in many black communities throughout his public prosecutions (O'Connor 2002). Dave also refers to more local heroes such as WBO cruiserweight Johnny Nelson and the middleweight Herol 'Bomber' Graham, the champions who trained at the same gym. The boxing body is, or has the potential to become, the heroic body. Boys and young men might aspire not only to being able to defend themselves and avoid being bullied, but also to identifying with the successful boxing hero and occupying the public space of boxing legends and stories and being part of boxing culture. The boxer's body is a heroic body which is configured around a particular version of masculinity, which is also linked to the possibility of overcoming fear of harm and physical damage to oneself as well as incorporating the possibility of inflicting such damage on one's opponent.

However, such successful embodied masculinities are not achieved without enormous effort. Boxing heroism is not easily won. The sport demands both rigorous training regimes and, for those who compete, facing the dangers and conflicts of the ring. The whole purpose of the enterprise in the ring is for one person to overcome the other by inflicting physical damage, whereby the victor prevents the loser from continuing, in many cases by a knockout, that is by rendering the opponent unconscious. Success in the sport demands control of one's own body, but success in the ring requires domination over the body of another. Boxing is a sport in which competition takes a starkly embodied, conflictual form. It is 'one on one; there's just you and him and one of you wins' (Brian, 18). Boxing foregrounds the centrality of embodiment in shaping the self and the aspiration to succeed through identification with heroic sport figures.

This chapter explores two aspects of the construction of the gendered self, focusing on the example of masculinity. These are, first, aspirations to heroism and to being part of the public representations of boxing, and, second, the importance of embodiment, which, I argue, are inextricably entwined. Using the example of a sport which has traditional associations with men and particular versions of heroic masculinity and gendered embodiment, this chapter interrogates the status of body practices in sport. Boxing is a sport which, par excellence, enables individuals to deploy their bodies to re-create and defend themselves. The gym abounds with stories of boxers who were drawn to the sport as a means of affirming their self-respect through body practices. Like Dave in the opening quotation, many boxers claim to have been attracted to the sport because they were bullied, either because they were small and skinny or because they were subject to racist taunts (or both) (Woodward 2004). Learning to box is part of a long tradition of learning how to 'look after yourself' through physical, sporting activity, which has been encouraged for boys in many families, especially by fathers and male relatives. This is recognised in the public stories and media representations of boxing heroes, even, or perhaps especially, at the amateur level. For example, press and television coverage constantly showed the amateur British boxer Amir Khan as accompanied by several members of his family at the 2004 Olympics. Women boxers are much more likely to have decided for themselves as adults to join a gym and take up the sport (Mennesson 2000; Lafferty and McKay 2004). Many boys report being taken down to the gym by their fathers. The British lightweight boxer Billy Schwer's experience is typical: 'My dad took me down the gym when I was eight' (BBC Radio 4 2006). Sometimes, although less frequently, it is mothers who deliver small boys to the gym on Saturday mornings (Woodward 2004). However, this phenomenon demonstrates how boxing is part of a cultural tradition and is recognised as providing a means of retaining respect for oneself and control over one's body and indeed of securing identity, especially masculinity (Woodward 2006).

Gendered identifications: masculinities

Which versions of masculinity continue to survive or are transformed within boxing? Boxing has a long tradition of attachments to traditional masculinities, although these might have passed unstated as taken for granted. However, it is no longer so easy for masculinity to be unmarked and assumed; it has become the subject of notice and of interrogation.

> Men are no longer the invisible, unmarked gender, the Archimedean point from which all norms, laws and rights flow; men are themselves the objects of the gaze of women, of other men and of a new critical scholarship that is deeply informed by the feminist insights . . . and scholarship of pioneers in the study of masculinity.
>
> (Nye 2005: 1938)

Men's boxing remains strongly configured around its associations with a masculinity that is constituted in polar opposition to femininity. Joyce Carol Oates expresses this most powerfully and starkly as 'Boxing is for men and is about men and is men' (1987: 72). This comment is not only an empirical observation about the people who actually box, which is supported by many who write about boxing (Sammons 1988; Sugden 1996), but it also refers to the dominantly gendered metaphors of the sport and its traditional associations with particular versions of courageous, tough, corporeal masculinity (Jefferson 1998a). There is a long history of women's participation in boxing (Hargreaves 1996) and women's boxing is popular in the contemporary world, especially in the US, but it is men's boxing that dominates the narratives of heroism, especially the myths of masculinity in which boxers, those who train at the gym, and spectators and followers of the sport invest.

Masculinity has been interrogated at a variety of different sites, for example within the social sciences and humanities, and outcomes have been framed within a range of negative, pessimistic positions and those observations which present more optimistic, positive understandings of change and possibilities of more democratic participation and equality between women and men. Some approaches which have acknowledged feminist theoretical frameworks have suggested that masculinities are being transformed and 'new' masculinities (McKay *et al.* 2000), along with new gender relations and transformations of intimacy, are emerging (Giddens 1992; Beck and

Beck-Gernsheim 1995). However, sport may offer more limited potential for gender equalities. In his analysis of men, masculinities and gender equality in the global arena, R.W. Connell suggests that the most positive and liberatory critiques have been located within the more marginalised masculinities and that sport occupies a more pessimistic space in terms of the subversion of het-erosexist, patriarchal orthodoxies, even though there is support for change among some men (Connell 2005). Michael Messner largely supports Con-nell's views in his extensive study, *Taking the Field*, and argues that, although conditions have improved, in some ways the gender inequities generated by sporting institutions and by the apparatuses of sport remain securely en-trenched (2002). Messner maps networks of collusion in the performance of violent masculinity, which is most frequent in the revenue-producing contact sports. Drawing upon US media coverage, he argues that status is accorded to conformity with a particular code of heterosexual masculinity, a 'man-hood formula' (2002: 123), which he describes as a script that is rehearsed and replayed by gendered performances. These performances incorporate pleasurable erotic bonds which are reinforced by the imperatives of sport and strengthened by the threat of failing to be complicit in such relationships (Messner 2002). This kind of analysis is written within a critical framework which addresses the ways in which traditional, gendered identities persist in order to demand change and to create its possibility. Whereas some work on masculinities points to existing transformations, for example in the sub-version of racialised, heterosexist norms, others also provide very useful deconstructions of traditional and even hegemonic masculinity in order to highlight more progressive alternatives and to make explicit that which had been assumed and therefore unchallenged (Whitehead 2002).

Some of the work that has been conducted on masculinities has pointed to the complicity or collusion that takes place at particular sites, of which sport is a good example (Messner 2002). Connell's concept of hegemonic mascu-linity (1995) remains most useful for exploring some of the ways in which masculinities are constituted in specific, situated contexts. Recent work on masculinity has often been in dialogue with Connell's conceptualisation (Messner and Sabo 1994). Sport remains dominated by strong attachments to traditional masculinities (Messner 2002), although this is changing and many women are challenging these attachments through their participation in a wide range of sport (Scambler 2005). Boxing draws on stories of its heroes and anti-heroes, from a history marked by traditional masculinities that have been associated with physical strength and force and courage, and is thus a place where one might expect to find the entrenchment of tradition through the iteration of hegemonic masculinity and some resistance to the emerging 'new masculinities'. Hegemonic masculinity is an idealised concept premised upon men's supposed superiority over both women and those men who do not comply with its requirements. Although many, if not all, men do not achieve the apparent mental and physical status of hegemonic masculin-ity, many men and women behave as if it represented actuality. Hegemonic masculinity involves the configuration of gender practices which guarantee (or are taken to guarantee) the dominant position of men and the subordination of women and of those men who do not conform to its racialised and sexualised standards. For example, hegemonic masculinity is largely based on whiteness and, especially, heterosexuality. What remains useful about Connell's concept is not so much the actual dominance of men but the expectation and assumption that masculinity is superior and a focus upon the processes through which this masculinity is repeated and re-enacted. How might this be demonstrated in boxing?

Boxing offers a very useful example of the enactment of a traditional masculinity based on physical prowess, strength and courage, which the vast majority of the sport's followers could never achieve. In order to be part of this social world supporters have to adopt other strategies and practices, often as spectators, which enable them to be complicit with this masculinity (Woodward 2006). However, this version of masculinity, configured as it is around notions of physical strength and aggression, has to be addressed in relation to the ambivalence and anxiety which underpins it. This traditional masculinity has to be accommodated with other gendered identifications which are adopted in other areas of social life. Boxing has long been implicated in the politics of 'race' and class and has provided a route out of poverty for those who have been excluded through poverty and the processes of racialisation and ethnicisation. Social exclusion, as well as being part of the everyday life of boxers, for example through the experience of racism in routine encounters, has been formalised, for example in the US prohibition of fights between black and white boxers right up until the black boxer Jack Johnson defeated the white boxer James Braddock in 1937. Gendered identifications within the social world of boxing are complex and involve intersections of class, 'race' and 'ethnicity'. As Connell argues, hegemonic masculinity must embody a successful collective strategy in relation to women and a 'mix' of strategies is necessary (1995). Hegemony involves not total dominance but ascendancy achieved through a balance of forces. One set of such forces involves the public stories that are told about the sport.

Public stories: heroes and anti-heroes

Boxing heroes (and anti-heroes), like the former heavyweight champions Muhammad Ali (Marqusee 2005; Lemert 2003; Hauser 1991) or Mike Tyson (O'Connor 2002), figure strongly in the public representations of the sport and in the accounts of the aspirations and dreams of many of those who train in the gym. Such figures could even be seen as celebrities (Cashmore 2005). The relationship between heroism and more negative, transgressive configurations of masculinity is far from a simple binary; there is considerable ambiguity about the status of boxing heroes. They are often, if only temporarily, transformed into anti-heroes, for example through criminal activities both inside and outside the ring, as in the case of Tyson. The former lightweight champion Naseem Hamed, who had been associated with positive represen-tations of social inclusion, gained notoriety, rather than fame, in 2006 for his imprisonment for driving offences, although he still performed his release from prison, for a crime which left another person very severely injured, in the style of the boxing champion, punching the air as if he had just won a major fight. Boxing is linked to other more negative representations, for example of disasters in the ring, including the cases of Michael Watson and Gerald McClellan. Experience of the flesh in boxing can be of terrible injury. Damage ranges from the more personal experiences of minor injuries to pub-lic accounts in the global media of death, such as that of Bradley Stone, and brain damage, as in the case of Michael Watson. The first death of a woman in the ring took place in 2005 when Becky Zerlentes died at the age of 34, after being knocked out in an amateur bout in Washington (Walters 2005). More positively, some boxing heroes have triumphed against the odds and now occupy almost iconic status, such as Ali. Occasionally lightweight box-ers and amateurs hit the headlines, like Amir Khan, who won a silver medal for Britain at the 2004 Olympics and achieved considerable media coverage as a role model for multi-ethnic Britain. Boxing has strong links with the history of 'race' and its heroes are often seen as representatives of those who have experienced racialisation or ethnicisation and class-based social exclusion. Boxing and its heroes play a major part in the public stories of popular culture in the news media and in films, frequently in 'rags to riches' narratives, like the *Rocky* series and the 2005 film *Cinderella Man,* in which Russell Crowe played the part of the eponymous hero, James Braddock. Braddock's heroism, which still has resonance in the contemporary world, was based upon his self-reliance and resilience as the embodiment of US values of individualism and traditional masculinity manifest in his decision to support his family by returning to boxing, rather than to rely on welfare benefits. Women, such as Laila Ali, also figure in boxing stories of success but male figures dominate the sport's heroic narratives. Some of Laila Ali's status could derive from her being the daughter of Muhammad Ali as well as her competence in the ring and her status as a strong black woman.

The public stories of boxing often challenge civilised sensibilities. Oliver McCall suffered what was described as a nervous breakdown in the ring at his WBC heavyweight fight against Lennox Lewis in Las Vegas in 1997. 'At the end of the fourth round, when McCall threw just two punches, he was crying . . . and needed just 55 seconds of the fifth to see that the man's prob-lems were deep-rooted and mental' (Mossop 1997). McCall's body refused to respond from round four. This is conceptualised as 'mental failure', but what was evident is that McCall could not fight. This example illustrates the passive rather than the active synthesis of mind and body, which is visible in the broken body in the ring, in an unusual scenario and also a disjuncture. McCall became an object of pity in what was perceived to be a loss of control of his body. Decisions may be active, as I suspect Tyson's was last year when he remained on his stool in his last fight. Such instances demonstrate the centrality of questions about agency and the relationship between mind and body in the embodied identifications of boxing.

Boxing bodies

Bodies are central to boxing. The body practices of the gym cover a range of activities:

> There's pad work ... just shadow boxing, footwork, combination punching and there's easy bag work as well as sparring and of course you've got to work at keeping fit.
>
> (Johnny, 20)

The punishing regime of the gym is not only physically demanding; it also involves techniques of the self, expressed both through body practices and control in relation to others in order to satisfy the demands of the trainer and the sport. Professional boxers have to have annual brain scans. Boxers are classified by weight and to fight outside one's weight category invites disaster. Heavyweights carry the highest status (Oates 1987). Boxers are constantly having to meet the weight criteria and this may involve restricted diets, constant visits to the toilet and not eating before a weigh-in.

The embodied activities of boxing can occupy a special place in body stories. The technologies and practices of boxing involve classifications of the self by the body, not only through weight categories. Boxing bodies are saturated by disciplinary techniques and are highly regulated and self-disciplined through a set of routine practices and mechanisms. Thus the body becomes the inscribed surface of events combining the body practices and the traditions to which they belong. Boxing bodies are disciplined and regulated through techniques of the self (Foucault 1988). However, boxing bodies bleed, sweat and are injured. Although all sport focuses on corporeal engagement for practitioners, boxing involves more physical contact than most and crucially is premised upon the aim of the whole endeavour being to inflict as much damage as possible and knock your opponent senseless, while avoiding injury yourself. Boxing is physical for spectators too; they are drawn into the spectacle and, as Vivien Sobchack argues in relation to film (2004), spectatorship is a corporeal practice in which all the senses are implicated. You can smell, hear and see the experience and the spectators' reactions are also physical sensations. Boxing reminds us of the flesh at every turn.

The body clearly matters. Having to negotiate a body that is impaired creates a completely different experience of the world and of the self from having the previously experienced athletic, powerful body. The world reacts in different ways to the impaired from the way that it reacts to the fit strong body. The meanings of this body are not written on its surface, nor will the experience be the same for everyone. Following Simone de Beauvoir's use of the French philosopher Merleau-Ponty, the human body is ambiguous; subject to natural laws and to the human production of meaning. The body is crucial but it is 'not enough' to explain human existence even in such dire situations, situated as limited to the material body itself.

> It is not merely as a body, but rather as a body subject to taboos, to laws, that the subject becomes conscious of himself and attains fulfilment – it is with reference to certain values that he valorizes himself. To repeat once more: physiology cannot ground any values; rather, the facts of biology take on the values that the existent bestows upon them.
>
> (Beauvoir 1989: 76)

Boxers gain success and status by taking control of their bodies through rigorous training regimens. The risks of the sport and the very real threat of physical pain and possibly damage in the ring might suggest that boxers need to exercise enormous control, which could be expressed as 'mind over matter' in common-sense parlance. This relationship, between mind and body, is one that has concerned not only work that has been done on sport, but also the wider field of academic study of the status of 'the body' and bodies. Boxing offers an important site for the development of understanding about how 'we are our bodies' in a form of 'direct embodiment' (Wacquant 2004: 60) in which there is no distinction made between mind and body. Increasingly sociologists prefer the term 'embodiment' because it overcomes the problem of either having to separate mind from body or marginalising the physical dimensions of identification. It is not surprising that sports sociologists have drawn upon phenomenological accounts to theorise the body. Feminist critiques of the body and theories of embodiment have also deployed phenomenological approaches arising from the work of Merleau-Ponty, although their focus has been more rarely upon sport. Bodies are crucial to an understanding of selfhood and the processes through which people position themselves and are positioned within the social world.

> The body is not a thing, it is a situation: it is our grasp on the world and a sketch of our projects.
>
> (Beauvoir 1989)

Beauvoir's approach, which has significant parallels with Merleau-Ponty's, informs many such critiques and focuses upon having a specific kind of body and the meaning which that body has for the situated individual. However, Beauvoir foregrounds the gendered dimensions of the situation *and* the situated body, unlike Merleau-Ponty, which means including the body as object, situation, lived experience, gendered myths and embodied sex/gender, rather than 'simple' sex/gender or mind/body binaries (Beauvoir 1989). This approach provides a way of bringing together the natural, material body and the situation through which the lived body is re-created. Bodies are not 'just' in a situation, nor just objects of empirical or scientific inquiry, although of course science can both describe and treat bodies and sport is a key site where this happens, but it is not enough; bodies are more than this. Beauvoir's analysis of the 'lived body' provides a means of enabling

> a situated way of seeing the subject based on the understanding that the most important location or situation is the roots of the subject in the spatial frame of the body.
>
> (Braidotti 1994: 161)

However, the deployment of Merleau-Ponty's phenomenological approach within the field of boxing has focused more upon the body and its practices than upon the situations, especially those that are gendered, of the lived body. Loic Wacquant adopts a practice-based approach which is strongly influenced by Merleau-Ponty's (1962) phenomenological account in order to address not only the question of how boxers engage in their sport but why. Wacquant deploys this approach, through which Merleau-Ponty sought to overcome mind/body dualism, in order to understand boxers' 'willing embrace and submission to the pain and rigour of their chosen sport' (Wacquant 1995a: 88). He claims that for the boxer:

> There is an *unconscious fit between his (pugilistic) habitus and the very field which has produced it* . . . The boxer's *desire* to fight flows from a *practical belief* constituted in and by the immediate co-presence of, and mutual understanding between, his (re)socialized body and the game.
>
> (1995a: 88; emphases in original)

This 'practical belief' is not simply an effect of mind, that is of deciding to engage in the sport and exercising the necessary rational powers of decision-making to put it into practice. 'Practical belief' is not a state of mind but rather a 'state of body' (Bourdieu 1990a: 68).

> The boxer wilfully perseveres into this potentially self-destructive trade because, in a very real sense, he is inhabited by the game he inhabits. A veteran middleweight who has "rumbled" on three continents for over a decade and who reported breaking his hands twice and his foot once, persistent problems with his knuckles (because of calcium deposits forming around them) as well as a punctured ear drum and several facial cuts necessitating stitches, reveals his . . . acceptance, made body, of the states of pugilism when he fails to find cause for alarm in his string of injuries: "Sure you do think about it, but then you regroup yourself, start thinkin', you can't, *it's in your blood* so much, you can't, you been doin' it so long, you can't give it up.
>
> (Wacquant 1995a: 88)

Mind and body are one through 'the shared belief in, and collectively manufactured illusion of, the value of the games (real) men play – becomes progressively instilled and inscribed in a particular biological individual' (Wacquant 1995b: 173).

Wacquant's account is persuasive in describing the processes of embodied attachment which take place, for example, in training regimes and the commitment of boxers to their sport. Boxers *are* their bodies and only become boxers through practice and physical engagement. It is not possible to differentiate between mind and body or body and self. Such ethnographic accounts, which draw upon Merleau-Ponty's notion of embodiment, give high priority to body practices in the making of attachments and demonstrate how engagement in the pugilistic activity of boxing works. This could, of course, apply to any activity in which practice is so effective that actions are carried out without reflection. Thinking might impede the action. (Like serving in tennis or bowling in cricket; once you start thinking about it you fail to operate effectively.) Wacquant's account assumes rather than explores associations with masculinity and suggests a universal embodiment which fails to accommodate the specificities of gender. A generic and universal mind/body elision is assumed. The absence of gender difference is one of the criticisms of Merleau-Ponty's approach as taken up by Wacquant. This has been addressed in different ways. For example, within the tradition of phenomenology, Iris Marion Young (1990, 2005) challenges the determinism of accounts based on body practices and suggests that actors might exercise more agency than is implied in accounts such as Wacquant's.

Young's phenomenological approach, which deploys the phenomenological concept of embodiment, attempts to redress the imbalance in Merleau-Ponty's work by focusing on gender and, in particular, the specificities of women's embodiment. Young challenges the universal account of the gender-neutral body implied by Merleau-Ponty and claims that the female body is not simply experienced as a direct communication with the active self, but it is also experienced as an object. She suggests that there are distinctive manners of comportment and movement that are associated with women. Young attributes these different modalities, first, to the social spaces in which women learn to comport themselves. In terms of sport this involves constraints of space and learning to act in less assertive and aggressive ways than men. Conversely, from this it might be deduced that men acquire those embodied practices, as in boxing, which are aggressive. Second, Young suggests women are encouraged to see themselves through the gaze of others including the 'male gaze', as developed in the work of Laura Mulvey (1975) and to become more aware of themselves as objects of the scrutiny of others. Similarly, the aspirations to the heroic body of the successful boxer might be viewed as informing the dreams and the practices of men who box. Whereas young women practise the comportment of femininity, young men engage in the techniques of masculinity, embodied in the 'hard man' image of the boxer. Women's boxing has been described as conforming to the 'softer' regimes of the bodily practices of femininity (Lafferty and McKay 2005).

Iron Mike: case study

If women have been associated with 'soft boxing' and men with turning their bodies into weapons (Lafferty and McKay 2005), Mike Tyson, 'Iron Mike', certainly offers a good example of a 'hard man'. The figure of the hard man, which combines physical toughness and determination, is present throughout the history of men's boxing, especially in the heavyweight division. Mike Tyson was not, however, always so tough, as Tony Jefferson records in his paper, 'From "Little Fairy Boy" to "the Compleat Destroyer"' (1998b), in which he analyses Tyson's transition from lisping, bullied youth to hard man and world champion. Tony Jefferson uses the case study of Mike Tyson to illustrate some of the psycho-social dynamics of attachment to a version of racialised, embodied masculinity which presents Tyson at different times as both hero and villain.

Jefferson challenges the universalising principles of Wacquant's phenomenological approach to embodiment. Wacquant argues that men willingly embrace the sport with its pains and rigours and take all these aspects for granted. He rejects the economic arguments of the route out of poverty and the ghetto and a culturally determinist view which sees boxing as an example of 'normative compliance to some cultural dictate' (Wacquant 1995a: 88) and suggests that there are unconscious forces in play in the embodied attachments that are made in boxing, especially in the practice of a sport that is 'in the blood'. However Wacquant does not offer any discussion of the dynamics of these unconscious forces, although he acknowledges that this is another dimension of the processes of attachment taking place within this social world. Jefferson suggests that Tyson's decision to box can be partially explained in terms of his experience of being bullied as a child. Many boxers cite this reason for their decision to box as being to defend and 'look after' themselves (Woodward 2004, 2006) as illustrated in the introduction to this chapter. Wacquant does acknowledge this vulnerability of masculinity in his review essay on body builders, 'Why Men Desire Muscles' (1995b), but it is not part of his analysis of embodiment in boxing. Anxiety poses problems for his theory of the merging of mind and body, because the desire to defend the vulnerable self and the feeling of anxiety that this involves presuppose a source of these feelings which precedes the body practices through which bodies and selves are made. This would reinstate a mind/body split whereby there is consciousness of vulnerability which comes before the boxing body practices which are the remedy. Jefferson brings together phenomenological embodiment and psychoanalytically derived discussion of anxiety.

> Tyson . . . can somehow both identify with and embody the hard man. To do so . . . there has to be a set of social and psychic congruences, which add up to a compelling satisfaction in or desire to inflict punishment and thereby triumph over the threat of having it inflicted, that are neither wholly specific to him, nor are they shared with every man. The

social legacy of being a poor, ghetto born Afro-American with few options or images beyond the tough, sexual, "bad-ass" athlete performer,
combined with a painful psychic legacy of emotional neglect and the
resulting pattern of anxiety, in which . . . primitive defences would be
characteristic, produced the sort of ability to split off or deny parts of
himself, for example, that provided this particular route to being able to
embody, or "live" hardness.

(Jefferson 1998a: 94)

Jefferson's account does not privilege social over psychic factors but argues that the two domains are inextricably linked. The anxieties that are
presented as providing some of the explanation for individuals taking up
boxing, apparent in the stories of being bullied or subject to racialised abuse,
are all part of the psychic investments that are made in boxing masculinities.
Although Jefferson is arguing not for universal psychic investment in a particular masculinity but for the need to focus upon specific situations and circumstances, it has to be stated that very similar social, cultural and economic
circumstances inform the experiences of boxers. They may not be universal,
but poverty and racism play very important parts in boxing stories; the understanding of boxing as providing a route out of the ghetto and the promise
of 'rags to riches' narratives permeates any analysis of identification with the
masculinities in this social world. These stories constitute part of the appeal
of the sport as a solution to the problems of disempowerment, whether they
derive from economic or social exclusion and deprivation or an embodied
self-consciousness and physical, corporeally based anxieties.

Conclusion

Bodies and selves are inextricably interwoven and the example of the sport of
boxing explored in this chapter demonstrates the centrality of embodiment
in shaping the self. This self is not one which can be easily split into separate
entities of mind and body, and corporeality is crucial to an understanding
of, for example, the ways in which gender identities are reconfigured and
experienced. Some of the developments of phenomenological approaches to
embodiment, especially those that have been applied to boxing, have emphasised the bodily practices, for example as expressed in the training regimens
of the gym in order to establish the synthesis of mind and body. However, I
have argued that these practices have to be situated both in the wider field
of social relations and in the context of the dreams and aspirations of those
individuals who engage in the sport. Embodiment and bodily practices are
situated and subject to the play of power structures which shape the social
world. Thus I have suggested embodiment is also marked by gender, which
has been a major concern of this chapter, and other dimensions of difference.
The theories of embodiment that have been explored in this chapter suggest

that not only are bodies necessarily intertwined with situated selfhood, but also the material body is involved in the agency that selves can effect.

Bodies are gendered, not only in their materiality as living, breathing entities, but also, and as importantly, in the manner in which bodies are experienced and how they are situated. Sporting bodies are lived and experienced through the public stories, for example expressed through media accounts, popular culture and traditional narratives, through which people make sense of their embodied lives and corporeal selves. The example of boxing presents a particularly gendered focus on the identification processes that are involved in linking personal investments and the more public stories that dominate the wider cultural field.

The masculinities that are enacted and experienced within boxing appear to represent a contemporary version of hegemonic masculinity that seems clearly bounded and draws upon traditions of powerful, physical masculinity. However, not only does this particular identification have to be accommodated with 'new', more ambivalent versions of masculinity that feature in other areas of social life, for example in relation to parenthood, employment and femininity, but also the appeal of traditional masculinity may lie more in its weaknesses than in its apparent strengths. Boxing as a sport and the masculinity that is implicated in its embodied practices have to be understood as situations of vulnerability and ambivalence. Thus boxing may not be such an anomaly in the twenty-first century and it may even be not so surprising that increasing numbers of young women are not only 'doing' the masculinities of the sport but reconstructing them through identifications of their own. The situated approach to embodiment adopted in this chapter demonstrates the possibility of reconfigurations of embodied selfhood through sporting practices even if such transformations might be slow to arrive in boxing.

4 Girls, bodies and pain

Negotiating the body in ballet

Angela Pickard

When I'm dancing it's like I'm free and floating, I'm me. I have always wanted to be a ballerina and I will be. When I started ballet classes at 3, I think I took it more seriously than the others. Everyone else saw it just as a fun thing. My teacher suggested that I audition for here. At the audition, the teachers, without saying anything particular, just seemed to make me work really, really hard and I didn't seem to get tired, I just kept going. I was excited and was enjoying what I was doing. The time went very quickly. I remember having to do the splits and all the people saying 'go on, try a little harder' and it really encouraged me so I got lower down and it didn't really hurt. I get better all the time. I love it here. The first two years were fun though also disciplined, now it's harder and everyday it gets more harder. When I started *pointe* I was scared of the pain of blisters and the bleeding but it is ok. You get used to it. If you want to be a dancer, you just learn to be tough and strong and put up with the pain. You have to deal with knock backs sometimes when things don't go so well. I do seem to cry a lot but it's worth it to prove to myself what I can be.

(Megan, 12 years)

This 12-year-old child has been identified as talented in dance, particularly ballet, from a young age. She has had some success in annual audition processes and regular assessments in order to gain and maintain access to a place at an elite dance training institution. She now participates in a non-residential ballet training programme that includes a weekly class and performance opportunities alongside her local ballet classes. She dances for at least eight hours a week in the evenings and at weekends. Megan wishes to become a ballerina. She is able to articulate that the journey towards becoming a professional ballet dancer is not always pleasurable and expects and accepts pain and 'knockbacks' as part of that journey in order to 'prove to herself what she can be'. She appears to be dancing for herself, to be self-motivated and determined and to be gaining from her achievements, affective engagement and developing identity as a dancer. Yet this is a painful pastime. Megan, from an early age, has set her goal on a highly competitive career that is plagued with injuries and physical and emotional discomfort (Brinson and Dick 1996; Buckroyd 2000). Such features are often associated with traditional male sports (Young 1993; Young *et al.* 1994; White *et al.* 1995; Connell 2000; Gard and Meyenn 2000; Roderick *et al.* 2000), although, according to Cole (1993), physical education and sport, despite being based on hegemonic masculine principles, can challenge passive constructions of femininity and offer scope for the development of 'progressive practicalities' for girls and young women.

So does the pleasure outweigh the pain? Is the sense of achievement in being able to push the body to the limit and control the pain motivating? Are these words autonomous with the beliefs of Megan or has she become influenced, seduced by and socialised into the culture of ballet which she inhabits? How realistic is her dream and is there a cost? Contemporary Western society tends to promote the view that children are to be kept sheltered out of the reach of harm, that they need protection from injury, to be nurtured and comforted by adults (Furedi 2002), that childhood brings innocence, happiness, pleasure and certain freedoms with supported and guided risk-taking, development and growth (HMSO 1989, 1998; DfES 2004a,b). Yet in Megan we have one of many children (myself as a child included), not to mention the more numerous young athletes, who are engaged in a regular commitment that is disciplined, structured and painful; a hobby or leisure pursuit that is taken more seriously, that matters more, that becomes an aspiration.

This chapter draws on work in the fields of dance, sport and health and examines themes relating to the body, pain and pleasure within the context of ballet education and training programmes at elite ballet schools. Ballet as gendered practice, definitions of pain and the notion of positive pain, aesthetics and perfection are discussed, particularly in the context of the cultural tradition of ballet. The lived experiences of young female ballet dancers, aged between 10 and 14 years, all of whom wish to become professional ballet dancers, are explored, as they develop their ballet bodies and learn how to negotiate the ballet body in pleasure and pain.

The ballet body

The professional dancer's body is trained to be strong and flexible. In dance technique training the young female dancer gets to know every part of her body and how she can use it for the greatest effect. Pain is simply seen as a means of improving technique and performance. Dancers learn how to push the boundaries of pain and gain a high sense of pleasure, enlightenment and achievement through experiencing moving in particular ways. Dance is lived not only through the body but also *as body* by performer and perceiver (Fraleigh 1987) and can reveal the infinite possibilities of the body in movement and stillness (Thomas 2003: 214) whilst providing a site for examining the limitations and extraordinary potential of the physical body.

Wainwright and Turner (2004), in their study of former ballet dancers and staff, comment upon the 'sheer physical hard work of the professional ballet dancers' (2004: 314), which is similar to the physical training undertaken by professional athletes.

Transforming the body into what could be perceived as a structured, high-performance, controlled and disciplined machine (Foucault 1992) takes much commitment and effort. Those wishing, and considered to have the potential, to become professional ballet dancers engage in audition processes and, if successful, commence training at an early age, leading to specialisation as pre-pubescent children. Body shape, size and physical attributes are often the starting point in any audition process:

> One has to obviously start I suppose with the physical aspect because without that everything is a struggle. It [ballet] is such a visual art that you need to be pleasant to look at. You need to have the right physique because if you're struggling with a physique that is wrong you can't get past it. You can still be a brilliant dancer but your physique might not be right for classical ballet companies but it will be enough for other companies. You can be stunning but won't get into classical ballet companies.
>
> (teacher)

Similarly, from an early age, young dancers become aware of the expectations of the ballet body physique, the idealised ballet body and performance demands. 'The dancer's ideal body may specify size, shape, proportion of its parts as well as expertise at executing specific movements' (Foster 1997: 237). Jane shares her view of how a ballet body should look:

> Not fat but not too thin, just right. Slim and nice. You have to look perfect and be perfect. Long legs, but *pointe* shoes make your legs look longer, long neck, good tidy feet.
>
> (Jane, 14 years)

There may be pressures placed upon the young dancers to be thin; incidences of anorexia nervosa and bulimia and experiences of control and sense of achievement in maintaining low weight are well documented (Abraham 1996a,b; Schnitt and Schnitt 1986; Nixon 1989; Yannakoulia *et al.* 2002; Sundgot-Borgen *et al.* 2003). Much of the literature points to the high incidences of dancers' eating behaviours such as elective restriction of food, binge eating, purging and the maintenance of extremely low weight through use of laxatives. Some studies (Abraham 1996a; Le Grange *et al.* 1994), have explained the eating disorders of ballet dancers (gymnasts and some other athletes) as reactions to requirements and external pressures to remain thin. This may seem too simplistic but many symptoms of anorexia (e.g. amenorrhoea, strict diet control) appear to be common and even adaptive in the ballet community (Garner and Garfinkel 1980; Garner *et al.* 1987). Other authors (Abraham 1996b) have suggested that dancers have simply learned poor eating habits that persist and may be reinforced in professional ballet companies.

During puberty, genetic potential in terms of physique will start to become apparent. This may make it clear that a particular body shape may not fit the requirements to become a professional ballet dancer. Unsurprisingly, research has demonstrated that those dance trainees most vulnerable to eating disorders were those whose natural shape did not conform to the requirement to be very slim (Hamilton *et al.* 1988). As Green argues, the body is 'mechanised or habituated into an ideal form that represents the teacher's/school's learned belief system and presumed ideas about what the body should be and do' (2001: 156). Dancers may also give their body over to the teacher/school in a sense of belonging and identity (for example, T-shirt or kit identifies the body as affiliated with or belonging to the school) as they are then moulded and strive for a particular, specific and acceptable look. There is also the suggestion that a dancer's lack of individual ownership and largely powerless stance in the ballet world reflects their resolution of the human tendency to assume either dominant (sadistic) or submissive (masochistic) roles: 'the dancer's body provides an object on which others impose, and express, their creative ideas . . . in which the choreographer says "Jump," and the dancer asks only, "How high?"' (Sartre 1971: 34, quoted in Gray and Kunkel 2001).

Dancers, then, in order to be successful, appear to need to cultivate conformity as public property, be deprived of their identity and become impersonal commodities of their companies (Gray and Kunkel 2001), implying that they are passive recipients of all that is being done to them and are simply bodies. 'Classical ballet is predictable and conservative in form and in preserving a particular style and code of manners, usually at the expense of much self-expression, originality or experimentation . . . dancers frequently labor in large, anonymous corps de ballet' (Abra 1987/8: 33).

Phenomenological approaches (Merleau-Ponty 1962; Bell 1991; Hughson and Inglis 2002), however, draw upon the view that the dualist conception of the mind and body divide is misleading and that one cannot live an experience separately from either mind or body. The theme of pain then is especially interesting as it could be the case that dancers (trained from an early age) do learn to think of their bodies as machines, which need to be controlled and to which pain, injury and harm are acceptable because 'they' (the subject; the dancers) are not hurt. It is just their bodies.

At the same time, the status derived through social understandings of a 'dancer's' body could be seen to provide additional buffers to counter the negative aspects of pain. Bourdieu (1977, 1990b, 1993) suggests that the body can be expressed as 'cultural capital', according to which a particular type of body appears to carry more cultural weight in a particular context or 'habitus'. Habitus can be considered as cultural background in which a multitude of behaviours constitute a form of cultural identity:

> The habitus, as the word implies, is that which one has acquired, but which has durably been incorporated into the body in the form of permanent dispositions. So the term constantly reminds us that it refers to something historical, linked to individual history, and that it belongs to a genetic mode of thought, as opposed to an essentialist mode of thought.
>
> (Bourdieu 1993: 86)

Although the habitus appears to be intrinsic to culture and innate, it is rather like a property or a form of capital which is embodied by the person in that culture. The habitus is reproductive and productive; it is sometimes referred to as learning the rules and getting a feel for the game. These rules are learnt through explicit teaching as well as practice. In relation to speech, acts occur through linguistic habitus and power is expressed through the use of what constitutes appropriate language in the linguistic market. The body is the primary means of expression and representation in dance so dancers experience and engage in dance through their bodies. The development of physical acts, competence, behaviours and social relations that occur through the habitus of dance (in this case the focus is on ballet) enables individuals to achieve understanding of this social world through bodily practice: 'the meanings and implications of dance, indeed of all art, are embedded in the experiences of the art itself – learning, teaching, creating, performing and watching' (Bull 1997: 270).

The style and manner of social performance, such as gesture and stance, relates to 'hexus' and demonstrates the importance of the body and the individual within the habitus. Bodily hexus combines with the social and mediates a link between an individual's subjective world and the cultural world. For Bourdieu, the body is the device upon which the culture is imprinted and encoded in a socialising process (Jenkins 1992). So powerful are cultural factors over the individual that the individual, without knowing it, is constrained to act in certain ways by the system's rules and categories.

Ballet has a long, historical tradition, beginning with Renaissance spectacles, moving to France, where the foundations for classical ballet were laid at the royal court with Louis XIV. The Academie Royale de Musique began in 1671 and by the early nineteenth century technique had been codified. Ballet therefore cultivates status that means the visual art of ballet tends to be seen as high art and that one will sacrifice and suffer for one's art, as seen in the film *The Red Shoes* (1948). The status of cultural capital is shown to an audience in the form of disciplined, sylph-like, mesmerising objects of beauty in female ballerinas during performance. Here, the ballet body is portrayed as an elegant, *en pointe* fantasy creature encompassing all that is deemed feminine by ballet society and audiences alike.

Conversely, the reality of the ballet body aesthetic is that it seems to eradicate all marks of the feminine, that is, the ideal, female ballet body should be breastless and hipless, 'adolescents frozen on the border between childhood and adulthood' (Gray and Kunkel 2001: 16). The ballet world's reverence for the wispy ballerina reflects, as Bordo (1997) argues, paradoxically massive internalisation of distain for feminine qualities, although ballerinas are also viewed as flights of imagination and whimsical visions of desire that seem to 'entail hyper-feminisation' (Gray and Kunkel 2001: 21).

Ballet as gendered practice

Ballet can be seen as gendered practice as it can portray the dominant versions of what constitutes masculinity and femininity (Segal 1997). For Connell (1995) the body and the relationship an individual has to his or her own body is the central means through which gendered identity is constructed:

> Gender is (among other things) a certain feel to the skin, certain muscular shapes and tensions, certain postures and ways of moving, certain possibilities in sex. Bodily experience is often central in the memories of our own lives, and thus our understanding of who and what we are.
>
> (Connell 1995: 53)

A central focus of attention and scorn in feminist dance scholarship was directed initially towards classical ballet, with its emphasis on gender-differentiating *pas de deux* form (Carter 1999). This distinction between male and female behaviour and roles presents the acceptable version of gender in ballet where the male supports the female. Ballet classics are odes to sentimentality and to the romantic vision of women: they are beautiful and delicate. Both men and women dancers require considerable strength and bodily control; however, in the main, male dancing exerts energy, force and strength whilst demonstrating a capacity to occupy space. The movements of women must be effortless, weightless and graceful:

> Princes and princesses are manufactured from the ways male and female bodies interact in physical terms. Support, initiation, strength, adaptability, delicacy, directness – all occupy their richness on the continuum of gender identity.
>
> (Goldberg 1997: 307)

The body then is the starting point through which social definitions of gender can be read; at the same time, as the individual experience of the living body is recognised there is the potential for a form of agency in the form of practice.

The ballet body in pain

Ballet dancers are more likely to experience higher rates of pain and injury, particularly those associated with overuse and overtraining (fatigue), than other dance styles. They are also more likely to ignore pain and what they consider to be minor injuries, regarding them as manageable nuisances (Hamilton and Hamilton 1991; Liederbach and Compagno 2001). Dancing, in the world of the professional ballet dancer, is not simply something you do but something you are, and thus being a ballet dancer is an embodiment of identity (Bakker 1988, 1991; Turner and Wainwright 2003). Dance training involves a willingness to tolerate a considerable amount of discomfort, tiredness and probably pain and hunger (Buckroyd 2000). The rules of the ballet body in pain are that dancers are:

> constantly operating on the edge of their pain tolerance level in order to express beauty or powerful emotions. One does not see the pain; unspoken, it lies hidden in the biography of the individual dancer – behind the movements. Pain is a powerful expression of emotion and aesthetics . . . an emotional condition that is beautiful.
>
> (Roessler 2006: 44)

Interestingly, this does not fit with social expectations and patterns of behaviour of a heterosexual feminine way to respond to pain. It has been suggested that females have a lower pain threshold than males but there is no current biological explanation for this (Criste 2002). It may be that (non-dancer) women generally are more likely to share the fact that they are in pain because historical social constructs have allowed them to be more expressive than men. Consequently, it may be that female pain is seen as exaggerated and is less likely to be taken seriously (Hoffmann and Tarzian 2001). However, it is also noted that, if a woman is not expressive about her pain, then she is not in pain. Historically, 'physical exertion and assertion were considered to be harmful to girls' overall development and the social understanding of "motherhood" dictated that girls were seen as passive carers rather than as active providers' (Wellard *et al.* 2007: 79). Though engagement in a physical activity which is painful 'undermines women's categorization as people who avoid pain and need protection from pain wherever possible' (Lock 2006: 164), thereby challenging the norm.

In ballet training, pain is seen as an expected and integral part of becoming a professional ballet dancer, 'posing inviolate demands such as turn-out and ear-threatening leg extensions that break every rule of human anatomy' (Abra 1987/8: 33). Posture, internal abdominal muscles, metatarsals and turn-out are developed and structured at the earliest opportunity, as is an understanding of one's own body and its limitations, as illustrated by Sima:

You soon get used to aching, sometimes all over. I'm doing my exercises to switch on my tummy muscles and get a better turn-out. I'm learning how far to push myself and everyday look forward to how much more I can do.

(10 years)

Foucault's (1977) concept of 'docile bodies' is relevant. In this, the body is viewed as a training instrument through techniques that require habituated movement patterns and control in which the dancer is removed from having any sense of ownership of their own body. The dancer wishes to conform to specific standards to be seen as a 'good' dancer by teachers, choreographers or artistic directors so may learn to discipline him- or herself to conform through self-regulation and unconscious habit through fear of criticism or rejection.

Unfortunately, this habituation often leads to a disconnection from inner messages of the body as well as loss of ownership. This could lead to injury, physical strain, pain and a general lack of confidence and well being.

(Green 2001: 164)

Is the dancer passive in the dance experience? Is the dancer's body simply given over to become manufactured like a machine? Does the need to be a successful dancer mean that the dancer will do anything/be anything to achieve the success? Is success as a dancer, even though a dancer is apparently passive in the experience, the motivating force that means dancers will, and expect to, experience high levels of pain?

Definitions of pain

Pain has been defined as 'an unpleasant sensory and emotional experience associated with actual or potential tissue damage' (International Association for the Study of Pain 1979). Levels of pain are notoriously difficult to distinguish, as the severity of each individual's pain will always be relative. Since the early 1990s there has been increased interest in pain and injury from physiological (Brinson and Dick 1996; Krasnow *et al.* 1994) and psychological (Anderson and Williams 1999; Fawkner *et al.* 1999; Petrie 1992; Liederbach and Compagno 2001; Mainwaring *et al.* 2001) perspectives, and with regard to its social importance, particularly within the disciplines of sport sociology and anthropology (Nixon 1992, 1993; Young 1993; White *et al.* 1995; Howe 2004).

It has been suggested that athletic pain is recognised as playing a role in defining men as masculine (Nixon 1992, 1993, 1996; Young *et al.* 1994; Pringle 1999; Roderick *et al.* 2000; Howe 2001) and that male pain is rendered legitimate and visible. More recently pain has been placed at the intersection between biology and culture (Bendelow 2000). Any investigation of pain, however, is problematic as it can be seen as a highly subjective, cultural phenomenon and construct (Howe 2004). Pain can be inscribed with meaning based on the socio-cultural context in which it is situated. The experience of pain may be normalised by some groups and problematised by others (Curry and Strauss 1994; Nixon 1992, 1993; Young 1993). Socio-cultural contexts can make the infliction of pain and suffering acceptable and even admirable. The acceptance and endurance of pain are seen as necessary to succeed as a dancer. The body is seen as more or less a productive tool and 'pain is not an obstacle to, but a means towards liberation and salvation' (Loland 2006: 54). According to Melzack (1973), the concentration of a dancer is focused not on pain but on dance, particularly so that the audience is not aware of the physical pain behind the dance. In this way, cultural capital is accrued through the ability to function with (sometimes intense levels of) pain. This may be the mobilisation of individual inner strength with the help of 'willpower' in order to change the intensity of the pain (Sauerbruch and Wenke 1936). Coping and managing pain can be seen as a litmus test for acceptance into sporting/dance subcultures – that one is tough enough (Kotarba 1983).

In relation to wider social expectations of gender and pain thresholds, birthing for example is an exclusively female pain, constructed as a sacrificial pain that women are expected to fear and suffer, and they may be vocal about it. Bergum argues 'the offer of medication confirms the fear that, yes indeed, we will not be able to stand it' (2004: 5). In affirming the fear, there is a suggestion that a woman's capacity to control pain is lower than that of men. Medication is an indication that a woman is too weak to bear the pain. Birthing can be seen as symbolic of the female role of sacrifice for and caring of others: 'The significance of the sacrifice is that it marks a woman as self-less, giving of her-self and giving up her-self in order to nurture the child' (Lock 2006: 162). Pain as embodied is fundamental to exploring pain as a social psychological dimension (Turner 1992). A holistic view of pain leads us to an understanding that pain is more complex than a simple mechanical process of stimulus and response (Melzack 1973; Melzack and Wall 1996). Mind and body are considered to be fully at one while pain is present – physical experience is inseparable from its cognitive and emotional significance. Pain can be used to describe physical agony, emotional turmoil and spiritual suffering but is also connected with will power and passion (Roessler 2006).

Positive and zatopekian pain

Without pain our bodies are 'taken for granted' and pain may signal impending or actual injury. Positive pain is a term used to describe the fatigue that an elite sporting participant goes through in the course of trying to enhance performance. It is believed that all properly structured athlete training schedules should be developed to maximise this component of pain – the notion of a 'no pain, no gain' culture (Stamford 1987). Exposing sporting participants to pain, while they are injury-free, in the process of training is believed to raise their pain threshold (Carmichael 1988). Pain is constructive only when it is limited to periods of intense training that are followed by no negative side effects from training and/or involvement in competition or performance:

> Fatigue and muscle soreness are quite different from overtraining or staleness, although they may exist during such states. They are normal physiological elements of what may be termed the training process, which is defined as a set of interactions between a stimulus and a response intended to initiate adaptive (beneficial) physiological changes.
>
> (Martin and Coe 1991: 254)

Zatopekian pain is considered to be positive fatigue and muscle soreness, but it is difficult to distinguish these from a pain which may be a marker of injury and negative. It is important that dancers be in tune with their bodies. Zatopekian pain or positive pain is seen as a useful way to increase the body's immunity to pain and pain threshold. Children may be particularly vulnerable to exacerbating pain and injury because of partial or limited knowledge (Gaffney 1993), or thinking that they must endure pain in order to be successful. Some previous research has considered children's definitions and understanding of pain and injury prevention (Gaffney and Dunne 1986, 1987; Harbeck and Peterson 1992; Nemeth *et al.* 2005). One young dancer Lie (14 years), shares her developing understanding of her body and determination to continually increase her pain threshold and push the boundaries set by her aching body:

> Sometimes my body gets so tired and it aches and I think 'I'll never do anymore' but I do and I feel good. You have to find the determination to do the best you can, you want to prove yourself all the time, to push all the time, sometimes a little 'cos you're scared about how much it is going to hurt but you realise there's more there and it's ok. You might be stiff but you know eventually it'll wear off. You push through it and gain that much more.

It is important to develop the ability to distinguish negative pain (as a signal of impeding injury) from positive pain (soreness from exertion), and this can be increased by knowing and listening to the body and determining when the body is tired (Buckroyd 2000). However, as Buckroyd (2000) argues, dancers may desensitise and ignore what is happening to their bodies. As Traccy (13 years) argues 'You mustn't give into the pain, the muscles will release if you keep pushing them.' Tajet-Foxell and Rose concluded 'the meaning of pain, the importance of acknowledging pain and of learning how to respond to it should be targeted as early as possible in a dancer's training'

(1995: 34). The sensation owing to exertion is often not seen as pain or painful but is related to a sensation of sore muscles, muscle stiffness, momentary pain or feeling very tired and these can be seen as good indicators that those involved had been working hard. How much, though, can we rely on children and teenagers (those featured in this chapter are passionate about being professional ballet dancers) taking a duty of care for their own bodies, being able to judge their limitations and understanding the consequences of injury if they push too far? How far is too far?

> They have to learn what pain they can work through and what hurts. I think stretching is a nice pain but they don't all seem to. When they say 'ow!' we have to work out if it is that the muscles really aren't going to do it and are in danger of snapping or whether it is just that they have to get used to that feeling of lengthening. Most children would have been through a certain amount of pain to get here anyway so therefore they should know themselves if it's a nice hurt or if it's an agony. I think most of the pain is good and as dancers you expect pain to be good and doing good. It is difficult with children though as their bones are growing and not their muscles.
>
> (teacher)

Rite of passage – *en pointe*

Rites of passage have often been described in relation to boys becoming men. In traditional hunter-gatherer societies this tended to be characterised by pain through battle scars (Messner 1992; Burstyn 1999; Connell 2000). Putting on the *pointe* shoe signifies an important transition towards becoming a ballerina (Carter 2000). *Pointe* work, or dancing on the tip of the toe in specially designed *pointe* shoes that have been stiffened with glue, enables the dancer to balance her entire body weight on a tiny flat surface. This is traditionally restricted to female dancers. *Pointe* work is seen as a clear goal, rite of passage and achievement by many young female ballet dancers. Young dancers tend to begin *pointe* work at around 12 years old as ankles, toes, feet and abdominals need to be strong enough to take the weight of their body. Many young female ballet dancers claim that they look forward to their first experiences of *pointe* work, as often they see this as an acknowledgement that they are 'being a real ballerina' (Sima, 10 years).

> I love being on *pointe*. You look so graceful and elegant and the music just carries you. You just have to learn to pull up out of your *pointe* shoes, then it doesn't hurt.
>
> (Tracey, 13 years)

Some young girls, though, fear their *en pointe* experiences as they often bring discomfort, but the girls can learn to find strategies for overcoming the pain:

I was excited but also really worried about first going on *pointe* but it didn't hurt as badly as I thought it would. It's really after you stop you realise how much it hurts. We do a little bit of *pointe* work each time and build up. Now I put my feet in mentholated spirit to toughen them up. I strap my toes tightly and use these cushion pads in the toes of my shoes. I also bang and squash my shoes to make them softer. I'm not sure any of it helps as I always get lots of blisters and rubs. When we all take our shoes off it's funny that we all compare how many sores or blisters we have and whether there's blood, then we all limp home.

(Leah, 13 years)

A dancer can 'live' totally within a performance in which the dancer can be totally absorbed and 'transcend distinctions between body and mind, and between self and the social and physical environment' (Loland 2006: 56). During this time the dancer 'is' her body and is unlikely to 'feel' or think about pain until the performance is disrupted, for example when the dancer moves off stage, during scene changes and intervals.

Pointe work 'bestows bunioned and blistered feet decidedly at odds with that glamorous persona' of a ballerina (Abra 1987/8: 33) and tends to mean potential discomfort such as regular bruising of nails: 'common causes are improper maintenance, fungus and getting stepped on or dropped hard during partnering' (Novella 1994: 1). Further injuries such as sprains, fractures and tendonitis are also common. The potential pain of being *en pointe*, a core part of the role of the female ballet dancer, and the development of pain threshold when blisters, rubs and open sores are evident can be seen in relation to Bourdieu's cultivation of cultural capital. The routine of strapping of toes and the expectation to suffer for the art appears to be seen as an integral part of learning 'the rules of the game' (Bourdieu 1977). During *pointe* class and performances *en pointe*, discomfort or pain is not seen or shared but afterwards the wounds are paraded almost like a trophy as 'proof that you've worked hard' (Lie, 14 years).

Bodily pleasures

Although I have discussed aspects of the constructions and negotiations of bodies with a particular focus on pain, illustrated with the perspectives of young female ballet dancers, greater recognition must be given to the benefits of bodily pleasures, confidence and knowledge that are gained from the engagement in ballet as a physical activity. Perhaps the 'high' and physical pleasures that many of the young female dancers described is simply adrenaline and endorphins from being physically active, but Csikszentmihalyi (1990) relates rich experiences to the concept of deep engagement and flow. He discusses pleasure and fun. Pleasure is described as a conscious state when a biological or socially conditioned need is satisfied. Fun is when the activity matches and challenges ability. During the fun state, there is a clear focus, goals and regular feedback, the worries and frustrations of life do not intrude, self-consciousness is considered to be absent, sense of time is altered and the participant has a clear sense of control. After the activity, the sense of self is stronger.

Relating skilful action, personal competency and empowerment to intrinsic pleasure or 'flow' in physical education has been considered further by O'Reilly *et al.* (2001). Bond and Stinson (2000/1) have documented young people's positive, affective and 'superordinary' experiences in dance. Stinson *et al.* (1990) suggest that dance as a structured activity enables teenage dance students to receive discipline and to enter a transcendent state: 'When I dance, I'm more of a soul' (1990: 17). Similarly, Hamera (2005) examined how adolescents appeared empowered by tactically deploying the discipline and pleasure of ballet technique as a form of escapism to navigate the pressures of parental expectations. Autobiographical and biographical works of professional dancers in relation to the joy of moving and dancing in and through space have also been evidenced (Wulff 1998).

Indeed the girls themselves described the sensation of dancing as liberating and 'free', 'exciting' and 'like I'm floating or flying'. Buckroyd (2000) suggests that part of the process of developing a sense of self lies in the development of physical capabilities that enable us to control our bodies and use them to achieve our own ends. It has been suggested that if children and young people are helped to realise their bodily potential then they can experience a sense of pleasure, bodily power and well-being in relation to physical development and competence (Theberge 1987; Gilroy 1989; Davies 1995; Wright and Dewar 1997). Pronger (2002) interprets limits in law and, drawing upon Drusilla Cornell's (1992) 'philosophy of limit', describes the potential, or 'puissance' (2002: 66), to be found in bodily pleasures that exist 'outside' the boundaries of conventional thinking.

Finding pleasure in being physically active has been recognised as having emancipatory potential (Theberge 1987; Gilroy 1989; Wright and Dewar 1997; Garrett 2004a) providing opportunities for young women to experience physical skill and expertise: 'A physically active lifestyle can be empowering for young women allowing them to resist many of the dominant and limiting discourses around femininity and gender' (Garrett 2004: 223). Women will invest in their own bodies if they experience their bodies as strong and powerful and as a source of kinaesthetic or sensual pleasure (Wright and Dewar 1997). The young female dancer's enthusiasm for risk-taking, the thrill of pushing the limits of the body and the enjoyment of exceeding expectations and boundaries are discussed by Wellard *et al.* (2007), challenging traditional thinking in relation to girls' bodies and their physical potential and limit.

The ballet dancer can be intrinsically motivated and choose to take risks, push boundaries and try new movement. Even though the discipline, structure, rules and conventions that are imposed are acknowledged by young dancers, paradoxically feelings of freedom were often noted, implying that the dancer cannot be passive in the experience but is actively constructing meaning and associated positive feelings within the body:

> I love everything about ballet, the music, the grace, the little and large movements, the feeling that I can do this with my body. It's me and it's just beautiful. I love that it's so hard but then, when I've got it, I can make it look easy. I love moving through the space when I'm travelling and it's like I'm free and flying when I'm jumping. I can really express myself through my arms and my face. It's like I'm in a dream.
>
> (Jane, 14 years)

These young, female ballet dancers are able to explore the potential of the body, both physically and artistically, in ways that go beyond other forms of experience found in traditional sports. Those dancers with longevity in the profession may be the ones who are intrinsically motivated and gain most from the pleasure of the experience. The 'thinking dancers' (Clarke 2002; Duerden and Fisher 2002; Morris 2006) who can express, live in the experience as active agents and meaning-makers, responding in creative and artistic ways, as well as the physical as 'articulate bodies' (Parry 2006), to the choreographer's intention, are likely to be those who will last in the profession and be inspiring to watch. Duerden and Fisher state that the term 'thinking dancer' is a tautology and that 'dancing and thinking are not separate activities' (2002: 10). Although referring to modern dancing, Gill Clarke, admired for her own technique and artistry, epitomises the 'thinking dancer' and explains that by learning more directly from her own proprioception she 'gained greater control, articulation, strength – those qualities we label as criteria of technique' (2002: 13) and of performance.

The lived experience of ballet bodies

Ballet dancing can certainly be liberating but ballet bodies are also strained, bleed and can be broken, as there are high rates of pain and injury. Female ballet dancers must be tough and strong. To the spectator the female body is graceful, strong, elegant and objectified in the form of performance in high art entertainment.

> Such dancers radiate a public image of ethereal, unworldly glamor and romance. Witness the ballerina. Barely in contact with all things crassly physical, lightly she skims across the earth on her toes, leaps effortlessly into a space to hover breathlessly, or tarries aloft, borne by an ever-doting cavalier. All the while, unseen musicians, placed symbolically at her feet, emit the glorious sounds that impel her every move.
>
> (Abra 1987/8: 33)

One may ask, if being a ballet dancer is so painful and uncomfortable, why would anyone do it? Are those children and teenagers featured in this chapter really just volunteering and sufficiently aware of what they are doing to and with their bodies? One could ask the same question of any physically challenging and potentially harmful activity and probably of any programme of athlete development.

> Sometimes it's the frustration, anger and pain you feel that keeps you going 'cos you won't give up until you've got something right or perfect. Then you can really perform it and express yourself and feel high and great and proud of yourself and then you relax – until the next time.
>
> (Leah, 13 years)

Perhaps mastery of the discipline of ballet does not necessarily mean rule-bound constraint and lack of identity where the body is seen for public consumption, but greater confidence, freedom to play and express oneself. Certainly the strength, desire and determination portrayed by these dancers, in both body and mind, appear to be motivating. Conceivably, the sense of belonging to a community and relationship to a body of dance knowledge, the pleasure and liberty in moving, the satisfaction, sense of achievement and challenge that only the few succeed and survive as professionals, outweighs or balances the pain.

5 Being 'able' in a performative culture

Physical education's contribution to a healthy interest in sport?

John Evans, Emma Rich, Rachel Allwood and Brian Davies

'Ability' matters

How 'ability' is configured within physical education practices in schools reflects distributions of authority in society, the nature of power and principles of social control. Definitions of 'ability' are neither arbitrary nor immutable, and what counts as success and achievement changes over time. Although 'ability' is always configured in relation to class and gender, these features are often disguised within school cultures attempting to privilege equal opportunities, though historically deeply embedded in education policies and practices. As such, they tend to define the cultural fabric and thinking and action of teachers and pupils. In this discussion we examine the environments created by recent policies relating to PE and health (PEH) and how they influence teachers' and young people's understandings of 'ability'. Such policies increasingly determine dispositions recognised, endorsed and valued as 'ability', or valid forms of 'cultural capital' in PEH.

To illustrate how such processes occur and influence young people's attitudes toward their bodies, physical activity and health, we draw from research which has centred on the lives of some 40 girls and young women (aged 11–18), all of whom have suffered anorexia nervosa and/or bulimia. All are resident at a centre for the treatment of such conditions. We have used a variety of techniques, for example formal and informal interviews, diary keeping, focus groups and mapping techniques, to register their stories about how formal education figured in the development of their disordered behaviours and relationships with their own and others' bodies and physical activity. We have also interviewed teachers who work with them. Only relatively few young people are impelled to take such dramatic action, but they vividly reveal features of contemporary school culture that have been nurtured through recent education and health policy to which all are subject and which generate increasing levels of less dramatic body disaffection and dissatisfaction.

Teachers' and pupils' thinking on 'ability' and 'intelligence' arises from a variety of sources including family life, experience of schooling, initial teacher education and the discourse of policy texts. In the UK in recent years these last have increasingly framed how teachers are expected to think and behave toward pupils in schools, their underlying assumptions having a powerful bearing on how teachers and other responsible adults act toward pupils and how the latter act toward themselves (Evans and Penney 2008; Penney and Hunter 2006; Burrows and Wright 2004). The following analyses invite us to consider who is privileged through such policies and whose interests they reflect and serve. What are the social bases of the criteria which underpin curricular selections in PEH and the rationales which justify and legitimise them? How do these processes relate to the epistemic communities and particular social and political contexts of which they are part? Specifically, we will consider what embodied predispositions, body shapes and forms are recognised and policy privileged as being of value in schools (Evans and Davies 2004). Is there a dominant 'ability', or 'image' of value, such that some students are unable to recognise themselves as having a 'body' or 'self' or 'ability' of any value? What body dispositions are included or excluded by the dominant images of the school? Whose body is seen and heeded? In Bernstein's (2000: xxi) terms:

> A school metaphorically holds up a mirror in which an image is reflected. There may be several images, positive and negative. A school's ideology may be seen as a construction in a mirror through which images are reflected. The question is: who recognises themselves as of value? What other images are excluded by the dominant image of value so that some students are unable to recognise themselves? In the same way, we can ask about the acoustic of the school. Whose voice is heard? Who is speaking? Who is hailed by this voice? For whom is it familiar?

These are important issues because the distribution of knowledge, including that of and about 'the body', is likely to carry unequal value, power and potential. Distribution of material, financial and spatial resources also tends to follow the 'abilities' and images, such that for those with the 'right' image or 'ability' to perform there may be more time, space, opportunity, attention and reward, both emotional and material. As Bernstein pointed out, an unequal distribution of images, knowledge, possibilities and resources is also likely to affect rights of participation, inclusion and individual enhancement of groups of students. As we shall see, PEH teachers' practices are implicated in such processes in which 'success', 'failure' and achievement are produced, defined and rationalised, affecting not only young people's attitudes toward physical activity and sport but also their corporeal and intellectual health. Before addressing these issues empirically, we first consider in more detail how 'ability' is defined in and through contemporary policies of PEH.

P/policy, performativity and accountability: re-configuring 'ability' in physical education and health

The actions of teachers in schools in the UK are increasingly constrained by two forms of P/policy: state- or government-sanctioned Policy (such as the National Curriculum Physical Education – NCPE), which we highlight with an upper-case 'P' to signify that its features and requirements are laid down as, and endorsed through, *legislation*; and what we refer to as institutionally based 'pseudo policy' (represented with lower-case 'p'), state- or government-sanctioned *but non-legislated* initiatives taken by schools themselves (for example, around the sale of certain foodstuffs from vending machines, or the content of school dinners) reflecting frameworks of expectation prescribing how young people and teachers, as well as all others responsible for students in schools, should behave, especially toward issues of 'the body' and health (Evans *et al.* 2008). Together, these P/polices are having significant impact on the nature of teaching and how and what children and young people learn, in terms of not only instructional but regulative features of classroom life, shaping what they learn about their selves, embodied identities and 'abilities'. In the UK, education P/policy has nurtured and endorsed a strong emphasis on 'performativity'; a culture which celebrates competition, comparison and accountability and centres attention on manifest aspects of 'performance' in sport and physical activity and 'corporeal perfection', usually defined as 'the slender ideal', rather than other more holistic educational values and virtues.[1]

Such reforms are not arbitrary but reflect local, national and increasingly global trends and issues, some reactions to concerns over the health of populations in respect of what we now commonly refer to, in the Western (and westernised) worlds, as 'the obesity crisis' or to what others see as the putative capacity of populations to meet the skill and knowledge requirements of a fast changing high-tech world (Hargreaves 2003). Indeed, in the UK, PE teachers, perhaps more than others, have had to operate within what can be best described as a P/policy-saturated context. Their actions have been subject to a great deal of legislation, as well as many initiatives from government departments specifically concerned with education (for example, the Department for Education and Skills) and others concerned with sport (the Department for Culture, Media and Sport) and health (the Department of Health). Policies from each of these, sometimes in the form of joint initiatives, have wrought significant change not only to the content of physical education and rationales for its teaching but also to notions of where PE should occur and who are its stakeholders. Education Policy has increasingly reached out into community interests, creating positions (e.g. 'Sport Coordinators') to manage networks of relationships between providers of sport in and outside schools, as we shall see below. Such changes have been underpinned by a powerful culture of individualism which has celebrated the notion that everyone, irrespective of background, has equal capacity to succeed and 'get on'

in work, sport, leisure and health through the pursuit of excellence, self-im-
provement, individual initiative and personal responsibility, at the expense
of acknowledging how these processes may be conditioned and constrained
by the social and material conditions of people's lives.

The National Curriculum for Physical Education (NCPE) (DfE and WO
1992; revised, DfEE 1999) reflected these pressures and, in certain respects,
represented the most significant changes to have occurred in PE in the UK
for over 40 years. It not only set legal requirements (entitlements for pupils aged 5–16) for what was to be taught in schools in England and Wales
but issued teachers with a new language and, thus, potentially new ways of
thinking about educational purposes and the business of teaching. They were
now to talk and think in terms of 'key stages', 'programmes of study' and
'levels of attainment'. Their attention was to focus on assessment and 'differentiation' of 'performances' of children from a very early age, now even
reaching into the preschool and, thereafter, throughout their school career.
PE was to concentrate on sport performance and identification of 'the gifted
and talented', in a context of 'inclusive education' (defined as 'providing
opportunities for all pupils'; DfEE 1999: 28), signalling an intended radical
departure from established practice. Initially, in certain respects, introduction of the NCPE reflected no more than a gradual shift from 'education
through physical activity' (though never a consensus philosophy in the UK)
to 'education in and through sport'. A strong commitment to games teaching
(sport) has been not only retained but privileged in National Curriculum
(NC) legislation, specifically in terms of the time to be afforded to games in
schools. Subsequent P/policy has consolidated this emphasis, for example,
through initiatives designed to focus attention on, and raise the level and
quality of, participation in sport both in schools and in the wider community.
For example, in October 2002 the UK Prime Minister launched the National
PE, School Sport and Club Links Strategy, announcing that the government
would be investing £978m, plus £686m lottery funding between 2003–4
and 2007–8, a total of £1.5 billion, in its delivery (teachernet 2006: 1). This
initiative, typical of P/policy in recent years, not only further defined the
orientation of physical education toward sport but also altered the structure
of provision of PE, weakening boundary relationships between primary and
secondary schools and between schools and community sport. Emphasis on
high-level performance, talent identification and participation was not to be
confined to secondary schools but to extend into primary school practice
and coaching in community sport. Such changes have been officially justified
in terms of their direct contribution both to elite performance and participation and, as a by-product, to young people's health. Although few would
contest that such investment has enhanced the rather insecure place of PE in
the school curriculum, what is of interest here is the way in which these and
subsequent P/policy initiatives have been configured within a wider discourse
of individualism and 'performativity' in UK schools and its implications for
how teachers perceive 'ability'.

Whereas recent education P/policy change in other countries has endeavoured to *reduce* pressures on teachers and students in schools (for example, see Kakuchi 2006), in the UK, the National Curriculum and associated assessment measures have reflected much narrower political ideals which have intensified pressures on teachers and students. Testing and assessment are now routine features of life for students throughout their school careers. For example, National Curriculum SATs (Statutory Assessment Tests) ensure in England that at the end of Key Stage 1 (age 7) a child will sit national tests in English and Maths, and at the end of Key Stage 2 (age 11) and Key Stage 3 (age 14) in English, Maths and Science. They will then sit public examinations at 16 and, if they stay on at school past the minimum leaving age of 16, again at 17 and 18, making children in England amongst the most nationally tested and assessed in the world. The ever-increasing number of exams and tests which pupils take and the distortion of educational practice caused by pressure on schools to do well in league tables means that some in education feel that many young people are being 'tested to destruction' (Professional Association of Teachers 2000). Furthermore, systems of accountability, largely through inspection by the central government's official agency, Ofsted (Office for Standards in Education, Estyn in Wales), have been put in place to ensure that these processes occur and schools in England can be placed/positioned in 'league tables' according to their 'performance' at effecting test or examination success.

Although SAT testing does not occur in PE, differentiation according to 'levels of attainment' set out in the NCPE is now a routine feature of its culture and practice, bringing pressure to define the purposes and success of the subject, its teachers and students, in terms of either NC performance outcomes or high levels of performance and participation in school and community sport. Indeed, we might look upon the search for the 'gifted and talented' as the high water mark of performative culture within PE, fuelled by a less than subtle, even fatuous notion that such measures are needed to correct the putative mediocrity and 'dull uniformity' of 'bog standard' state comprehensive schools. We are pressed to assume that pupils would be better off in schools designated as having 'specialist' subject (including PE) status. As Benn (1982: 52) pointed out, however, the giftedness movement 'put itself forward as an antidote to a disease no one had yet caught', for there was little, if any, evidence to suggest that the 'gifted' were being ignored or disadvantaged in PE or any other subject area in state schools. Having 'created a demand for itself', it went on to involve us all in 'trying to define the nature and extent of the problem of giftedness'. Recent changes to health policy in schools in the UK now also reflect this wider culture of instrumentality and performativity, since 2005 monitored as part of school accountability by Ofsted inspections of 'healthy school programmes' and to be reinforced by the introduction of measures, such as annual body mass index (BMI) 'weight' checks, a scheme piloted in 2006.

It is difficult here to convey either just how powerful and pervasive this culture of 'performativity' in UK schools is or articulate how severe the pressure is that it imposes on teachers and students as it regulates their work. Teachers and pupils are both constrained within this culture and constructed as 'able' performers or otherwise through its demands. They are constantly assessed, asked to strive for better grades and reach 'gold standards' that, no sooner achieved, are likely to be denigrated or changed. Though they are not without power, children and young people are less able than adults/teachers to resist or contest the intensified conditions of their work, modify or challenge conditions of schooling that may damage their academic well-being and general health. Although the value of 'competition' within education has long been subject to debate, what concerns us here is the way in which the dominance of these discourses in schools leads to a culture which impacts upon social relations among teachers and pupils, the latter becoming valued for their productivity or performance alone. These texts play their part, as Ball (2004) put it, in 'making us up'; they produce new modes of description of ability and achievement and new possibilities for action and despair. Authentic relationships between teachers and pupils are replaced by judgmental relationships engendering feelings of alienation as individuals are constantly required to make themselves different and 'distinct' through 'the micro practices of representation', judgment and comparison (Evans *et al.* 2004).

Whereas some have been tempted to read 'performativity' in PEH simply as further expression of 'hegemonic masculinity' (Connell 1995), crudely stated a dominant/dominating 'male culture' celebrating competition, hierarchy, a technicist view of the body as an object to be worked on and implicitly benefiting boys and men, our intention is to move beyond viewing performativity merely through a crude male/female lens. If nothing else we need consider not only how the 'abilities' of boys and girls are differently configured, recognised and (dis)advantaged in performative culture but also the subtleties of processes as to how gendered individuals fare in virtue of culture and class. What little research evidence we have suggests that levels of participation in school sport are more or less 'equitable' in gender terms; we are now less likely to find sexist and differentiated practices, for example boys doing soccer and girls netball, of a magnitude such that once defined and blighted the PE curriculum in the UK and elsewhere. Yet we do know that a good many children and young people disengage from physical activity before they leave compulsory schooling and even more once they leave it. In addition a growing body of literature suggests that vast numbers of young people leave school thoroughly disaffected with their bodies. Class and gendered patterns of participation and health stubbornly refuse to go away, despite surface progress in schools, not least because young people feel they do not have the skills or aptitudes to engage in physical activity or because they feel they do not have the correct embodied dispositions, especially size, shape and demeanour, to display them appropriately. Schools do not determine opportunities for leisure and health – individuals' class positions and relations to the nature of paid and unpaid employment are contenders for being even more powerful prime movers in doing that in the UK – any more than teachers set out to alienate pupils from engagement in physical activity and sport. However, as we shall see next, in trading on notions of body perfection within a culture of performativity, schools do strongly influence whether or not individuals are likely to engage with and derive pleasure from either or both.

Health P/policies in a performative culture

Education Policies are not the only and, perhaps, not even the most important influences currently acting upon PE in schools. In recent years governments in the UK, as in many other countries, have increasingly felt the need to respond to growing concerns about the health of the population, in particular, to what is purported to be an increasing risk to health from poor diets, lack of exercise and sedentary lifestyles. Together, these are believed to be generating an 'obesity epidemic' to which children in particular are deemed to be at risk. As a result, barely a day passes in the UK without the population being told that it is overweight or obese and that measures (diets, exercise regimes) ought to be taken. Authoritative international voices, such as that of the World Health Organization (WHO 1998), corporate voices in the UK, such as the British Nutritional Foundation and its Obesity Task Force, and charities, such as the British Heart Foundation, have been co-opted increasingly as spokespersons for government thinking on measures to be taken to improve the nation's health. Unlike education Policies, such as a National Curriculum, the recommendations of such agencies rarely enter schools directly but, rather, indirectly through popular media (TV, press coverage; e.g. *Daily Mirror* 2004) before entering the school system formally as Policy (see below) and/or informally as frameworks of expectation forming pressure to regulate behaviours around lifestyle, diet and food. This remains a powerful rhetoric driving the 'rationale' for PE within the UK curriculum for, even though 'Health' is not part of its nomenclature and there is only relatively incidental reference to health education in the NCPE, most teachers would now rationalise its provision and emphasis on sport in the curriculum with reference to their capacity to help resolve health concerns, invoking unproblematically the equation more sport = more health.

Although such concerns may be justified and important, they have, we suggest, become inescapably 'linked to the incipient madness of the requirements of performativity' earlier described (Ball 2004: 147) in a discourse in which complex health issues have been reduced to focus on weight, diet and exercise and individuals' responsibility to exercise and become thin. Health, it seems, is now relevant only in so far as it can be measured and evidenced in schools' capacity to ensure that students (and their guardians) achieve specific things (weight loss, proper diets and exercise regimes). Such concerns are driven by what might be described as 'new health imperatives' which prescribe the lifestyle choices that young people should make, particularly in relation to physical activity and diet. These imperatives are strongly embedded in a number of fields, including consumer culture, health education, the biosciences and the policy documentation of health organisations. Furthermore, they share a number of distinctive features which separate them from other health discourses. Firstly, reflecting a culture of individualism, as earlier described, health imperatives around 'eating well', exercising regularly and monitoring our bodies carry powerful moral as well as educational overtones and, as such, are very difficult to resist or contest. Young people, teachers and their guardians are implicitly held personally responsible and accountable for their own health, particularly prevention of obesity and certain associated conditions (e.g. diabetes) by knowing and avoiding relevant 'risk' factors. Secondly, these imperatives do not treat health holistically, that is to say as being subject to social, political and physical contingencies, but are perceived reductively as strongly associated with body size and appearance, such that the thin or slender body is taken to represent not only a state of 'good health' but also an outward sign of self-control, virtue and being a 'good citizen'.

These imperatives are a powerful force, driving major P/policy initiatives on health and education in a number of countries in the Western world. In the UK, as elsewhere, flooding schools with P/policy initiatives geared towards helping children and young people lose weight, become more active and change their eating patterns has made it hardly surprising that teachers take for granted that these imperatives are both unproblematic and inherently a 'good thing', given that they are supported by significant government investment. Reflecting this, in the UK, a public service agreement (PSA) target has been established,[2] which seeks to halt the year-on-year rise in obesity among children under the age of 11 by 2010. Part of the agreement includes arrangements already referred to for children to have their body mass index (BMI) measured annually in schools, with subsequent 'advice on lifestyle' given to those deemed 'at risk'. From 2006, primary school children will be weighed and measured (using the BMI) at ages 4 and 10 and their parents told if they are 'obese'. Equally, non-legislative policy interventions, such as those in the UK by the celebrity chef Jamie Oliver, have pressed schools to respond in particular ways (improving lunchtime menus, altering vending machine offerings) in an effort to regulate young peoples' bodies and health and are now being turned into legal requirements. Large sums of money invested by governments in efforts to reduce assumed escalating rates of childhood obesity and associated ill health are far from confined to the UK. For example, in 2004 the Australian Prime Minister, John Howard, announced that his government would spend $116 million over four years on addressing declining activity and poor eating habits among children through both official educational Policy measures and non-legislative initiatives (Lundy and Gillard 2003).

We can here dwell on neither the nature of 'obesity discourse' nor the merits of the measurement tools (particularly the BMI) or statistical techniques used to define and describe children's 'health' (Evans 2003; Gard 2004a,b; Gard and Wright 2005). But we do need to acknowledge that a growing body of research increasingly points toward the problematic nature of both the tools and the science which feeds this discourse and has highlighted both the uncertainty and the fragility of the claims made within the knowledge base from which health initiatives are being developed (see Rich *et al.* 2004; Monaghan 2005; Aphramor 2005; Gard and Wright 2001, 2005). Considerable investment has been made in development and dissemination of policies and programmes associated with new health imperatives. Thus far, however, the main interest of governments and researchers has been in determining 'measurable outcomes', that is changes in lifestyle practices, specifically physical activity participation and food choices. Such an approach assumes a simple relationship between knowledge/awareness and improved behaviour, while research across a range of fields and disciplines has documented that those between weight, diet, physical activity and health are far more complex and uncertain than is currently suggested within public health discourse and associated policy (Biddle *et al.* 2004; Evans 2003; Gard and Wright 2005). It is, therefore, unsurprising that P/policy interventions show 'disappointing' outcomes in terms of subsequent physical activity (European Youth Heart Study 2006).

Despite these uncertainties, schools in the UK and elsewhere are being pressed to respond to the notion of an 'obesity crisis' with certainty and in quite distinct ways. P/policy initiatives reach into and regulate both the 'formal' curriculum (e.g. warranting a greater emphasis on health education in PE) and the 'informal' environments of schools, for example individual and peer group student activity during playtimes, lunch breaks and in corridors (e.g. around the purchase of foodstuffs and drinks from vending machines). As others have noted (Burrows and Wright 2004), these new health imperatives are legitimising actions in schools, related to the control and regulation of young people, which in other social contexts would not be considered permissible or 'just'.

Performative health policy

Until recently, in the UK 'health education' has largely been taught either outside PE (for example, in personal, social and health education) or incidentally within PE, a context orientated powerfully towards competition and sport (Penney and Chandler 2000). As governments have responded to pressure to confront 'the obesity epidemic', health has come to be considered a 'whole school issue' (DfES/DH 2005), the responsibility of all concerned with the education and well-being of young people, across a variety of sites. For example, in 1999 the government launched the National Healthy Schools Programme along with National Healthy School Status (NHSS) as vehicles to support delivery of personal, social and health education (PSHE), in our initial 1988 National Curriculum a 'cross-curricular theme', now rehabilitated as a curriculum 'subject' in secondary schools (DfES/DH 2005). Initially this programme gave priority to improving health in 'the most disadvantaged areas', though government has since stated that it expects that 'half of all schools will be "healthy schools" by 2006, with the rest working towards healthy status by 2009' (DH 2006: 1) and 'new guidance' was issued in 2005 to bring 'a more rigorous approach to the programme' (DfES/DH 2005: 1). Since September 2005 schools have had to meet a range of criteria in four core themes (see below) to satisfy the requirements of National Healthy School Status (NHSS). What is important here, however, is that this initiative clearly is couched in a language of performativity; schools are now required to provide visible 'evidence' in the core themes of PSHE, healthy eating, physical activity and emotional health and well-being, 'using a whole school approach involving the whole school community' (ibid.: 4). It is hoped that schools will be able to work at one of three levels. At level 3 (the highest) schools will have demonstrated 'a more intensive level of involvement by having undertaken a process of auditing, target setting and action planning'. Again, a language of performativity pervades this text as it continues:

> The impact of activities is assessed through school monitoring and evaluation, with a particular focus on pupils' learning outcomes [. . .] in order to achieve national consistency at level 3, schools are expected to fulfil specific criteria drawn from the NHSS and have evidence of the impact of development work for each criterion. This requirement is in line with current practice in schools where evidence is collected for celebration of success through the local healthy schools programme. The national evaluation of the NHSS, which is under way, will build on these criteria to provide more refined indicators for the future.
>
> (teachernet 2006:1)

A school might achieve level 3 involvement when there is a range of 'evidence of impact', demonstrating that all criteria have been met.

This culture not only pervades activities across many sites inside schools but reaches across the sector. It is reported that 'since the final rounds of accreditation were attained in April 2002, Local Education Authority Participation in the NHSS programme has reached 100 per cent'. In effect:

> over 14,000 schools are taking part in the healthy schools scheme at level 2 and 8,000 are working intensively at level 3 to achieve the standard. Half of these schools serve deprived areas [. . .] All schools in England with 20 per cent or more free school meal entitlement should be recruited to the programme by 2006.
>
> (teachernet 2006: 2)

We cannot here provide further detail on this policy initiative or document its many criteria but merely highlight its distinctive features. The NHSS represents a coming together of health and educational concerns and associated P/policy agencies and agents so as to effectively accommodate health discourse in education discourse, configuring and subsuming (or is it consuming?) it in the latter's powerful logic of 'performativity'. In the process there is a conflation of what we have elsewhere described as 'performative' and 'perfection codes' (Evans and Davies 2004), so that work on 'the body' is now perceived in much the same way as any other academic work in schools: as something to be managed, regulated, measured and weighed to provide evidence of meeting specified behavioural ideals. For example, in order to achieve healthy school status in 'healthy eating' a school has to meet six criteria including involving:

> pupils and parents in guiding food policy and practice within the school [. . .] and ensuring healthier food and drink options are available and promoted in breakfast clubs, at breaks and at lunchtimes
>
> (DfES/DH 2005: 7)

and providing evidence that 'conversations with pupils, teachers, parents/ carers and professionals about how Healthy Schools work has had an effect' (ibid.: 11) while more generally aiming 'to develop an ethos and environment that supports learning and promotes the health and well being of all' (ibid.: 5).

Together, these and other far-reaching criteria for action and 'success' create unprecedented levels of surveillance of students' and teachers' behaviour across almost every aspect of school life, in classrooms and corridors, including lunchtimes and playtimes, as well as reaching into and regulating behaviours in communities and homes. In effect, every school is now required to become, adapting Bernstein's (2001) concept, a 'totally pedagogised microsociety' (TPMS) in which health is everyone's concern, everywhere. And, though criteria for success are many and varied, health is reduced essentially to that which can be measured, so that weight, exercise and diet become 'gold standards' by which 'successful health' is defined. Indeed, it has recently been mooted that a school's success should be defined and measured by Ofsted in terms of not just its academic performance but how well it has reduced the 'collective waistline' of its student population as measured on BMI scales. In a performative culture, it seems one needs to possess not only the right physical skills to perform successfully in physical activity but the correct weight and shape.

Our point here is that these systems of regulation and control become ubiquitous when expressed within a 'totally pedagogised society' (Bernstein 2001) in which methods of evaluating, monitoring and surveying the body are encouraged across a range of contemporary cultural practices and there is convergence of pedagogies, not only in schools but in popular media (Burrows 2005), new technologies (e.g. the internet (Miah and Rich 2007) and health organisations. As Burrows and Wright (2006) suggest, in effect, across all of these sites, children and young people are being offered a number of ways to *understand* and *change* themselves and *take action* to change others and their environments. Self-assessment and self-monitoring become key aspects of these emerging pedagogies (Burrows and Wright 2006), which become means either to subjugate/control or to liberate populations via construction and definition of body forms, shapes, sizes and dispositions. In the totally pedagogised micro societies which schools have become, teachers' practices are thus constituted and encoded by this culture of performativity and bio-power that defines what the 'good' professional and 'good' student should be in contemporary schools. Particular notions of 'body perfection' (Evans and Davies 2004) are thus generated in which 'weightism' – a 'prejudice about people of heavier weight and about body fat' (Steiner-Adair and Vorenburg 1999, quoted in Piran 2004: 4) – may feature prominently. This particular prejudice can have as serious, damaging consequence for individuals' lives as those related to race, sex or social class, particularly when impacting upon social and economic opportunities and individuals' sense of value, dignity, wealth and health (Piran 2004).

Being 'able' in a de-formative culture

Performance and perfection pedagogies do not, however, impact upon the lives of young people independently but intersect, creating a culture which ensures that some pupils are privileged and derive pleasure from physical activity while others cannot, and are alienated, not just from it but from their own bodies. In effect, new hierarchies of the body are created as, by virtue of their own class and culture, children differently perform or display 'ability' or willingness to subscribe to the culture and values of performativity and its requirements. Children come to physical education deeply socialised into particular ways of seeing and doing physical activities, with images already worked out about what is appropriate for their respective genders and classes and cultures. Years of socialisation, differential resourcing and practice have also differently predisposed them with skills and abilities necessary for competent performance in particular activities. Armed with this social and cultural 'habitus', a deeply sedimented package of physical as well as social attitudes, skills and competences, teachers and pupils enter into pedagogical processes. A cycle of social and cultural reproduction is thus set in motion which recognises, sieves and sorts skills, shapes and demeanours through actions authorised in the putative interests of health and/or excellence in sport. Thus, although boys and girls may enjoy equal access or opportunity with respect of activities they will be differently resourced socially, emotionally and physically to access them by virtue of their culture and class, not just in terms of skills but lifestyle (including diets and exercise regimes) to achieve the correct corporeality (weights, shapes, demeanours) for the display of 'ability' now required in schools. As one of the girls in our study stated, reflecting sentiments expressed by many others:

I want to be like toned, but I feel flabby [. . .] I never really joined in any clubs of extra-curricular activities because I wasn't very confident and I felt I'd be really bad at anything I tried. I did join in the sports clubs because I liked the exercise. [. . .] Because like even though I felt really fat I knew I was skinny. I was really skinny but I felt really fat but, now I just know I'm like normal so I really hate PE and like everything about PE is just really awful, and like swimming, it's not that bad because you're in the water and everything but I hate like having nothing to wear apart form the costume.

(Vicky)

Of course, not all children hold such negative attitudes toward PEH, nor are such assessments of it always deserved. But what such views indicate is the ways in which a discourse of health shapes how 'abilities' are recognised and celebrated within PE and sport. Wider social understandings of the nature of 'ability' within sport and physical activity connect strongly with these new health imperatives, where 'ability' is read by both teachers and pupils not simply via the skilled 'performance' of the body but via the *physicality* of the body, its size, shape and form:

Well, not really but in PE a lot of girls were like self-conscious . . . when were getting changed and stuff . . . and like people who are good at sports are like the ones who are all like slim and . . . can run and they . . . I think a lot of girls were a bit put out by PE as well.

(Kate) (note: . . . indicates pause)

Just as those girls who were seen to be 'able' were 'thin' and, therefore, seen as 'healthy' within the context of these new health imperatives (exercise = improved performance and weight loss), so they worked to define those girls who were not 'able', therefore, not 'healthy':

I wanted to do exercise 'cos I liked exercise but then I thought everyone would think I was like lazy 'cos I'm not very good at it.

(Jane)

Here a discourse of 'ability' was intimately bound up with the way in which it was perceived or read. 'Ability' is not ring-fenced as 'skilled' sports performance but viewed as an inherent feature of whether someone is 'taking responsibility' for their body by repeatedly engaging with physical activity and hence, with practice, would presumably become more 'able'. This may further consolidate discourses associated with performance and techno-scientific views of the bodies which are drawn upon in selecting, labelling and positioning some, rather than others, as 'able'. The body no longer has to simply perform in terms of what it may achieve, how quick, strong and flexible it may be; ability needs to be inscribed *onto* the body, to embody the 'athletic' and 'able'. Health discourse may in this sense be helping to shape both theoretical and wider public constructions of 'performance'. Health discourse recontextualised via sport practices and initiatives and thereby as a feature of physical education may come to shape the social construction of 'ability' and the ways in which particular knowledges of the body are transmitted and 'received' within its pedagogical practices and the cultures of which they are part.

Being 'able' in these contexts achieves narrow meaning and may fundamentally change physical activity experience itself, inhibiting children's opportunity either to display *various* physicalities or participate in particular activities. Opportunity to explore sport and physical activity in what Pronger (2002: 273) refers to as alternative spaces that represent the body's potential for 'transcendence', as in the feeling of *freedom* one has while swimming, running or cycling, or in other pursuits that allow us to throw our bodies through space and time with some amount of skill, may, thus, be diminished as health imperatives press young people towards increasing modes of performance and away from emphasising creativity, diversity, exploration and the joy of movement (Miah and Rich 2007). As Susie recalled of physical education, 'I thought "oh yeah, this is really good for burning 'cos we did circuit training"'.

No longer is physical activity and associated 'ability' a means of discovering the pleasure of movement but, rather, a mechanism for fulfilling the requirements of health imperatives. Although these emerging (re)constructions of 'ability' impinge upon all young people they may be particularly damaging for young women. The relationship drawn between the body, thinness and the values espoused through obesity discourse asks them to constantly scrutinise their own and others' bodies in terms of their sizes, shapes, detail and form:

> Yeah, and I hated doing PE cus you had like shorts and a T shirt on.
>
> (Vicky)

> If you've been out all day for a lesson then you're gonna have communal showers and that just puts more emphasis on everyone like looking at each other . . . or like communal changing rooms, I just think that's terrible.
>
> (Rebekah)

Students thus get to know their bodies, their 'illness' and 'health' through the language of performativity, and some are deeply affected psychologically in the process. They cannot escape 'body perfection codes', structures of meaning defining what body size, shape, predisposition and demeanour are and ought to be and how, if not meeting these ideals, they should be treated, repaired and restored:

She [teacher] picked out this girl who was literally like this thick [pointing to a pole in the room] and she said 'now this looks like a girl who is the right weight'. That really upset me because I just thought I have to get [my weight] down quick, so yeah that probably had a big effect on me.

(Lydia)

It had been nigh impossible for these young people to either escape or avoid the normalising effects of obesity/health discourse. There were constant pressures to evaluate and judge their bodies against unattainable social ideals and of being routinely evaluated, judged and on display. Consequently, particular body shapes were recognised as being of high status and value so that some were unable to recognise themselves as having a body and 'self' of any value at all (see Evans *et al.* 2004). Given the social sanctions that went with this discourse, the bullying, stigma and labelling that young people, especially girls, talk of in association with being defined by their peers as 'fat', it is hardly surprising that we read of rising levels of 'body disaffection' in the population (Grogan 1999) and that some young people take such drastic action to lose weight that they become ill and seriously depressed. For some, pressures to perform 'ability' result in unhealthy drives toward corporeal perfection, whereas others adopt attitudes of apparent apathy and indifference as their preferred strategies, knowing that these corporeal ideals cannot realistically be achieved.

When I'm at home I do loads of exercise 'cos I get really obsessed with it but then I can't like manage the amount of calories to make up for how much exercise I do.

(Jane)

Given the power and biomedical authority of performative culture when constructed in and through health discourse it is hardly surprising, then, that at the same time as we are presented with a stream of data and imagery on 'obesity' and its ill effects, a parallel research literature reports increasing numbers of the population as experiencing significant dissatisfaction with their bodies. Some people are not eating enough, or not at all, and becoming dangerously thin. The very specific consequences of discourses associated with relationships between body shape, eating and exercise has been well documented for some time in the literature on eating disorders (Bordo 1993; Malson 1998; Frost 2001). The Eating Disorders Association UK, for example, cautiously reports that '[U]sing the prevalence figures . . . the combined total for people diagnosed and undiagnosed with an eating disorder in the UK is an astounding 1.15 million' (EDA 2004). A large volume of literature suggests that eating disorders often involve associations of negative body image, fear of fat, and feeling powerless and insecure (Levine and Piran 1999), and have strong risk periods during adolescence. These clinically defined eating disorders are, therefore, categorised as serious psychiatric illnesses, conditions seen to include psychological problems, as well as concerns around dieting, weight and body image.

However, changes in health P/policy do not impact only the vulnerable few who may experience severe eating disorders. Within a totally pedagogised society (and TPMS) health imperatives now reach a much wider spectrum of the population. Indeed, the reported levels of 'body disaffection', especially among women and young and girls, is higher than ever and not just in the UK (Grogan 1999). Many young people are now seen to exhibit disordered forms of eating or weight loss but might not meet all of the strict diagnostic criteria as defined by the *Diagnostic and Statistical Manual of Mental Disorders* (DSM-IV). These behaviours are now being recognised as new conditions of disordered eating, rather than clinically defined eating disorders. These include *orthorexia*, an obsession with eating healthy foods, and *anorexia athletica*, which involves compulsive over-exercising, often alongside restrictions on food intake. Although athletes experiencing these conditions may not experience severe health threats, such as those associated with anorexia or bulimia, they may nonetheless experience psychological distress, body dissatisfaction and problematic relationships with embodied identities and be exposed to health risks (Beals 2000). Evidence is emerging that girls as young as nine are concerned about their weight and restraining their food intake (Burrows and Wright 2006). Similarly, we are seeing an increase in body dissatisfaction and eating disorders amongst young men (Anderson 1995; Cohane and Pope 2001). These are hardly mental states conducive to the further involvement of young people in physical activity in and outside schools. To make matters worse, in a culture of performativity failure to succeed either in gaining good *performance* in sport, or *corporeal perfection* in fitness and health, is likely to be explicated in terms of the individual's lack of 'ability', or as familial, or sectional pathology. Pupils, parents or teachers, rather than curriculum structures, policy content, resources, system failure or government policies on education, become the loci for blame and shame.

Conclusion

We can only speculate whether reductionist conceptions of 'ability', such as those mentioned above, are merely emerging or already endemic in PEH. As we have elsewhere argued (Evans *et al.* 2004), with the fashionable search for the 'athletic gene' endorsing the belief that 'ability' is given at birth and differentially 'fixed' in both quality and form in the identities of women and men, we can only be on our guard against such P/policy developments and tendencies in PEH in schools, Initial Teacher Education PE (ITEPE) and the biological, behavioural and health sciences. We might reasonably ask what potential damage is done to pupils' sense of confidence, competence and embodied selves when subjected to pedagogical and discursive practices which consider 'health' to be an individual responsibility while regarding the 'ability' to achieve it by engaging in appropriate health-promoting physical activities as both fixed and unevenly distributed amongst individuals and social groups. Are parents and guardians differently positioned by virtue of their social class and culture to invest in, nurture, for example, through out-of-school leisure activity and personal coaching and endorse forms of 'physical capital' (Bourdieu 1986) required of children if they are to display 'ability' in schools? Most of the girls referred to above originated from middle-class families and had 'enjoyed' opportunity, resource and, in some cases, sometimes inadvertently, even encouragement to meet the requirements of performativity and perfection, and take them to damaging extremes. Some ultimately subverted them, their embodied actions saying, 'look; now I have no body, now see and treat me as a person, for who I really am'. Most from similar backgrounds will not take such radical measures and are likely, at least on the surface, to subscribe to and benefit from their 'ability' to meet performative ideals, even at the expense of enduring body disaffection or dissatisfaction and damaging levels of examination anxiety and stress. Others, including the 40 per cent of predominantly working-class children exiting state schooling at 16 with few or any qualifications to their name, may have neither cultural resources in terms of lifestyle diets, incomes and exercise opportunities nor the desire to meet these damaging ideals. They, along with those who may seek a more holistic attitude toward the body's education (Zaman 1998), may reasonably assume that formal education as currently configured and what PE represents within it is not meant for them.

Deconstructing categories of 'ability', 'success' and 'failure' endorsed in P/policy and largely taken for granted in education and PEH may help reveal their socio-cultural and economic origins, enabling us to see more clearly some potential consequences of our curricular and pedagogical actions for pupil learning opportunities and identities. We need to pursue the relationships between these phenomena and socio-cultural and economic interests, hierarchies and ideologies prevailing both in wider school settings and outside society, exploring issues of whose voice and values matter and where power, authority and control are located. Unsurprisingly these questions may seem nihilistic and damaging to conventional ways of understanding education, especially to those with vested interests in sustaining an inequitable status quo. All educational realities, categories and subjects stand in need of exploration; the task is to do so through asking which persons, interest groups and processes are sustained by which forms of knowledge, discourse and organisation, status and identity in schools and PEH.

6 Gender and secondary school National Curriculum Physical Education

Change alongside continuity

Ken Green, Andy Smith, Miranda Thurston and Kevin Lamb

Introduction

Measured in terms of organisation and content, PE is the most sex-differentiated and stereotyped subject on the school curriculum, particularly at secondary level. Although it purports to be a single subject, PE contains two distinct sex[1] (or, rather, gender) subcultures. This is unsurprising given that contemporary PE is built on a history of sex segregation: distinct male and female traditions expressed in quasi-separate boys' and girls' departments, teaching differing activities to sex-specific teaching groups and holding, by degrees, differing perceptions regarding suitable content and teaching methods.

Despite the introduction in 1992 of the National Curriculum for Physical Education (NCPE) in England and Wales – establishing the principle of an equal opportunity to access a 'broad and balanced' PE curriculum as a statutory entitlement for all pupils – traditional gender-differentiated patterns of provision remain largely unaltered (Evans *et al.* 1996; Flintoff and Scraton 2005; Kirk 1992; Scraton 1992, 1993). In this regard, contemporary PE appears little more than a continuation of customs and practices shaped into conventions over the course of the century or more history of PE (Fletcher 1984, 1987; Flintoff and Scraton 2006; Kirk, 1992, 2005a; Scraton, 1992).

Persistent criticism of the traditional multi-sport-based approach to organising NCPE (see, for example, Flintoff 2005; Kirk 2005a,b; MacPhail *et al.* 2003; Penney and Chandler 2000; Penney and Harris 1997) has, in part, been predicated on the perceived relationship between the gendered nature of NCPE and young people's (especially young women's) supposedly declining levels of participation in sport and physical activity. But to what extent are the levels of participation and, for that matter, the number and range of activities undertaken in the contemporary NCPE differentiated according to gender? In order to answer this question, this chapter draws upon data from large-scale surveys of participation among 11- to 16-year-olds in England and Wales (SCW 2003; Sport England 2003), as well as the findings of a recent study of 1,010 15- to 16-year-olds attending seven secondary schools in the north-west of England and north-east of Wales (Smith *et al.* 2007).

Levels of participation in NCPE

An abundance of research over the last three decades has greatly enhanced our understanding of young people's involvement in PE and sport. The picture emerging from research into patterns of participation as well as young people's experiences of PE and sport can often appear complex, not to say contradictory. It has, for example, been amply demonstrated in Britain (see, for example, Biddle *et al.* 2005; Cox *et al.* 2006; Flintoff and Scraton 2001; Hargreaves 1994; O'Donovan and Kay 2005, 2006; Scraton 1992; Sport England 2003), the USA (Wallhead and Buckworth 2004) and Europe (Brettschneider and Naul 2004; Pfister and Reeg 2006) that girls' participation in leisure sport and, albeit to a lesser extent, PE declines quite sharply during adolescence. This decline appears most marked in the upper secondary school years and a good deal more substantial for girls than for boys of the same age. Reporting upon the national project Girls in Sport – a project aimed at increasing girls' participation in sport and PE in England – O'Donovan and Kay (2005, 2006) highlighted the persistence of relatively low levels of participation in sport among girls and their associated reluctance towards physical activity. Sport England's (2003) typology of young people in relation to sport identified four main types: 'sporty types' (those who enjoy sport: 25 per cent of 5- to 16-year-olds); those with 'untapped potential' (who like sport: 37 per cent); the 'unadventurous' (who do not mind sport: 14 per cent) and 'reluctant participants' (who actively dislike sport: 24 per cent). It was noticeable that young females were disproportionately over-represented among those with 'untapped potential', and 11- to 14-year-old and 13- to 16-year-old females were to be found in relatively high numbers among the 'unadventurous' and 'reluctant participants' respectively. Indeed, secondary-aged girls were especially prevalent among the 'couch potatoes' – a sub-category of the 'reluctant' group – who disliked sport intensely.

Nevertheless – and notwithstanding the fact that, for some observers, reports of a growth of participation are exaggerated – a good deal of research into young people's (particularly girls') participation reveals a trend towards substantially greater participation in PE (in terms of numbers participating, frequency of participation and time spent on activities) than is often thought to be the case (Coalter 2004; Flintoff and Scraton 2001, 2005; Flintoff 2005; Green *et al.* 2005; Smith *et al.* 2004). The findings of large-scale studies of participation in PE conducted in England and Wales (SCW 2003; Sport England 2003), for example, suggest a trend towards increased participation in sport and physical activity among young people. In particular, these studies indicated that, in 2002, over three-quarters of 6- to 16-year-olds participated frequently (at least ten times in the past year) in sport and physical activity via NCPE (SCW 2003; Sport England 2003). It was also apparent that, whereas there had been a 'small, but notable' (Sport England 2003: 5) increase in the numbers of young people not taking part in sport frequently, in 2002 there were 'fewer young people spending less than one hour, or no time, in a week doing sports and exercise than was the case in 1994' (Sport England 2003: 58).

It was not only the frequency with which young people participated and the time spent doing so which had increased, however. The data from the Sport England (2003) studies pointed to the ways in which PE teachers had, over time, focused more on increasing the range of sports that young people took part in frequently and less upon the number of times they participated in particular sports (Sport England 2003). Indeed, the range of sports and physical activities undertaken during lessons hardly differed between the males and females in secondary schools. Nor, for that matter, were there any sex differences in the proportions playing no sports at least ten times in school lessons or in the proportions playing seven or more sports this frequently (Sport England 2003). In a more recent study of the PE participation of 1,010 15- to 16-year-olds in England and Wales (Smith *et al.* 2007), approximately four-fifths of young people (87 per cent of males; 78 per cent of females) reported participating frequently (defined as at least ten times in the past year) in at least one sport and physical activity in NCPE, with both males and females undertaking an average of three activities frequently in the past 12 months. Confirming the findings of Sport England and the SCW, Smith *et al.*'s (2007) study also indicated that female 15- to 16-year-olds were more likely than males to report participating in various NCPE activities occasionally and to participate in a wider range of activities when doing so, whereas the opposite was true in relation to frequent participation in NCPE. The average number of sport and physical activities in which young males and females in that study reported participating in frequently in NCPE was three and two, respectively (Smith *et al.* 2007).

The kinds of activities undertaken in NCPE

Although there appears to have been an increase in participation among school-aged youngsters in NCPE over the last decade, in particular, males and females were not necessarily participating in the same sports and physical activities (Sport England 2003). Despite the fact that participation rates and forms sometimes differ markedly within as well as between the sexes, secondary school PE remains distinctly gendered. In this regard, NCPE has a tendency to reinforce, more than challenge, existing sex-differentiated patterns of provision and participation in sport and physical activity (Colwell 1999; Evans *et al.* 1996; Flintoff and Scraton 2001, 2005; Hargreaves 1994; Kirk 1992; Penney 2002a; Scraton 1992; Waddington *et al.* 1998). As Penney (2002a: 113) has noted, this is particularly so with regard to traditional team games which remains an area of NCPE 'associated with sex-differentiated patterns of provision' in the form of sports stereotypically regarded as exclusively 'male' or 'female'. For example, although males and females were participating more or less equally during NCPE lessons in England in 2002, males played significantly more football, rugby union, cricket and basketball and participated in more multi-gym activities both occasionally and frequently than females (Sport England 2003). The latter, in turn, were more likely to participate in stereotypically female activities, usually in female-only settings, playing significantly more netball, hockey, rounders and tennis, and more likely to take part in dance, gymnastics and aerobics classes. Activities such as athletics, swimming, cross-country and badminton, by contrast, tended to be undertaken by roughly the same proportion of both sexes on an occasional and frequent basis (Biddle *et al.* 2005; Cox *et al.* 2006; Flintoff and Scraton 2001, 2005; Sport England 2003).

A similar pattern is discernible in the participatory profiles of males and females in curricular PE in Wales. Here, female participation in particular had significantly increased in a number of sports and physical activities in school PE, prominent amongst which were football, gymnastics, circuit-training, aerobics and athletics. At the same time, there were significant increases in males' participation in activities such as circuit- and weight-training, football, basketball and tennis (SCW 2003). These increases notwithstanding, it remained the case that, although males and females were participating more or less equally in sport and physical activity both occasionally and frequently during PE lessons, as with their counterparts in England, they were not always participating in the same activities. For example, football and rugby as well as cricket were played both occasionally and frequently in lessons by many more males than females, whereas netball, hockey and dance became major participatory activities among females, but were played by far fewer males (SCW 2003). As in England, participation in activities such as athletics, badminton and swimming was unrelated to sex and females were doing as much, and as many, sports and physical activities as males in school lessons, both occasionally and frequently, and were being offered a wide range, encompassing activities played mainly by females and others that were played by both sexes (SCW 2003).

The persistence of sex differences in terms of the kinds of activities in which young people participate within PE lessons was also evident in the participatory profiles demonstrated by the 15- to 16-year-olds in Smith *et al.*'s (2007) study. This was especially so in relation to participation in 'traditional' sports – especially competitive team games – experienced as part of NCPE. Males were more likely to report participating frequently in sports such as football, basketball, cricket and rugby union, whereas females were more likely to report frequent participation in activities such as netball, hockey, dance and aerobics. It was also clear that the largest difference between male (80 per cent) and female (48 per cent) frequent participation was in invasion games, whereas similar proportions of both sexes reported participating in striking games, racket games, outdoor and adventurous activities and athletics and gymnastic activities. Females, however, were much more likely than males to participate frequently in dance, whereas males were more likely to do so in swimming and diving than young women (Smith *et al.* 2007).

Despite the continued sex-differentiated provision characteristic of NCPE, particularly in relation to team games, the findings of several studies reveal that males and females of secondary school age in England and Wales have roughly the same participation rates in those activities that have witnessed the most dramatic increases in participation (particularly, though by no means exclusively, in leisure), namely 'lifestyle activities' (such as swimming, cycling and walking). Lifestyle activities are characterized as individual or small-group activities that are flexible in nature, usually less competitive and tending to be pursued more recreationally than competitive team-based sports (Coalter 1999, 2004). The data from Smith *et al.*'s (2007) study, for example, revealed a number of similarities between males and females in those lifestyle, recreational activities undertaken as part of NCPE. Badminton, for example, was participated in frequently by approximately two-fifths of males and females, and tennis was reported by two in ten young men and women. Frequent participation in other individualized activities such as multi-gym/fitness, circuit-training and squash were all undertaken by similar proportions of males and females (Smith *et al.* 2007).

The data in Smith *et al.*'s (2007) study also provided a further indication of how PE in secondary schools in England and Wales has been characterized by a measure of change alongside continuity. The NCPE participatory profiles of the 15- to 16-year-olds reflected the prevailing tendency for curricular PE to be dominated by games, especially competitive performance-oriented team games. The increase in girls' participation in sport and physical activities within the PE curriculum in Wales has been 'generated by increases in traditional sports as well as activities which promote general health and fitness' (SCW 2003: 4) of the kinds added to PE curricula in recent years. Nevertheless, the data also supported claims that traditional team-games-oriented PE curricula had been supplemented by a broader range of partner and team sports and individualized, lifestyle activities of the kinds that have become central features of young people's leisure-sport lifestyles (Coalter 1999, 2004; Green *et al.* 2005; Roberts 1996a; Smith 2006; Smith *et al.* 2004).

All told, although sport and team games remain a dominant feature of NCPE for a large proportion of pupils, their experiences of the subject have been broadened to include activities from several activity areas (Green *et al.* 2005; Roberts 1996a; Smith *et al.* 2007; SCW 2003; Sport England 2003). The sporting experiences of the 15- to 16 year-olds in Smith *et al.*'s study were also more 'balanced' in terms of the relative proportions of lifestyle, recreational activities (such as swimming, dance, multi-gym and aerobics) and team and other kinds of games and partner sports (such as football, basketball and badminton). In this regard, the renewed emphasis given to sport in schools in general and team games in particular as central aspects of government policy over the last decade or so (DfES/DCMS 2003; DCMS

2000) does not appear to have radically altered a trend under way for several decades; namely, the tendency for secondary school PE teachers to respond to young people's changing sport and leisure styles and preferences, providing what they view as 'sport for all' alongside competitive sport in PE (Green *et al.* 2005; Roberts 1996a,b; Smith 2006).

School-based differences in participation in NCPE

Many of the existing studies on NCPE participation among young people have been based on nationally representative surveys as well as more locally based studies and have revealed little about the extent to which participation varies between, as well as within, individual schools. Valuable as they have been, these studies have tended to present a partial picture of the levels, forms and patterns of participation among young people in any one school, and have precluded the possibility of exploring institutional differences in terms of the ways in which a school's particular blend of provision might shape young people's participatory profiles. This is particularly surprising for, despite its statutory nature, it was explicitly recognized in the guidelines to implementation that NCPE would not, and could not, be applied in a uniform manner across all schools. It was acknowledged, in effect, that young people – within as well as across schools – not only could but in many cases would experience PE differently (Penney 2002a,b; Penney and Evans 1999). Nonetheless, much of the research to date has tended to be based on the assumption that NCPE would, indeed, vary between schools without providing any empirical evidence to substantiate – or even challenge – that assumption. With this in mind, a recent study by Smith *et al.* (2007) explored the influence of the school setting (see Table 6.1) in shaping the participatory profiles of 15- to 16-year-olds (Smith *et al.* 2007). They noted how, although higher proportions of males were participating frequently in NCPE in all schools compared with females in the same school, these differences ranged from 4 percentage points in School C to 20 percentage points in School D (Table 6.2). However, as Table 6.2 indicates, alongside this pattern of within-school sex differences there were variations between schools. For example, the highest proportion of 15- to 16-year-olds who participated frequently in at least one sport or physical activity in NCPE was found in School G (overall, 92 per cent; males, 97 per cent; females, 88 per cent). The lowest proportions were found in School F overall (73 per cent) and for males (77 per cent) and School D for females (64 per cent). These intra- and inter-school differences meant that, although females were always less likely to participate frequently than males in the same school, females in some schools (for example Schools A, B, C and G) were more likely to participate frequently than males in School F. Inter-school variation was also evident in the proportions of young people who did not take part in any sport or physical activity frequently. For males, this varied from 3 per cent in School G to 24 per cent in School F, and for females the proportion ranged from 14 per cent in School C to 36 per cent in School D (Smith *et al.* 2007).

Table 6.1 Key characteristics of the participating schools in Smith et al.'s (2007) study

School	Single/ mixed-sex	Age of pupils (years)	School type	Specialist status	5A*–C GCSEs (%)[e]	Pupils taking GCSE PE (%)	Religious affiliation	Type of governing	Pupils eligible for free school meals (%)[f]	Index of Multiple Deprivation (IMD) score[g]
A	Mixed	11–16	Comprehensive	None[a]	27	22.5	Non-denominational	Community	41.9	39.64
B	Mixed	11–18	Comprehensive	TC[b]	55	19.2	Non-denominational	Community	19.4	25.32
C	Mixed	11–18	Comprehensive	MCB&E[c]	70	20.2	Non-denominational	Community	4.3	8.65
D	Mixed	11–16	Comprehensive	None	15	13.7	Non-denominational	Community	39.7	44.53
E	Mixed	11–18	Comprehensive	None	66	27.2	Non-denominational	Community	7.4	12.2
F	Mixed	11–18	Comprehensive	SSC[d]	29	89.3	Catholic	Voluntary	31.0	44.56
G	Mixed	11–18	Comprehensive	SSC	70	13.4	Non-denominational	Community	6.3	5.78

Notes
All schools are state funded.
a At the time that the study was conducted, this school was in the process of applying for Specialist Sports College status. The school has since been granted such status.
b Technology college.
c Mathematics, computing, business and enterprise college.
d Specialist sports college.
e Based on the results for academic year 2003/4.
f Based on the total number of pupils on roll for academic year 2003/4.
g Based on 2004 IMD Scores for England (ODPM 2006), with the exception of school E, which is based on Rank of IMD for Wales (National Assembly for Wales 2006).

Table 6.2 Number of sports and physical activities (%) done frequently in National Curriculum Physical Education by sex and school

School	Overall		Males		Females	
	One or more	None	One or more	None	One or more	None
A	82.0	18.0	87.8	12.2	77.1	22.9
B	82.0	18.0	85.9	14.1	79.2	20.8
C	87.5	12.5	89.6	10.4	85.7	14.3
D	75.8	24.2	83.1	16.9	63.9	36.1
E	76.3	23.7	85.4	14.6	68.1	31.9
F	73.3	26.7	76.6	23.4	68.5	31.5
G	92.0	8.0	96.7	3.3	87.6	12.4
Total	86.7	13.3	82.1	17.9	77.6	22.4

Source: Smith *et al.* (2007).

In terms of the average number of sports and physical activities that 15- to 16-year-olds undertook frequently as part of NCPE during the previous year, there were significant variations by school, ranging from an average of 5 in School G to 2.5 in School D ($P < 0.0005$) (Table 6.2). Overall, those 15- to 16-year-olds who attended Schools A, C and G in Smith *et al.*'s (2007) study were significantly more likely ($P < 0.0005$) to participate in a larger number of activities than those in the other schools. For males, however, this applied to those who attended Schools A, B and G ($P < 0.001$), whereas females who attended Schools G and C were significantly more likely to participate frequently in a larger number of activities than those in other schools ($P < 0.001$). The only significant sex-related, intra-school differences observed were for School B, where males participated in a larger number of activities than females ($P < 0.001$) (Table 6.2) (Smith *et al.* 2007).

In addition to these school-related differences in participation, it was also clear that the involvement of 15- to 16-year-olds in different sports and physical activities in NCPE during Years 10 and 11 varied, sometimes substantially, according to the school they attended. As Table 6.3 indicates, those males attending any of the schools were most likely to participate frequently in football, whereas their participation in badminton, basketball, athletics and tennis – the remaining four sports in the top five for the male sample as a whole – differed markedly between schools (Smith *et al.* 2007). For example, males attending School G were almost three times more likely to play badminton frequently than those attending School E and to play tennis than males attending School F. Interestingly, even though it was the fifth most commonly played sport overall, tennis did not appear in the top ten in Schools D and E. Males at School G were four times more likely to participate frequently in athletics than those at School D, whereas those attending School F were three times more likely to play basketball than those attending School E (Smith *et al.* 2007). It was also apparent that males in every school were more likely to have participated in invasion games than any other activity area. However, as Table 6.4 indicates, frequent participation in invasion games varied between schools from 70 per cent in School B to 96 per cent in School G. Further variations in participation by activity area and school were also evident, with males who attended School A being more likely to participate in striking games and dance than those attending any other school, and those at School C more likely to participate frequently in swimming and diving than elsewhere (Smith *et al.* 2007). Similarly, males attending School F were more likely to participate in outdoor and adventurous activities than the others whereas those at School G were more likely to participate in racket games and athletics and gymnastic activities. It was noteworthy, however, that although the variation in frequent participation between schools was quite marked in six of the seven activity areas, invasion games were the only activity area where there were consistent participation rates among males across all schools.

In Smith *et al.*'s (2007) study, the school-related differences in NCPE

Table 6.3 Top ten sports and physical activities participated in frequently by Year 11 males during National Curriculum Physical Education by school (%)

Ranking	Overall	School A	School B	School C	School D	School E	School F	School G
1	Football 71.8	Football 80.5	Football 59.2	Football 63.6	Football 76.3	Football 75.6	Football 63.6	Football 85.6
2	Badminton 40.0	Badminton 39.0	Badminton 47.9	Badminton 41.6	Basketball 30.5	Circuit-training 36.6	Basketball 41.6	Badminton 51.1
3	Basketball 33.4	Tennis 34.1	Table tennis 47.9	Basketball 35.1	Badminton 25.4	Rugby union 22.0	Multi-gym 33.8	Rugby union 51.1
4	Athletics 25.6	Volleyball 34.1	Basketball 46.1	Athletics 31.2	Swimming 25.4	Athletics 18.3	Athletics 31.2	Tennis 48.9
5	Tennis 20.9	Cricket 31.7	Athletics 28.2	Swimming 31.2	Trampolining 18.6	Badminton 18.3	Badminton 27.3	Athletics 42.2
6	Rugby Union 18.1	Basketball 29.3	Cricket 28.2	Volleyball 28.6	Athletics 10.2	Swimming 18.3	Swimming 22.1	Basketball 40.0
7	Cricket 15.9	Trampolining 24.4	Rounders 22.5	Multi-gym 18.2	Running/jogging 10.2	Table tennis 17.1	Gymnastics 18.1	Cricket 28.9
8	Swimming 15.7	Hockey 22.0	Rugby union 22.5	Squash 18.2	Cricket 8.5	Gymnastics 15.9	Cross-country 15.6	Running/jogging 20.0
9	Multi-gym 13.5	Athletics 17.1	Squash 21.1	Running/jogging 16.9	Rounders 8.5	Basketball 14.6	Climbing 14.3	Circuit-training 16.7
10	Running/jogging 13.1	Running/jogging 14.6	Tennis 21.1	Tennis 15.6	Cross-country 5.1	Multi-gym 13.4	Tennis 14.3	Rounders 14.4
Total	497	41	71	77	59	82	77	90

Source: Smith et al. (2007).

Table 6.4 Frequent participation (%) by males in the seven different activity areas by school

Category of activity	Overall	School A	School B	School C	School D	School E	School F	School G
Invasion games	80.1	85.4	70.4	76.6	76.3	82.9	71.4	95.6
Striking games	26.8	48.8	40.8	36.7	11.9	13.4	7.8	24.5
Racquet games	48.1	56.1	63.4	50.6	27.1	35.4	35.1	66.7
Swimming and diving	16.1	14.6	5.6	32.5	25.4	19.5	22.1	2.2
Dance	0.6	24.3	0.0	0.0	5.1	0.0	0.0	0.0
Outdoor and adventurous activities	5.2	4.9	2.8	3.9	0.0	3.7	16.9	0.0
Athletics and gymnastic activities	45.3	46.3	36.6	46.8	10.2	48.8	48.1	53.3
Total	497	41	71	77	59	82	77	90

Source: Smith et al. (2007).

participation were also true for 15- to 16-year-old young women, particularly when the five activities most 'frequently' undertaken activities – badminton, netball, rounders, trampolining and dance – were considered. For example, as Table 6.5 shows, females attending School A were more than twice as likely as those attending School D to play badminton, and those attending School G were three times more likely to play netball and trampoline than those attending School B, and nearly four times more likely to play rounders than in School E. With regard to dance, females attending School B were more likely to participate frequently in this activity than those attending School D, and dance did not appear in the top ten most common NCPE activities reported by young people attending Schools C, E and G (Smith *et al.* 2007). It is also apparent from Table 6.5 that notable variations were also found in females' participation in less common NCPE activities (that is to say, those not within the top ten most common activities for females), with those attending School A, for example, being more likely to participate frequently in volleyball than those attending any other school, and young women attending School B were more likely to engage in table tennis and gymnastics than those elsewhere. Females at School C were more likely to participate frequently in squash than other young women, and those attending School D were more likely to participate in basketball. Females attending School F were more likely to participate in trampolining, climbing and football, and those at School G were more likely to participate frequently in circuit training and running/jogging than young women attending the other schools (Smith *et al.* 2007). In contrast to the school-related differences in males' participation in the activity areas comprising NCPE, the pattern of frequent participation among females was more differentiated across the seven schools and activity areas. It can be seen from Table 6.6, for example, that females attending School G were more likely to participate in invasion games and athletics and gymnastic activities, and females at School F were more likely to participate in swimming and diving and outdoor and adventurous activities than those at other schools. Similarly, those attending School C were more likely to participate frequently in outdoor racket games than those attending any other school, and young women attending School B were more likely to dance than those attending elsewhere. In contrast to males however, the variation in frequent participation in invasion games between schools was particularly marked, with those attending School G being nearly three times as likely to participate frequently in invasion games as the young women attending School B (Smith *et al.* 2007).

Beginning in the early 1970s there was a tendency among PE teachers to offer a broader, more varied sporting and physical activity diet – particularly for older pupils, who were often allowed a degree of choice of activities (or 'options' as they are commonly referred to) – than that currently experienced by young people in schools. To some extent this tendency was curtailed by the advent of NCPE in 1992 and the stipulation of particular activity areas to be covered at each Key Stage of schooling. Nevertheless, despite the

Table 6.5 Top ten sports and physical activities participated in frequently by Year 11 females during National Curriculum Physical Education by school (%)

Ranking	Overall	School A	School B	School C	School D	School E	School F	School G
1	Badminton 38.4	Badminton 50.0	Dance 41.7	Badminton 42.9	Netball 38.9	Netball 40.0	Netball 46.3	Netball 61.9
2	Netball 38.2	Netball 37.5	Badminton 24.0	Rounders 40.7	Trampolining 33.3	Badminton 38.5	Multi-gym 35.2	Rounders 42.3
3	Rounders 23.0	Trampolining 35.4	Netball 18.8	Multi-gym 34.1	Aerobics 27.8	Aerobics 30.0	Swimming 25.9	Trampolining 38.1
4	Trampolining 22.4	Dance 33.3	Tennis 17.7	Tennis 34.1	Badminton 22.2	Hockey 26.4	Trampolining 25.9	Tennis 34.0
5	Dance 20.7	Rounders 27.1	Rounders 17.7	Netball 33.0	Athletics 11.1	Circuit training 18.7	Hockey 16.7	Athletics 27.8
6	Tennis 19.7	Athletics 14.6	Aerobics 16.7	Squash 27.5	Basketball 11.1	Gymnastics 11.0	Dance 14.8	Aerobics 27.8
7	Hockey 18.7	Multi-gym 14.6	Table tennis 15.6	Hockey 26.4	Circuit training 8.3	Rounders 11.0	Tennis 13.0	Circuit Training 26.8
8	Aerobics 17.5	Volleyball 14.6	Gymnastics 14.6	Swimming 25.3	Dance 8.3	Tennis 10.0	Rounders 13.0	Hockey 24.7
9	Athletics 16.6	Tennis 8.3	Trampolining 13.5	Trampolining 24.2	Football 8.3	Swimming 10.0	Climbing 11.1	Running/jogging 19.6
10	Multi-gym 14.2	Running/jogging 8.3	Athletics 12.5	Athletics 23.1	Swimming 8.3	Athletics 7.7	Tennis 11.1	Swimming 14.3
Total	513	48	96	91	36	91	54	97

Source: Smith *et al.* (2007).

Table 6.6 Frequent participation (%) by females in the seven different activity areas by school

Category of activity	Overall	School A	School B	School C	School D	School E	School F	School G
Invasion games	48.3	45.8	26.0	52.7	36.1	48.4	48.1	72.2
Striking games	26.5	37.5	16.7	42.6	7.7	11.0	13.0	45.4
Racquet games	47.0	54.2	46.9	64.8	22.2	42.9	11.1	59.8
Swimming and diving	11.7	6.3	3.1	25.3	8.3	9.9	27.8	2.1
Dance	20.7	33.3	41.7	0.0	8.3	1.1	14.8	39.2
Outdoor and adventurous activities	3.5	10.4	0.0	3.3	0.0	4.4	11.1	0.0
Athletics and gymnastic activities	48.9	47.9	41.7	58.2	47.2	37.4	46.3	60.8
Total	513	48	96	91	36	91	54	97

constraints of NCPE, PE teachers are continuing to provide young people in the later years of secondary schooling with a degree of 'activity choice' in order to increase participation levels in PE (as well as in later life) – by making the subject more enjoyable, leisure-oriented and recreational (Bramham 2003; Flintoff and Scraton 2001; Green 2003; Roberts 1996a,b; Smith 2006; Smith and Parr 2007). The provision of activity choice and more individualized, lifestyle activities at Key Stage 4 tends to be justified by teachers on the grounds that it allows PE to become more recreational, leisure-oriented and enjoyable in a manner is perceived by PE teachers as helping to increase participation rates, particularly in schools in relatively deprived regions (Green 2003). The shift away from skills-oriented forms of PE at Key Stage 3 towards more recreational and leisure-oriented forms of PE at Key Stage 4 is popular with pupils not least because the latter begins to resemble more closely their sporting and leisure lifestyle preferences – in terms of the activities offered, the form in which they are provided, and, more crucially, the provision of opportunities to have fun with friends in a relatively informal setting in school (Bramham 2003; Flintoff and Scraton 2001; Smith 2006; Smith and Parr 2007). The point about activity choice is that, despite its widespread popularity among PE teachers and pupils alike, it continues to be more prevalent for males than females (Flintoff and Scraton 2001; Smith 2006; Smith and Parr 2007) irrespective of the school setting.

Summary

There have evidently been changes over several decades in the diet of sports and physical activities experienced by all young people – and girls in particular – within and beyond school PE. These changes are, in part, attributable to changes to PE provision made by PE teachers in light of their experiences of teaching (and, for that matter, managing) older pupils with changing leisure lifestyles and leisure-sport tastes. This is particularly true for female PE teachers with the main responsibility for a section of the school population – girls – who have a tradition of diminishing engagement with PE and sport.

The NCPE has further constrained PE teachers to introduce young people to a wider range of activity areas and, in many cases, activities themselves than was hitherto the case. Nonetheless, the flexibility built into NCPE – enabling teachers to choose some areas and activities over others – has meant that, in reality, the prevailing tendency to provide young males and females with gender-appropriate sports and physical activities (for example, netball and dance for girls, and football and basketball for boys) has not been fundamentally challenged let alone undermined. This flexibility to NCPE begins to explain why the extent of gender stereotyping to be found in the provision and practice of PE varies within as well as between individual schools. The between-school differences also suggest that further changes to the PE curricular diets and experiences of boys and girls are perfectly feasible. Young people are bound to experience what is offered in the name of PE by their teachers and, although this has undoubtedly changed, there remains a relatively high degree of mismatch between the preferences of the former and what the latter are inclined to provide.

All things considered, neither changes in NCPE since 1992 nor the broadening of PE curricula by teachers have resulted in the displacement of competitive sports or 'traditional' team games. Nonetheless, the implementation of NCPE in England and Wales has involved the introduction of a broader range of newer team and individual games and lifestyle activities within school PE and has occurred alongside rising levels of participation in sport and physical activity both inside and outside schools. Similar proportions of young males and females are now participating in these kinds of activities. Although NCPE may have met with only partial success in breaking down traditional, gender-stereotyped PE provision, the provision of more individualized, less competitive, lifestyle activities may have provided scope for challenging sex-differentiated patterns of participation among males and females (Colwell 1999; Flintoff and Scraton 2001; Smith 2006; Smith *et al.* 2007). To this extent, the NCPE experiences of boys and girls reflect a substantial element of change alongside the evident continuity.

7 Inflexible bodies and minds

Exploring the gendered limits in contemporary sport, physical education and dance

Ian Wellard

Practices should allow for multiple physical identities and multiple ways of being physical as well as challenging narrow and limiting conceptions of gender and the body.

(Garrett 2004b: 236)

Although it is apparent that different masculinities are constructed in a range of social spaces, bodily practices formulated in sport continue to reinforce hegemonic masculinity at the expense of other versions and consequently contribute to gender and bodily based discriminatory practices. At the same time, the pressures which are placed upon young people to accommodate socially prescribed gendered identities prevent the possibility to experience a broader range of 'ways of being' (Hunter 2004).

From a historical perspective, sport has emerged into its current form as both a powerful institution within broader political contexts (Hargreaves 1986) and a social space which continues to be considered male territory (Park 1987; Messner 1992). The prioritisation of hegemonic forms of masculinity results in continued discrimination against women and also those men considered unable to present the appropriate hegemonic displays. During this process it becomes evident that the body, gender and sexuality are central factors in the construction of contemporary understandings of sport.

In contemporary mainstream sport a version of masculinity based on a particular kind of bodily performance continues to prevail (Wellard 2002, 2006a). As such, contemporary sporting practice produces and promotes an environment where displays of traditional masculinity, those which present competitiveness, aggressiveness and toughness, are seen as normal and necessary. It is the perceived understanding of a traditional, 'natural' version of masculinity which dominates sport and continues to hold immense power. Connell (1995) notes that in many schools a version of masculinity championed through competitive sport is hegemonic and, consequently, sporting prowess becomes a test of masculinity. Even those who do not like sport have to negotiate, usually with difficulty, a relationship to it.

Sport also powerfully interacts with discourses of sexuality. The popular understanding of the professional sportsman is one of athleticism, strength, virility and attractiveness. This is promoted as the ideal form of masculinity, not only for men to aspire to, but for women to find attractive. The athlete's image is constructed through a discourse of physical and bodily performance. Most professional sports, particularly football, boxing and rugby, are highly physical, often involving contact with other men and there is generally a practical requirement to be physically strong. Often there are also expectations for exhibitions of hegemonic masculinity, on and off the field, such as excessive drinking and brawling. Sport, therefore, not only provides a site for learning social codes relating to gender but can be considered a prime site in which hegemonic masculinities are made and remade. Consequently, sport is a significant part of a social arena in which, as Butler (1993) would suggest, masculinities and femininities are constructed, learned and structured in relations of domination and subordination.

Through bodily practices individuals achieve an understanding of sport and the wider social world. For Bourdieu (1990b) an important aspect of learning about the social world relates to hexis, which can be considered as forming the style and manner in which actors perform, such as gait, stance or gesture. Hexis presents a social performance of where the individual is located within the habitus. It also demonstrates the importance of the body in Bourdieu's conceptualisation of the habitus. For it is in bodily hexis that the idiosyncratic (the personal) combines with the systematic (the social) and mediates a link between an individual's subjective world and the cultural world into which he or she is born and which she or he shares with others. Thus:

> For Bourdieu, the body is a mnemonic device upon and in which the very basics of culture, the practical taxonomies of the habitus, are imprinted and encoded in a socializing or learning process which commences during early childhood. This differentiation between learning and socialisation is important: the habitus is inculcated as much, if not more, by experience as by explicit teaching.
>
> (Jenkins 1992: 76)

In habitus, power derives from the taken-for-granted aspects of the performances. Socially competent performances are produced through routine, in the sense that the actor's competence is demonstrated in their not necessarily knowing what they are doing. For example, it could be claimed that many men may perform hegemonic masculinity competently, but would not necessarily be able to recognize their actions clearly or describe the concept of masculinity.

Feminist studies (for example Firestone, 1979; Beauvoir 1989; Wolf 1990; Butler 1990, 1993; Segal 1997) have highlighted the problematic nature of masculinity and how certain forms of masculine performance have maintained their cultural dominance. It is also these prevalent forms of masculinity which continue to provide the formula through which men construct an understanding of their bodies and gender identity. Assessing the extent of male bodily practices in the construction of gender is only apparent if we are aware of these dominant forms. For example, Segal (1997) is critical of the dominant versions of masculinity which preside at the expense of women and alternative forms of masculinity. In these, there is a social understanding of 'manhood' which still carries greater symbolic weight than 'womanhood' and one of the problems resulting from this is a constant focus on the divisions or differences between men and women. Constant focus on heterosexual masculinity causes an emphasis on presenting a distinction between male and female behaviour and, in turn, presents to others the accepted version of gender. The use of binary distinctions of gender creates a distorted understanding of what 'being' male or female entails. For example, within sports there is the constant assumption that men are more able to take part than women. Often in this setting, the language used to describe sportsmen is presented as powerful and dominant, whereas for women it is weak and subservient (to men). Consequently, it is suggested that subordinate forms of masculinity have the potential to challenge these taken-for-granted assumptions and also provide the opportunity to expose the inequalities and limitations of positioning heteronormative masculinity as the model form.

Men, in general, still have greater access to cultural prestige and political power than women have, but it is only particular groups of men who occupy positions of power. For Segal (1997), class and race are the chief factors for inequalities between men, but it is gender and sexuality that present the major threat to hegemonic masculinity. The position of power occupied by heterosexual men is justified through a biological determinist understanding of gender based on natural difference. These power relations are continually reinforced through institutional practices such as heterosexual marriage. Consequently, gay men pose a threat in terms of their blurring of these gendered binary distinctions. As such, according to Segal:

> There is nothing at all surprising about homophobia and the reassertion of men's rights and traditional masculinity operating in tandem. Both are a defence of the dominant form of masculinity enshrined in marriage, a 'masculinity' which is – despite its rhetoric – less a state of mind or body, than the various institutionalised routines for preserving men's power over women and over men who deviate from masculine ideals.
>
> (Segal 1997: 158)

Segal analyses masculinity in order to assess the relationships of gender in contemporary society and how constant reinforcing of gender binaries establishes an uneven balance between the sexes. There have been attempts within post-structuralist feminism to move beyond the limitations of these binary distinctions by highlighting ways in which normative assumptions can be disrupted. Butler (1990) does this by focusing more specifically on alternative sexual practices as well as gender.

Butler (1993) describes how normative gender is produced through language and how, in consequence, bodily performances create a social demonstration of normative behaviour. However, rather than being a theatrical performance or reproduction of learnt, existing, set social practices in the interactionist sense (Goffman 1972), these bodily performances constitute a discursive 'act' and thus, according to Butler, power is formed within these acts. For Butler, performance presumes a subject is already at hand or in existence whereas performativity contests the very notion of the subject and has the ability to create meaning. Butler starts with the Foucauldian premise that power works in part through discourse and to produce and destabilize subjects but goes on to contemplate performativity (particularly in speech acts but also through bodily performance, in which she uses the example of drag as a means of highlighting performances where gender is questioned) as the aspect of discourse which has the capacity to produce what it names (Butler 1993: 225). Performativity is based on an expectation of what is considered gendered behaviour. The expectation ends up producing the very phenomenon that it anticipates. Butler also notes that performativity is not a singular act, but a repetition or ritual, which achieves its effects through its naturalisation in the context of a body.

Butler (1997) also draws upon some of the theories of Bourdieu in order to explore further the role of the body. She focuses on how the habitus is formed over time and how this formation produces a belief in the reality of the social field in which it operates. Through this process of formation there is a sense that bodies are being animated by social conventions and in turn reproducing and ritualising these conventions into practices. For Butler, this means that the habitus is both formed and also able to form.

> In this sense, the habitus is formed, but it is also formative: it is in this sense that the bodily habitus constitutes a tacit form of performativity, a citational chain lived and believed at the level of the body. The habitus is not only a site for the reproduction of the belief in the reality of a given social field – a belief by which that field is sustained – but also generates dispositions which "incline" the social subject to act in relative conformity with the ostensibly objective demands of the field.
>
> (Butler 1997: 155)

Butler applies Bourdieu's concept of bodily hexis and doxa in which the notion of the taken-for-granted world located in the doxa corresponds, to an extent, with Butler's interest in normative practices. Both theorists are keen to explain the relevance of ordinary language and the way in which the body is invested more heavily in ordinary or everyday language. However, Butler is critical of Bourdieu in that his suggestion that the individual is coerced into acting into conformity reduces the potential of agency.

Butler (1994: 34) presents the argument that in the case of heterosexuality, or any other dominant form of ideology, crafting or determining a sexual position always involves becoming haunted by what is excluded. A more rigid position and greater reluctance to accommodate alternative forms creates a problem: the stance needs to be defended and invariably becomes hostile to those alternatives. Thus, for her, the greater the binary distinctions which promote social understandings of male and female as separate, opposite gender positions, the greater the intolerance generated through these practices. For Butler, this can be seen in contemporary heteronormative practices and in the way institutional practices shape social understanding of the body. For instance, the social understanding of pregnancy, which is associated with a biological understanding of gender rather than a discursive framework, produces acceptance of it being a feminine space (1994: 33). The same could be applied to sport, which the discursive framework rationalizes as an arena where male physical activity and performance is considered natural in comparison to women's sporting performance. Butler is critical of the discursive framework which positions heterosexual men in a binary opposition to women. The binary also positions gays as opposite to heterosexual men and alongside women. This distinction creates a normative understanding of the heterosexual male as superior to women and gays.

For Butler, transformative possibilities are to be found in queer acts which provide the opportunity to oppose and destabilize normative understandings of gender behaviour. According to her, the concept of performativity is the aspect of discourse which has the capacity to produce what it names. Through repetition and continued citing, in the case of speech acts, this production occurs. Thus, as Butler states, 'performativity is the vehicle through which ontological effects are established' (1994: 33).

In terms of sport, male PE students taking part in dance presents the initial opportunity for what could be (loosely) considered a queer act. This is because the understanding of sport is established within heterosexual discourse where dance is equated with feminine or failed masculinity and, consequently, not considered a part of it. A successful sporting male taking part in dance (who is heterosexual and with sporting capital gained in traditional sports) may provide cause to reconsider broader understandings of sport and gender in the same way that Butler provided 'drag' as an example of a performative queer act. However, as Butler states, the performative only works if it is constantly repeated and recited. Therefore, in terms of a male dance group, any queer acts would have to destabilize the performance of sport and PE as well as gender because the act of men taking part in dance would not necessarily call into question the ontological effects already installed within sport discourse.

In some ways, Connell (1995) provides a stronger theoretical position than those which focus solely on either the individual or discourse as there is the recognition of the role bodies have in social agency and the influence they have in generating and shaping social conduct. For Connell, the body is the central means through which gendered identity is constructed.

Connell attempts to incorporate the role of the biological in the social construction of gender and also applies a sociological reading of the social world where social actors are exposed to the restrictions created by social structures. Connell incorporates the corporeal to cultural definitions of gender in order to demonstrate the socially constructed nature of masculinity and femininity. The body, then, is the starting point through which social definitions of gender can be read and, at the same time, as the individual experience of the living body is recognised there is the potential for a form of agency in the form of practice (Connell 1995: 65).

Consequently, any questions relating to gender construction, sexuality, sporting participation and performance, I argue, need to incorporate the role of the body within these social processes. It is important to stress that, like Connell, I am interpreting the body from within what might broadly be described as the theoretical position of social constructionism. The acknowledgement of the physical body is important as an aspect of a neglected area within this position. However, and equally important, this concept does not in any way embrace biological determinism.

Connell acknowledges a form of complicity among men in his version of hegemonic masculinity, in which, even though only a small percentage of men rigorously practice it, a majority of men still gain from it. They profit from what he calls the 'patriarchal dividend' (Connell 1995: 79) and, as I have agued elsewhere (Wellard 2002, 2006b), many gay men, based upon their ability to perform hegemonic masculinity, are also complicit with this. They are able to gain from the patriarchal dividend to the extent that they can achieve relative success in material terms. However, successful performances of hegemonic masculinity and returns from the patriarchal dividend are achieved at the expense of any momentum in the quest for gender and sexual equality.

Butler is, however, more radical than Connell because she is more determined to dismantle the apparent presumptions based on gender and sexuality and is quick to dismiss notions of naturalness in relation to gender. For her, queering language provides the opportunity to highlight existing assumptions of gender and sexual practice and expose the limitations of heteronormative gender based discourse.

Butler produces some compelling arguments, particularly in relation to the notion of performance and queer acts. Reiterative acts constantly reinforce the normative and maintain understandings of (hetero)normative sexuality. Butler, to an extent, ignores corporeality and individual consciousness, by allowing constructions of gender to be dictated by discursive structures. However, her ideas are important because she employs sexuality as a means to highlight the normative practices found in understandings of gender. For her, homosexuality demonstrates a contrasting performance of accepted gender and with it the idea that alternative sexual practices have the power to destabilize heterosexual hegemony.

The notion that the policing of gender contributes to reinforcing heterosexuality is a valuable argument and gains greater resonance if applied with Connell's description of the circuit of bodily reflexive practices. For it is within this circuit that the policing of the social operates at the same time as the policing of the body.

Physical education and school sport

Within the context of physical education it could be argued that the claims made by post-structuralists of 'fluidity' of gendered identities is markedly restricted and individuals have to quickly learn the importance of presenting appropriate (less fluid) gendered bodily performances (Wellard 2002, 2006a; Paechter 2003a).

It could also be claimed that there are still ways in which many young people are 'excluded' from taking part in traditional sports – and ultimately enjoying their bodies to their full potential. There does, however, remain a risk that simply 'including' an individual suggests that what they are being included in is unproblematic. In merely attempting to 'fit' young people into the existing framework there is little challenge to the notion that the location of 'that which is included' is more superior to 'that which is excluded.' It is generally assumed that the practices which operate in sport are less problematic than the individuals who would like to participate. However, rather than looking at 'problem' children and attempting to make them fit in, it may be worth considering the practices which may 'exclude' an individual in the first place, as well as the 'restrictions' which are placed upon those who are already included.

The process of selection or distinguishing those who are included and those who are excluded is rife in sport as well as PE. As Evans (2004) has already pointed out, talent selection in the UK already separates the 'able' from the less able in order to identify winners and losers. The consequence is that many young people will be excluded not only from the 'pool' of talent, but from taking part in sports in general. There is also an additional irony with this form of filter process, in that even for the 'winners' there is often a pursuit of what could be considered unobtainable goals which are potentially both physically and psychologically damaging (Heikkala 1993). Similarly, Connell (1995) describes how the idealized (or hegemonic) version of masculinity which is represented by the elite, traditional sports competitor is often the most insular and the least socially adept. More worrying, is the trend, identified by Miah and Rich (2006) to focus upon 'natural' ability, justified through genetic testing, which in turn has severe implications for PE. According to them, within schools, there is the potential 'for these sciences to create "regimes of truth" around the body' (2006: 269) which ultimately creates a hierarchy based upon those who can and those who cannot.

Miah and Rich apply Feinberg's (1980/1992) concept of an 'open future' and argue that contemporary scientific practices are ultimately violating a child's right to an unrestricted future. Another way of looking at the restrictions placed upon young people as they attempt to fully experience their bodies is by applying the concept of what is limited within a system. For instance, Pronger (2002), drawing upon the legal feminist scholar Drucilla Cornell's (1992) 'philosophy of limit' (which itself is a version of desconstructionism aimed at acknowledging materialialist critiques), describes the potential, or 'puissance' (Pronger 2002: 66), to be found in bodily pleasures that exist 'outside' the boundaries of conventional thinking – potential which, it could be claimed, is kept restrained by the barriers, often self-imposed, created through attempts to conform to perceived social expectations of normative gendered identity. For both Cornell and Pronger, questioning limits has been central to the work of activist movements, although, in comparison to other social institutions, sport and PE could be considered to have remained relatively unscathed by activist challenge.

Boys, men and dance

In the UK, traditional sports still provide the model for PE provision within schools (Kirk 2002) and through this (and broader definitions provided through the media and professional sport) it could be claimed that particular 'gendered' patterns are reinforced. However, there are instances when established gender patterns may be contested. The location of dance within physical education could be seen as one such area where there is the potential to challenge existing gender binaries. The differing gendered histories of traditional sports and dance provide the opportunity to explore the tensions which emerge and the strategies adopted by those who choose to take part in dance. In this case, the focus is upon men with previous experience of traditional sports who take up dance as part of a teacher training course. The questions which emerge relate to whether these men have to renegotiate their masculine identities in light of their previous sporting histories. It also highlights broader issues about abilities (Evans 2004) and the role that physical education may play in the shaping of young people's physical identities.

Recent research conducted with male physical education students undertaking a four-year PE degree (with Qualified Teacher Status (QTS)) who, as part of their programme, took part in an all-male dance group highlights some of the issues raised above. Observations and life history interviews (Plummer 2001) with ten of the dancers were conducted over a period of six months. All the men had experience of traditional sports, but little or no previous experience of dance. The paper attempts to explore the ways in which the men developed strategies to renegotiate their own sporting/male identities as well as redefine their understandings of the physical body. It also assesses the extent to which the men had to reconstruct personal and social interpretations of dance and physical education. The intention, therefore, is to explore whether the way in which these men negotiated different gendered and sporting spaces may offer lessons for physical education provision in a broader context.

In previous research I have explored the relationship of gender and bodily performances to the construction of masculinities and the extent to which this influenced levels of participation in physical activity (Wellard 2002, 2006a,b). Connell's (1995) concept of a 'circuit of body-reflexive practices', which describes how new constructions of self identity are formed through bodily experiences, was instructive during this research. For instance, a key theme which emerged during my research with straight and gay men who took part in sport was that they all expressed their enjoyment of taking part in physical activity, although within the context of sports there were contrasting levels of enjoyment or pleasure. What became clear was that specific socially prescribed performances dictated the nature of subsequent participation and contributed to the men's construction of sporting identities in terms of their own understanding of whether they 'fitted in' or not. The 'body-reflexive practice of sport' which Connell describes (1995: 63) created an understanding of normative identity for some men, whereas for others it established an identity based upon difference.

The research also suggested that the practices prevalent in sport maintain barriers which prevent alternative of varied forms of expression. Highlighting the 'limits' of conventional thinking about physical activity helps us explore not only who is excluded, but also the range of experiences that are available within the context of many forms of physical expression.

Additional research into the experiences of girls in physical activities (Bailey *et al.* 2004) highlights, unsurprisingly, that girls do enjoy engaging in physical activities but it is the practices inherent in sport that deter them rather than their willingness to take part. One activity in which girls have traditionally been associated with is dance and by exploring the embodied, pleasurable experiences of this activity it is also possible to explore the 'limits' of many formalized activities, such as mainstream sports, which continue to exclude 'alternative' practices or 'inappropriate' bodies. As such, dance is considered to be an established form of physical activity which incorporates different aspects to mainstream (male-based) sports, whilst demanding highly advanced physical techniques and practices by the dancer.

Analysing the experiences and everyday practices of a group of men who engage in physical education and sports pedagogy was intended to explore further questions which had arisen in the previous research. These related to the extent to which gendered bodily performances contribute to successful participation in sport, the significance of demonstrating sporting ability within the context of sport and the capacity of dance education to assist with creating a more inclusive experience in PE.

For the male students who took part in a BA Physical Education degree (with QTS) at a university in the south-east of England, a compulsory part of the course was to complete a dance module. Whilst taking part in this module, a number of men were selected to take part in a male dance group which would then perform to schools in the local area. In general, the majority of the men who enrolled on the course had very limited, if any, experience of dance. In most cases, they had expertise, or sporting capital, in traditional sports, such as football and rugby.

Although the interviews were used as the prime source of data for this chapter, the observations and informal conversations during the research period contributed to the overall 'story'. I am also aware that meaning is 'actively and communicatively assembled in the interview encounter' (Holstein and Gubrium 1997: 114). Given this, I attempted throughout the research process to remain aware that the interview itself is a rich social encounter and like any other research there is constant decision-making on the part of the researcher. Acknowledging these decision-making processes is part of the reflexive approach to the research (Bourdieu and Wacquant 1992). All participants were made aware of the study's aim, the procedures that would be undertaken, the nature of their contribution and the confidentiality of their responses.

Sport as a significant means of achieving cultural capital

Sport provided a significant way of achieving cultural capital for all of the men. Their ability to be physically active and participate in school-based physical activities was a recurring theme throughout the interviews. Sport had been and remained a central aspect of their lives and contributed to a large part of their formulation of masculine identity and their perception of how other men saw it.

> I think every lad thinks 'I'd love to be a professional player.'
>
> (Sam)

All of the men had been successful, to varying degrees, in sport during their childhood. This success was not necessarily related to specific documented sporting success, but more in that they were able to take part throughout their youth without any significant barriers. As such, they were all able to recollect how sport had been an essential part of their youth and at the same time demonstrate to me that they had the right credentials to take part.

> PE in our school was ability set and so I think because I was in all the sports teams I obviously had a higher level of ability, I was always in the top sets for PE, which always meant that, even though it wasn't favourit-ism, teachers preferred that because they are able to do more work.
>
> (Rob)

Their understandings of sport were clearly based within traditional formulations of heterosexual male-based sport (Messner 1992; Connell 1995) and they all presented themselves to me with this framework as a guide and distinguished between those who 'could' and those who 'couldn't'. In nearly all of the interviews, the men suggested that those who couldn't were generally 'girls and gays'.

Even though the context of the interview was set within the parameters of physical education, it became apparent that the men were able to use sport as a means of presenting 'legitimate' masculine and sporting identities to me in various ways.

For instance, evidence of sporting prowess and accounts of specific sports-related achievements marked out their legitimacy to me and within the field. At the same time, their understandings of traditional sport as a main aspect of physical education enabled them to bracket dance as something 'outside' their definition of sport. Consequently, their lack of experience and inability in dance became a reinforcement of their legitimate masculinity. This may have been a factor in what appeared to me as a general lack of real enthusiasm or commitment to dance in comparison to their enthusiastic accounts of their involvement in traditional sports.

Perception of dance

Dance was considered to be an activity 'outside' their definition of sport and an activity primarily for girls and with no real benefit for them.

> Mainly a girly way, as far as I'm concerned if you said dance, it's a girls activity, its something, it wouldn't be taught at my school.
>
> (Darren)

> I've had quite a sexist view, just for the girls really and girls and gays because that's what the opinion I had.
>
> (Jim)

The men were keen to present their own masculinity identity as distinct *from* women and other subordinate masculinities. As Epstein *et al.* (2003) found in their study of gendered identities within schools, boys performed in a particular way in order to establish themselves as unquestionably heterosexual and often used 'homophobia and misogyny, themselves closely related processes, as resources for the construction of masculinities' (Epstein *et al.* 2003: 128).

However, within the context of PE and the degree course they were taking, they were sufficiently aware of educational professional policies which promoted inclusive practices.

> I can go into schools and talk quite a bit now about dance and see the positive effect that it can have, like a lot of kids, we taught a lot of boys and you can actually see their opinions change just in an hour. Which is good, because it shouldn't just be a stigma of just being for girls and like for gays or whatever the stereotypes are. It shouldn't be like that because it gives a lot of opportunities for people that aren't necessarily games players, to do something, to be physically active like that.
>
> (Ben)

In this context, dance was still equated with an activity on the 'outside' which may act as an enticement for those non-sporting types to take part in sport. In terms of their own participation, however, dance was problematic. It was made easier for them by the fact that they could share the experience with other men in a similar situation.

> I was thinking well if my friends back home saw me doing this they'd be a bit like 'what's going on' but I mean everyone was in the same position. So gradually as the weeks progressed everyone sort of like for example you have to do your dance performance evening and all the lads are there, like lads who play rugby and they've got no interest in dance and everyone's in the same boat and you just get on with it and everyone claps everyone and says well done.
>
> (Rob)

The dance group was considered an activity which would look good in curricula vitae and would, subsequently, provide evidence that they were adopting inclusive educational practices. They were aware that physical sporting capital by itself was not necessarily enough to gain a job. For the men, taking part was considered advantageous not only for the successful completion of the course but also for future job prospects. Particularly, the men were aware that within the context of physical education, dance was considered as an area for encouraging girls to take part in physical activity.

At the same time, within the setting of the university, taking part in the dance group afforded the men additional social capital among other students, especially the opposite sex, and the men appeared to enjoy this aspect. Interestingly, on a positive note, several of the men did note, however, that there were additional benefits of taking part and approached participation in a positive way by broadening their educational skills base.

> I couldn't dance and dance was going to be my weakest subject so I thought that it would be a really good opportunity to develop that side.
>
> (Anthony)

Inflexible bodies and minds

Observations of the men taking part in dance rehearsals as well as the recorded conversations during the interviews suggested that there was a certain degree of inflexibility, not only in their physical capabilities but their general flexibility in accommodating broader interpretations of gender and sporting participation. To an extent, it could be claimed that the many years of taking part in traditional sports, although providing the men with sufficient sporting capital to successfully take part in sport and PE, had restricted their physical capabilities. For bearers of significant sporting and bodily capital, it could be considered ironic that nearly all of the men had difficulty displaying some of the basic levels of flexibility required for dance, for instance the ability to touch their toes with straight legs.

The sporting life histories also revealed a restricted view of the role of school PE. Many found it difficult to remember aspects of their PE lessons, particularly in primary school, and could only place specific traditional sports.

> I don't remember any specific sports other than football, that was the only recognised sport I can remember.
>
> (Nathan)

A narrow view of gendered participation was also reflected in their accounts of school practice. To an extent, the men were reflecting the discourses apparent within the classroom. Although, as already mentioned, the men were aware of the inclusive approaches to be found in the PE curriculum, they found it easier not to challenge discriminatory practices. There is the suggestion that the focus in schools upon who is able, or 'more suited' to taking part, creates a situation in which many young people are discriminated against on the grounds of their bodily performances rather than upon their willingness to take part (Wellard 2006c). As Fernandez-Balboa dramatically suggests, these attitudes constitute 'poisonous pedagogies' (1993: 146) which are adopted without critical reflection. For instance, Rob describes the reaction of some boys to including dance in PE.

> I heard one of the boys say 'oh my dad says this is gay and boys shouldn't be doing this'. So if his dad is saying that what chance, ok the PE teacher is meant to be inspirational, but if they're getting told that at home, I mean what sort of chance does he have?
>
> (Rob)

Conclusions

The responses from the men in this research suggest a shared 'lebenswelt' or life-view which conflicts with many of the inclusive practices that are meant to reside in the heart of any educational practice. Brown (2005), in his study of gendered practices within current PE teacher education, found that many practices in PE teacher education continue to refine and reinforce the gendered habitus. In a similar fashion, the men in the dance group were able to articulate an intellectual openness about the contribution of dance in a pedagogical sense. However, similarly to the findings of Brown, they had available to them physical capital which covers 'a number of the "core" masculine associated games that are highly valued capital and exclude Dance almost entirely' (2005: 13).

Likewise, accommodating or transforming dance into sport was also problematic. As Brown states:

> What was an alternative medium of body expression becomes re-appro-priated as conventional athletic activity in which symbolically masculine principles of athleticism are foregrounded and those more symbolically associated with femininity, including a concern with corporeal aesthet-ics, and emotional expressiveness are subordinated.
>
> (2005: 14)

Connell (1995) suggests that heterosexual men have less to gain from the breaking down of gendered hierarchies and may be, therefore, reluctant to embrace fully, if at all, the demands of those on the margins. For the men, the threat of 'subordinate masculinities' remained constant and there appeared to be a policing of their own and others' masculine identities, much in the way that Redman (1996) describes.

However, what became apparent in the study was that the men failed to grasp the possibilities of taking part in dance as a means of extending themselves, both in terms of the mind and the body. Dance had to be contextualised for the men in relation to their potential participation in education, rather than as an opportunity to extend their physical and aesthetic capabilities.

The men had developed an understanding of dance that was based upon social and historical formulations of sport as both gendered and class based. Within this discourse, dance was presented as 'other' and not considered as a part of traditional sport. Within the context of a group of trainee physical education teachers taking part in a dance group, this was more disappointing. Maybe naively, I had entered the research expecting to find evidence of challenges to the prevailing gender discourses which operate at the expense of many. The way the men constructed and performed dance was through a version which did not compromise their definition of normative masculinity and at the same time demonstrated their sporting prowess.

One of the problems identified by Brown is that dance, if it is incorpo-rated within the school context, is presented in a more 'sportified' form. The dance group in which the men took part presented a specifically gendered performance which highlighted the men's traditional sporting prowess, rather than a purely aesthetic form. Consequently, as a form of symbolic destruction, it became redundant. As Brown asks:

> how much symbolic and practical disruption to the gender order does such a practice really promote if the internalized habitus of such forms of instruction in Dance are shifted to appropriate a masculine sport-ing body habitus? Indeed, might not this approach reinforce the *libido dominandi*?
>
> (2005: 14)

Whereas Brown incorporates Bourdieu's theory of habitus, Paechter (2003b) draws upon Lave and Wenger's (1992; Wenger 1998) concept of 'communities of practice', which in effect operate as learning environments or 'apprenticeships' into specific ways of being. For instance, in PE, according to Paechter, within this community of practice the focus is on sporting competence, in which 'such competence confers membership of the community and power with it' (2003b: 143). Dance could be seen, for the men and within their construction of sport and PE, as a separate community of practice with a whole set of distinct membership criteria.

Recognising the structures of these communities of practice and with it their 'entrance requirements' helps us consider the potential impact upon young people during their introduction to physical activity and sport. The positive attitudes which are held by a majority of younger children towards PE and school sports (Bailey and Dismore 2005) are often tarnished by exposure to the practices adopted within schools and by PE teachers.

It is not, however, only those excluded who miss out. As Wellard *et al.* (2007) suggest, many of the practices which form the basis of dance incorporate many of the distinguishing factors used so often to describe performers or performances in elite male sports. Indeed, the combination of strength and grace has often been a factor in the descriptions of many male sporting 'heroes'. These qualities are core aspects in the development of the young dancers. It could be claimed that many young people taking part in traditional sports miss out on exploring and expressing their bodies fully, not only in terms of physical accomplishment, but also in terms of artistic and creative expression.

In many ways, sport could be seen as a last frontier in the battle for gender equality. Consequently, PE is implicated in this battle because of its continued allegiance with traditional sport. However, this battle should not been seen in terms of winners and losers. There can only be one winner, and that is sport in general. PE, in its capacity as a provider for young people, and a site in which children 'learn' about sport, should be a prime mover in this fight for change.

8 (Hetero)sexy waves

Surfing, space, gender and sexuality

Gordon Waitt

The surfie's sexuality is one of blatant male chauvinism

(Fiske 1989: 74)

In November 2004 I was conducting daily participant observation at Sandon Point, a suburban Wollongong reef break, in the Illawarra region, on the east coast of Australia, some 80 km south of Sydney (Figure 8.1). Locally and nationally, this is now considered one of the most prized surfing locations for shortboard riders, given this right-hand reef break consistently produces hollow, barrelling waves, four feet in height and over. Over the course of my observations, although at some breaks groups of young women on short-boards could often be seen, particularly in small surf (less than four feet) or attending surf schools, at Sandon Point, women's participation was almost absent. Here, riding high-performance shortboards is almost an exclusively young, white, able-bodied male activity. Shedding some light on the gen-dered dimensions of surfing are my observed reactions of how young males respond to the few young women entering this male-dominated space. For example, a young woman carrying her shortboard is apparently ignored by a group of young males evaluating the morning surfing conditions. Dressed in a skin-tight wet suit, she cannot conceal her body. She confidently passes the group of young men, crosses the rocks and paddles out in the rip tide. The group of young males seem surprised by her decision. One young male comments that: 'She's not local. I hope she knows what she's doin'.' Another remarks on the size of the young women's breasts. The group dissolves into laughter and wolf-whistles.

This chapter begins with this participant observation because I want to address the gendered dimensions of surfing, that is to couple a *spatial* with an embodied understanding of the gender order. In other words, I seek to interrogate the gender order and gendered subjectivities of young Wollon-gong surfers, not as fixed or pre-existing, but as fluid, contested, embodied, enacted, interpreted and spatial. The chapter explores the ways in which particular sets of social relationships that interact at particular surfing breaks

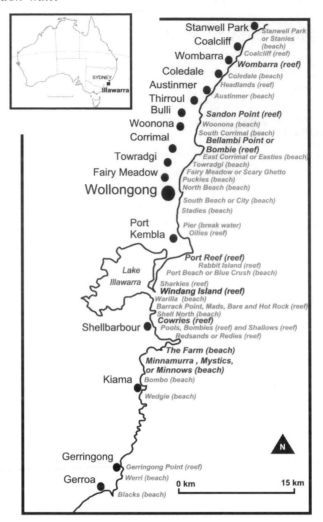

Figure 8.1 Map derived from the collective participants' knowledge to show the location and names of surfing breaks in the vicinity of Wollongong, New South Wales, Australia.

are essential for young men and women to construct a range of complex gendered subjectivities. As Ford and Brown (2006: 83) assert, 'there is little critically focused academic work on surfing that addresses explicitly the theme of gender relations.' They go on to warn us, 'on the surface many practitioners consider there is "no issue" with gender in surfing ... with women's participation seen as an unproblematic inclusion into a male sphere of activity'. Yet, as Booth (2001: 4) stresses, 'predictions of a more equitable gender structure in surfing are premature'. These uneven gender relations are examined during activities of surfing, illustrating how surfers take up

particular gendered subject positions through inhabiting the social relations
that help comprise particular breaks.

The chapter is divided into four sections. Initially, the chapter reviews research on sport as a means of constructing gendered subjectivities. Particular
attention is given to those authors who discuss how contemporary surfing
subculture is embedded within a web of heteropatriarchal gender power relationships. Next, the methodological process used to carry out the research
is explained. The chapter then presents interview data on experiences of
young men- and women-who-surf to examine how heteropatriarchal norms
of masculinity and femininity are made, remade and contested. The chapter
concludes that, for young people growing up in Wollongong, the spaces of
the surf culture are crucial in mapping out the contours of heteropatriarchy.
Gendered subjectivities of surfers are not only embodied, but also intimately
bound to the spatialities of the surf.

Sport, surfing, space and subjectivities

Women's absence from the prized surf breaks of Wollongong, and then being valued here by young men as sexualised subjects and objects, is bound
up with how sex and gender are on display at any sporting event. In Miller's
(2001: 17) account, 'the sporting body and sex have always been bracketed.'
Pronger (1990) argues that, in the West, the institutionalised myths of sports
from the nineteenth century still remain to preserve a polarised gender and
sexual order by emphasising the difference between 'girls' and 'boys', with
heterosexuality assumed the norm. Koivula (2001: 378) asserts that 'sport
has been, and continues to be a site for the construction, strengthening, and
naturalisation of perceived gender differences, and, further, that it serves
to reaffirm the gender dichotimisation and the gender order in which the
gender categories are differently valued.' The conventional practice of ex-
cluding women from participating in sport is based on biological myths that
women are physically inferior, psychically less aggressive and physiologi-
cally less able to withstand pain. Sporting masculinity, as Connell (1995:
54) warns, 'serves as symbolic proof of men's superiority and right to rule.'
Pronger (1990: 17) reminds us of how heterosexuality plays a crucial role in
constituting masculinity within institutionalised male team sports, in which
coaches are renowned for berating players with insults such as 'ladies', 'fag-
gots' and 'pansies'. Hence, in Western societies, sports are a privileged site
for defining, affirming, monitoring and resisting particular masculine subjectivities. In Australia, it is hard to ignore that surf breaks are also a site
where discourses of sexuality and gender intersect with the white history
of Australian masculinity, nationality and citizenship in terms of 'mateship'
(McGloin 2005). Probyn (2000: 15) reminds us that sports are often sites
where 'sex and nation explode.'

Recent feminist research on sport has troubled the essentialistic assumptions and dualistic categories of male/female and heterosexual/homosexual

that underpin the assumptions of sports as a natural heterosexual male domain (Wheaton 2004; Waitt 2003; Wellard 2006a). Here, the work of Butler (1993) and Connell (1995) has been particularly important. Butler's concept, that the sexed body is not necessarily biological in origin, contests the binaries operating in the regime of heterosexuality that legitimise the dominant position of men in sports. For instance, a common misconception existing within this regime is how higher levels of testosterone in men's bodies enable men to be more aggressive and competitive (see Pronger 1990). Instead, rather than assuming a pre-given biologically sexed body, her work points towards the impossibility of trying to separate gender subjectivities from those of sexuality. Butler offers possibilities to conceptualise how the gender/sex body manifests itself through bodily performance (bodily comportment, clothing, gestures and movement). This gives rise to the possibilities of female masculinities and male femininities (see Browne 2005; Johnston 2005; Longhurst 2005). Thus, her work also suggests that obliterating concepts of sexuality from understandings of gender can only lead to an impoverished understanding of the social relationships that comprise social sites, such as sports.

Alongside Butler's work, Connell (1995: 44) asserts, 'masculinity and femininity are inherently relational concepts, which have meaning in relations to each other, as a social demarcation and a cultural opposition. . . . Masculinity as an object of knowledge is always masculinity-in-relation.' Connell encourages us to think of masculinities and femininities as interpellated relationally by the dominant culturally ideology of a historically specific gender order, what she terms 'hegemonic masculinity'. Also like Butler, Connell takes the view that there are possibilities of multiple masculinities. Furthermore, if masculinity is historically produced in relations and culturally defined to the interests and needs of a particular social group, there are always possibilities for different types of hegemonic masculinities, across different sports (surfing, rugby, cricket and tennis) as well as at different times. Hence, Hall (1996) warns against conceptualising gender in sports as devoid of history, disembodied and de-eroticised, and treating gender and sex as biological rather than a cultural practice. Instead, Hall (1996: 31) appeals for research 'to focus on sport as a site for relations of domination and subordination (gender, race, class, sexuality and other forms) and how sport serves as site of resistance and transformation.' Rather than conceptualising gender and sexuality as an attribute of an individual, subjectivities are conceptualised relationally, the outcome of a particular culturally, temporally and spatially defined set of social relationships. Geographers have been paying close attention to the vital importance of how space is shaped through particular sets of social relationships, as well as the role of space in shaping particular subjectivities. Hence, the social spaces of the Wollongong surf are an outcome of a temporally, spatially and culturally specific set of social relationships that, in turn, help to contour the gender and sexual subjectivities of surfers.

Feminist geographers have demonstrated the reciprocal relationships between place, gender and sexuality (Massey 1994; Bondi 1998). Probyn (2003) highlights the 'spatial imperative' of subjectivity. She argues that our subjectivities are always multiple, and are hailed into existence by a range of ideological systems. Crucially, how subjects experience these multiple and often conflicting subjectivities depends on the site and space of its production. For example, given how the hegemonic construction of the Australian surfer is saturated with ideas and behaviours (and images) of a 'mate' identity that celebrates masculinity, heterosexuality, athleticism and whiteness, a surfer who is feminine, non-heterosexual or non-white would more than likely be interpellated by other surfers as somehow 'different', if not deviant, despite being a skilled surfer.

On the basis of Bell and Valentine's (1995) claim that little appears to be known on heterosexual geographies, geographers have also paid increasing attention to how heterosexuality plays a key role in the construction of masculinity (see Rose 1993; Hubbard 2000; Longhurst 2000). Insights into the importance of considering the spatial in the contestation, reworking and reaffirmation of patriarchal heterosexual subjectivities – differentiated by class, age, race and physical ability – are provided in a range of contexts including houses-as-homes (Robinson *et al.* 2004), sports stadia (Hall 2005), offices (McDowell 1997; Massey 1998), gyms (Johnston 1998), cars (Hartig and Dunn 1998; Gregson and Crewe 1998), trawlers (Waitt and Hartig 2005) and the 'rural' (Woodward 1998; Campbell *et al.* 1999, Cloke 2005). However, with the important exceptions of Ford and Brown (2006) and Preston-Whyte (2002), the geography of sport has paid little attention to either surfing or gender (see Bale 2003). Although Preston-Whyte's (2002) survey in Durban, South Africa, suggests that slightly less than 18 per cent of surfers there are women, he provided no consideration of how gender may operate in the territorialisation and communities that he identified operating out of these breaks.

Geographers, it seems, have assumed that how surfing bodies are gendered is outside the 'flags' demarcating its 'safe' disciplinary boundaries. Fortunately, however, there are exceptions beyond the disciplinary boundaries of geography. Vital has been the work of Douglas Booth (1995, 1999, 2001, 2004, 2005). Booth (2001) provides crucial insights to the history of the gendered dimensions of Australian surfing subcultures. Although he argues that all were/are male-dominated, he draws attention to the differences in surfing masculinities between the Australian lifesaver of the 1930s, the 'subversive soul-surfer' of the 1960s, the professional surfer athletes since the 1960s, and the most recent generation comprising predominantly groups of young men riding high-performance shortboards. Booth's (2001) analysis demonstrates the differences of surfing masculinities in Australia from that in Hawaii or California, the fluidity of surfing masculinities in Australia, and the possibilities for resistance and change, particularly with the introduction of new surfing technologies and new institutional organisations.

Through the 'subversive soul-surfer', Booth provides an insightful way to demonstrate how ingrained surfing masculinities were/are reliant upon competition, courage and toughness. Contradicting the conventions of the Australian Lifesaver, soul-surfers practised a surfing style that prioritised becoming part of the wave through movements that emphasised style and grace over aggression. Soul-surfers' bodies transgressed normative codes of surfing masculinity with their long hair, slimness, drug-taking and sexual practices. Their bodies, values and actions exposed the artificiality of surfing as a rule-bound, competitive and masculine sport. Pearson (1979) explains how the mainstream media marginalised soul-surfers by portraying them as 'bums', 'drifters' and 'useless' for going against the grain of hegemonic surfing masculinities.

Stedman (1997) and Henderson (1999, 2001) focus on the gendered and (hetero)sexed representations of surfing circulated within the globalism of sports media empires. Henderson provides an analysis of the representations of the advertisements and articles in *Tracks* magazine, an Australian niche publication, targeting a teenage male audience. She provides a fascinating instance of how the dominant ideological norms of hegemonic masculinity of global surf companies, international surfing associations and professional surfing are circulated. The multiplicities of local surfing masculinities are now in part (re)configured by how they intersect with global surfing commerce, international surfing associations and professional surfing. Given this, Henderson demonstrates how Australian surfing masculinity is constructed through inter-relations across geographical scales. Further, she demonstrates how masculinities are policed in *Tracks* in terms of the 'yobbo', 'rebel' and 'athlete'. As such, this magazine illustrates how understandings of surfing masculinity are framed within the strict conventions of the white, confident, courageous, able-bodied, athletic, virile and heterosexual man.

Evers (2004, 2005, 2006) presents an interesting account of the relationships between the body, surfing, masculinities and emotions. Drawing on the ideas of Elspeth Probyn, Gilles Deleuze and Marcel Mauss, he demonstrates the fluid masculine performances of white, able-bodied, heterosexual men-who-surf. Working at the scale of the body, Evers (2005: 113) explains surfing masculinities as dynamic processes that are 'never fixed because of the dynamic interactivity of the biological, psychological, and sociological'. For the purposes of this chapter, Evers raises four interesting points. First, he demonstrates how individual performances of surfing masculinities change in relation to not only the location of the break but also the surfing conditions, including the number of surfers at a break, the tide, swell, wave quality and height. These all help to dictate whether a body actually goes surfing, as well as the particular surfing styles and rhythm the surfer performs on the wave. For example, large, hollow waves facilitate riding short, narrower, high-performance shortboards, allowing tight, sharp turns. Second, Evers illustrates the hierarchical gender order both within groups of male friends who surf and between men-who-surf, through how prestige and respect can be earned in the Sydney surfing subculture. According to Evers (2004), in Sydney, groups of young men-who-surf shortboards together are complicit in embodying a hegemonic masculine norm that demonstrates skill, courage, muscular strength, aggression and toughness. Consequently, at the top of the hierarchy are aggressive shortboard riders. In Sydney, perhaps the benchmark is provided by the tattooed bodies of the 'Bra Boys', who claim ownership over the break at Maroubra. At the bottom of this hierarchy are bodyboarders – which some shortboard surfers term 'failed men'. Indeed, Evers (2004) documents how access to some breaks involves 'grommets' (often young bodyboard riders learning to ride shortboards) undertaking a 'rite of passage' to hegemonic masculinity. This initiation to manhood by the surfing group that claims ownership of a particular break sometimes emphasises enduring physical pain (grommet bashing), verbal abuse and/or humiliation, such as being denied access to waves. Evers notes how the performances of surfing masculinities and retaining a position within the social hierarchies of surfing is about more than just riding waves. Equally important are the bodily and verbal exchanges of surfers in the line-up and telling stories between 'mates' after a surfing session or 'out the back'. Often these narratives configure the legitimacy of heteropatriarchy in the social spaces of the surf through inciting both heterosexism and homophobia.

Finally, Evers (2004) points out how, generally, surfing bodies are constantly self-policing, managed not only by a surveillance informed by the gender order, but also by surfing rules that apply to all surfers who advance across the whitewash – the Tribal Law of Surfing (see Nazer 2004). These regulate how to enter the surf by a rip tide, how to handle your board, and who 'gets a wave' based on queuing principles that give right of way to whoever is closest to the breaking part of the wave. Breaking this rule is termed 'dropping in'. Despite these regulations now being posted at some Australian beaches, the 'laws of surfing' are neither transparent nor taught but experienced from inappropriate actions at specific breaks. Evers (2004) also reveals how groups of men-who-surf together with friends help add complexity to the social hierarchy layered over spaces of the surf. Males who bond together for surfing companionship form a surfing mateship. By a surfing mateship I mean an 'elite' group of self-proclaimed 'local' surfers who make territorial claims of ownership over particular prized breaks. Members may verbally harass, and in some instances physically assault, to 'defend' claims of ownership over 'waves' from 'tourists' or 'blow-ins'. The latter are anyone they are unfamiliar with in the line-up and take-off position of *their* break. In the context of this territorialism of waves, dropping in can therefore be understood as a strategy of power to exert authority over a break. Consequently, the regulations have their own place-specific peculiarities and have to be negotiated in practice each time when entering the surf. Each of these points was evident in my research of young people who surfed Wollongong breaks. However, first I turn to discuss the methodological processes for conducting this research.

Surfing methodologies

To address rigour and trustworthiness in this project a number of strategies were deployed. Data presented in this chapter were derived from data collection designed to study men- and women-who-surf in Wollongong. In an attempt to position young surfers as co-narrators rather than subjects of research, a semi-structured interview was designed with the help of young women- and men-who-surf to enable respondents to create narratives of their surfing subjectivity through the multiplicity of relationships with surfing technology, ocean, reefs and people. Drawing was included to encourage respondents to express spontaneously their associations with surfing and its embodied affects (Nairn 2002). Collection relied upon ten young women and a similar number of men, aged between 19 and 21 years old, trained in qualitative methods, to conduct semi-structured interviews. Some conducted up to ten interviews, and others only conducted one. These young interviewers, although all university students, were differentiated by their ethnicity, place of birth, nationality, gender and surfing experience. The involvement of a large number of interviewers enabled investigator triangulation. Each interviewer conducted an audit of their contribution to the project, writing a critically reflexive statement (Dowling 2000).

A total of 40 semi-structured interviews were conducted, 34 with men and six with women-who-surf. By age, the sample varied from 18 to 54 years of age. By ethnicity, only two identified as not being European, one as Japanese and one a Pacific Islander. All identified as being heterosexual. None identified as being 'disabled'. This sample was drawn from mainstream surf culture. These participants were recruited by inviting them to participate in a project titled 'Surfing the Illawarra' through a website, contacting local board riding clubs, personal contacts and presentations in several first-year classes at the University of Wollongong. No attempt was made to screen between various types of surfboard riders. In 23 cases participants gave their consent for interviewers to join them on their next surf, providing insights on activities and lived experiences. All interviews were transcribed.

Crucially, the spontaneous, relaxed and informal interactions at the surf often provided a richer source of materials than the semi-structured interviews. Further, narratives tended to differ depending upon the interviewee's previous surfing experience and gender. Interviewees unfamiliar with surfing tended to generate detailed narratives about surfing rules, whereas those who surfed and shared a similar understanding of surfing masculinity spawned more detailed insights into particular breaks, experiences, emotions and performances. Furthermore, it became apparent from the richness of interviews conducted by young men-who-surf that sharing stories amongst other men-who-surf is central to surf culture.

Although one must acknowledge the importance of the surfing experience of older women- and men-who-surf, as well as longboard and bodyboard riders, these were positioned beyond the scope of this chapter. To aid interpretation of the interview data I focused on the performances of surfing masculinity amongst the dominant social group in the interviews, 22 younger men- and five women-who-surf shortboards. My interpretations of the sketches and transcripts was guided by Rose's (2001) and Waitt's (2005) discussions of discourse analysis because my central concern was to explore the relationship between these visual and verbal texts, social practices of surfing and the (re)making of the gender/sexed surfer through the social spaces of the surf. Drawing upon representations and terms used within individual surfing accounts, discourse analysis enabled sketches and transcripts to be first coded and then compared with each other to generate dominant and counter themes.

In addition to the drawings and transcripts that were the mains source of data, I also familiarised myself with the dominant discourses of surf culture by compiling a folder of texts and images circulated by surf magazines including *Tracks*, marketed as 'the surfers' bible', surfing movies (including *Blue Crush* (2002), *Billabong Odyssey* (2003) and *Step into Liquid* (2003)), and information from internet sites discussing surfing or selling surfing products.

Finally, in the course of my everyday interactions on the beach, over a period of several months, I observed surfer board riders at a number of Wollongong breaks. On the one hand, I was struck by the diversity of masculinities being performed in the surf, their fluidity and contingency. Yet, watching and listening to the aggressive, hostile and sexist behaviours amongst the groups of younger men-who-surf at the most prized breaks, I was struck how surfing remains an initiation into a normative expression of European Australian manhood. For example, 'mates' will praise each other for successfully riding a particular wave with the statement: 'You killed it.' This metaphor of war is integral to Wollongong youth surf subculture. At prized breaks, by 'killing waves', young white, heterosexual, able-bodied males can secure their place, snug in the orthodoxy of a Western gender order. Seemingly, nothing is more manly than 'killing waves'. Moreover, surfing as a rite of passage into Australian manhood made me poignantly aware of my own estrangement from how normative sporting masculinity enables aggression, violence and sexism to be 'acceptable' in particular social spaces.

The heterosexy surf breaks of Wollongong as an initiation into hegemonic masculinities

Adopting a relational approach to surfing genders and spaces suggests that the introduction of new technologies, institutions and subjectivities will be integral to challenging discourses that maintain the gender order in the social spaces of the surf. In recent years, Ford and Brown (2006) suggest at least five opportunities for shifts in the gender order established in the 1980s following the introduction of the high-performance shortboard: (i) the commercialisation of surfing through the emergence of brands such as Quiksilver,

Billabong, Ocean Pacific and Roxy; (ii) the heightened global profile of participants in the contest-orientated pro-surfing, including professionals from the female and male circuits, such as Lisa Anderson, Layne Beachley, Tom Curren, Kelly Slater and Nat Young; (iii) in 1997 the International Surfing Association (ISI) becoming a part of the Olympic Movement with its patriarchal concepts of gender, stricter definitions of sporting rules and sense of national superiority, competition and domination; (iv) the emergence of 'big waveriders' pioneered by Laird Hamilton and Mike Bradshaw through developments of modified shortboards, use of jetskis and tow-in-lines; (v) the increased participation of female surfers. In this context, I now consider the changing masculinities and femininities in the gender order of young people whose surfing subjectivities are simultaneously displayed and constituted through the spaces of Wollongong surf breaks.

Imagined masculinities and femininities in surfing spaces

Participants' sketches are illustrative of their surf imaginings, and, as such, provide important insights into their imagined way of being a surfer. As representations of surfing spaces, these sketches offer insights into how surfing spaces are gendered and sexed through their depiction of who are present, what they are doing, and the imagined relationships between the people and objects present. Crucially, in this research, similarities and differences were apparent between the sketches of young men- and women-who-surf.

In the minds of female participants, the surf is portrayed as a domain for women. In this project, the surf is portrayed as a place where groups of young women can socialise together or surf alone. Considering the dominance of men in the surf, this is an achievement not to be undervalued. Yet, their sketches also suggest the difficulties of negotiating a space coded by masculine embodiment, fantasies and histories. My analysis of the sketches suggests there is a range of female positions occupied by young women-who-surf. For example, Belinda is a 20-year-old student who has five years' shortboard surfing experience, three of which are at North Beach. Belinda became interested in surfing through her involvement as a 'nipper' in the Surf Life Saving Association. She portrays an understanding of surfing femininity fashioned by a heterosexual male gaze of the normative heterosexual female body (tanned skinned, bikini-clad and passively lying on the beach (Figure 8.2)). When she is asked to explain her sketch, her idea appears deeply intertwined with normative discourses of heterosexual femininity in surfing:

Belinda: I think that surfing to me, because I'm not like a pro-surfer or anything, but it'd be a very, very sunny day. And, there'd be lots of sand, because I love sun baking. That's me on the towel with my bikini on. And, I don't like huge surf, but I hate small surf, so it is just medium. And, then, I just think that because I always surf

Figure 8.2 Belinda's representation of surfing.

with friends, it's just a relaxing way of getting some sun. Getting a good tan, and sitting out there on your board.

Belinda's description of surfing would appear to conform to very conventional beach discourses and practices of how women's bodies would embody a heterosexualised feminine subjectivity, including 'relaxing' and 'getting a good tan', wearing a 'bikini' and passively 'sitting' (see Fiske 1989). Belinda sketches a heterosexy 'femaleness'.

In contrast, Alice portrays through her surfing sketch of a group of women-who-surf together the possibilities of a female surfing masculinity (Figure 8.3). Alice is a 21-year-old student who has been surfing her local break at Fairy Meadow for over four years. She was introduced to surfing by her boyfriend but now usually surfs with female friends. As she explains:

Figure 8.3 Alice's representation of surfing.

Alice: So, it's good to hang out with friends before, during and after to compare rides. Not that I have a problem with surfing alone, I just prefer company.

Rather than challenging the domination of surfing masculinities, Alice and her peers borrow and approximate the social practices found within groups of young men-who-surf. As Alice went on to explain in regard to her reaction to the increased number of young female surfers she had experienced at her local break:

Alice: Well, obviously you never want new people at your break. It's not so much new surfers as little girls in their Roxy gear getting out there thinking that they are awesome. And, they just sit there or get in the way.

Alice echoes the discourses and practices of surfing male mateship: localism, overcrowding, and a surfing hierarchy structured on performance capital given to 'surfing like a man'. Yet, in Alice's narrative there is one important difference. Her exclusions specifically target inexperienced young women. Female surfing masculinities would appear to operate to bring their own gendered exclusions.

Conversely, all male participants represented the surf as an exclusive domain of men. Although over half of the sketches portrayed surfing as a solo male pursuit, others emphasised the importance of the presence of male

Figure 8.4 Ed's representation of surfing.

Figure 8.5 Eric's representation of surfing.

surfers who are friends – mates (Figures 8.4 and 8.5). For example, as Bill (a 21-year-old male, who has been surfing a shortboard with his male friends (mates) for 11 years) explains:

Bill: I'm drawing stick figures to make it basic. These are boards . . . This is you with your mates and you know it's just you guys out there in the water.

Similarly, Eric (a 21-year-old male, who has four years' experience surfing shortboards with his male friends) emphasises the importance of surfing mateship when interpreting his portrayal of surfing as big wave riding:

Eric: I have just come out of a barrel. That's the aim of the game, the ultimate. I've got some mates out the back and they are cheering me on. They've just seen my barrel and, yeah, its pretty cool when your mates are out there and they see you in a wave because, you know it's a good feeling. I guess it's just that you can share it together and um. I guess you get respect from people surfing out there if you get a good wave or do a good turn. People, like, give you more respect out in the surf.

Eric suggests that the importance of surfing with male friends operates at a number of levels: to share experiences, to witness heroic achievements, and as an audience that transforms physical capital into social prestige within the surfing hierarchy. His response reiterates Evers (2004) and Booth's (2001) explanations of why young men surf together.

Respondents' sketches, regardless of surfing experience or the presence or absence of mates, emphasised the embodied performances of masculinity of pro-surfers or heroic male big wave riders. When asked to describe their surfing sketches, male participants in Wollongong constantly described the 'perfect wave' in terms of 'smoking tubes' or 'big barrelling waves'. Furthermore, surfers' interpretation of their drawing suggests a contemporary expression of the surf as sublime: magnificent terror (Figures 8.6 and 8.7). For example, Jack (a 20-year-old student who has two years' surfing experience) discussed his sketch as follows:

Jack: I've drawn a picture here of some guy, probably me, coming out of a barrel, and doing a slash of the lip. I've drawn a barrel because you don't get too much of these out here. I've got birds here and sunshine, they represent peace and harmony.

On the one hand, the surf is a respected 'enemy' that enables surfers to 'slash' waves. On the other hand, the surf is represented as place of 'peace' and 'harmony'. For Jack, the surf would appear a harmonious place tinged with the fear of combat. These attributes resonate with a surfing masculinity

Figure 8.6 Jack's representation of surfing.

described by Fiske (1989) that relies upon physical prowess to subdue a nature as dangerous, wild and raw defined in binary opposition to culture as civilised and tame.

Similarly, Nigel (22-year-old Anglo-Celtic engineer with 13 years' surfing experience), when asked to explain his sketch, replied:

Nigel: That's the weather [pointing to clouds and sun]. Surfing is best when it's nice and sunny. That's a perfect wave [pointing to a barrel with an emerging surfer], which doesn't happen much around here.

Both Nigel and Jack suggest the inherent scarcity of 'perfect waves' along the Wollongong suburban coast. Equally, both provide interpretations of their sketches that suggest how at the core of Wollongong surf subcultures are the myths of the 'perfect' wave, big wave riders and paradisal origins (see Scheibel 1995).

Despite the regular absence of waves over six feet, there is a clear desire to emulate the big wave riders, who surf waves over 40 feet and are physically very strong, technically skilled and heroically brave. Simultaneously, big wave riding widens and confines performances of surfing masculinity through introducing an alternative performance but within orthodox conventions of heroic masculinities. Mediated by images of contemporary surfing films, magazines and commercial advertisements, the masculinity embodied in the heroic achievements of big wave riders appear highly prestigious amongst young male surfers in Wollongong. Bound up in the histories of surfing masculinities in Australia (see Shields 2004) and refashioned in the image of the shortboard pro and big wave rider, these young male surfers consider themselves seriously heterosexy in a heroic, aggressive, abrasive and physical

Figure 8.7 Nigel's representation of surfing.

way (Figure 8.8). Although challenging some of the previous ways of being a surfer embodied by the soul surfer, the heterosexuality of big wave riders is naturalised through being bound up with a particular muscular, heroic and skilled masculinity. The urge to surf larger barrelling waves is perhaps, as Booth (2004) suggests, one way young males can reassert the conventional gender order over the surf. Although most young male surfers aspire to embody performances of masculinity of big wave riders, in the next section I argue that the numbers of young male surfers who are active in this perform-

Figure 8.8 Sandon Point shortboard turn on the lip of the wave. Photo: Gordon Waitt.

ance of heroic masculinity are very small. Rather than embodying the surfing masculinity of big waveriders, I argue that the gendered and sexed attributes of the social spaces of the surf are largely retained in the Wollongong suburban breaks by young women- and men-who-surf becoming a complicit part of the existing gender order through not attempting to challenge or change the internal social relations of hegemonic surfing masculinities.

Performing surfing masculinities and femininities in relation to a spatialised gender order

Place matters in surfing. First, the materiality of place impacts the waveform depending on the ocean floor, climate, swell and tide. Second, different board riders embed subjectivities within sets of reciprocal social relationships that help to constitute some breaks as more valued than others. Analysis of the interview data suggests the importance of the gender order constituted by pro-surfers and big wave riders in terms of where young people choose to surf, and their surfing subjectivities. One outcome of performance capital, or social prestige, being achieved through demonstrating strength, competency and courage of riding large barrelling waves is that shortboard surfers generally prize certain reefs more than others. Prized shortboard breaks in the Illawarra included Sandon Point (Thirroul), Cowries (Shellharbour),

Oilies (Port Kembla), Stanie (Stanwell Park) and Wombarra (Figure 8.1). At these sites in particular all surfers' bodies are policed, and self-policed, by the normative construction of masculinity born of the quest for big waves. Consequently, the social relationships that comprise the most prized short-board breaks of Wollongong are spaces where the gender order and surfing masculinities of big wave riding are established through the layering of a temporary social hierarchy over the break by groups of young men and women. Through claims of ownership these surfers territorialise the break, with big wave riding as its ideological reference point. Although groups of young women do sometimes surf these prized breaks, groups of young men still dominate. Consequently hegemonic masculinity remains very powerful through how it operates to define, regulate and enforce social relationships at prized breaks. How the social relationships of hegemonic masculinity operate through the social spaces of prized breaks is illustrated by the spatial imperative of surfing subjectivities that operate to discriminate between men-who-surf, marginalise all non-heterosexual identities, and sexualise women who are athletic, tanned and smooth skinned.

The spatial imperative of surfing masculinities and femininities

The majority of male respondents imagined surfing as a solo pursuit. However, in practice, most young men surf with male friends in a surfing mateship. Indeed, most young males articulate a preference for surfing with young male friends. None surfed regularly with women. As Carl explained in response to the question 'Do you surf with friends or by yourself?':

Carl: I'd probably prefer to surf with my mates because when your there with your mates egging [encouraging] each other on, someone gets a good wave and you all rib him on [encourage him] or if you stack it [fall off] you pay each other out [embarrass]. So, it's good surfing with your mates and it's a good time to hang out . . . so I enjoy that side of it.

Enjoyment comes from measuring up to the conventional expectations of surfing masculinity. Competition amongst male friends enables social prestige to be gained from receiving praise from the demonstration of physical prowess and risk taking. Equally, Carl tells how shaming plays a crucial role in this process. For other sporting bodies, Probyn (2000) outlines how shame operates to make participants aware of their bodily limitations and inadequate performances of a particular masculinity. Being made aware of their gendered performances through surfing with male friends appears to pressurise many young surfers to reconfigure the body towards conventional ideas of sporting masculinity through training and competing harder.

From a relational perspective, surfing mateships are important to consider in an analysis of how spaces of the surf are gendered. Women- and men-who-surf are positioned, and position themselves, in relationship to the discourses of masculinity within the social bonds of surfing, and in opposition to multiple constitutions of femininity. Under the surveillance of the surfing gaze, informed by the quest for the big wave, all surfers paddling out to joint the line-up at a particular break are made aware of their position within the surfing hierarchy, a ranking prescribed not only by their surfing ability, style and type of board they ride, but also by their race, gender and sexuality.

How hegemonic masculinities inform the social relations of surfing mateships, which play out through the spaces of a specific break, enables particular groups of surfers to claim the subjectivity of a 'local' and 'ownership' over a break. For example, Ewan grew up in Shellharbour and has been surfing for at least five years at Warilla and Shellharbour beaches with a group of male school friends. Ewan clearly illustrates how maintaining his status as a 'local' is constantly negotiated through relationships with the ocean, break and surfers. He discusses this process in reflecting upon surfing rules.

Erin: At your local surfing location would you say there are any rules that you kind of have to follow?

Ewan: Well at Warilla and Shellharbour beaches, I mean, you can basically, you just go there and you just sit on a certain bar or spot with your mates. So, you'll just take it in turns. But definitely at Cowries and Red Sands and places like that, where there's crowds, there's definitely a line-up where certain people, certain locals who surf it a lot generally get right of way. If they want a particular wave, they'll generally take it.

Ewan, as a white, heterosexual, able-bodied male and skilled surfer, never questions his subjectivity in the comfort of the social relationships that constitute his local break. He and his friends are able to dominate the break: 'you just go there go there and you just sit on a certain bar or spot with your mates.' In the context of his local break, Ewan is actively maintaining the gender relationships that layer a surfing social hierarchy across the ocean structured by hegemonic masculinity. Away from his local break he demonstrates how ideas of self-discipline become important, explaining how he has learnt to give 'certain locals who surf it a lot' the 'right of way'. Here he becomes complicit with the rules of the dominant masculinity, given he risks subordination through not meeting the embodied expectations of the dominant masculinity at this break.

Indeed, the taken-for-granted practice of the most respected surfers is their ability to maintain a sense of territorial rights through aggressive surfing strategies. Discussing surfing rules at North Wollongong beach break, where he considers himself a local, Carl provides details about how his friends deploy jockeying and policing strategies to marginalise rogue surfers from the line-up.

Andrew: At your surfing location, are there any surfing rules?

Carl: I wouldn't say there are specific rules at our break. I mean, we don't own the break, but it's just the general surfing rules. We know the regular faces that surf there, but if someone else comes in, then, they don't get mistreated. But, if there's four of us and one of him then we'll get most of the waves because we'll just block him out.

Andrew: So, you can work with your mates to block other surfers out?

Carl: Yeah, it's intimidating too. If your surfing on your own in a new break and there's ten blokes surfing together, laughing and having a good time, and your on your own, you're not going to, or I don't, paddle in amongst them and say 'stuff you, I'm going to take off.' You've sort of got to show a bit of respect.

Clearly, regardless of gender, at prized breaks not everyone has equal access within the line-up. Carl clearly receives a lot of pleasure from how, with the help of his friends, he is able to discourage a sole surfer from a break. Carl's claims that surfers are not 'mistreated' can only be understood if he believes that through implementing successful jockeying strategies he occupies a much higher status in the surfing hierarchy. Through policing performances he and his friends secure respect for their peers through their aggressive and bullying behaviours. Earning 'respect' through the 'defence' of a valued surf break through intimidating surfing strategies defines the social space of the surf as hegemonically masculine.

Similarly, Derrick, a 21-year-old council worker with ten years' shortboard riding experience, explains how a beach break is gendered as a masculine space through social interactions that enable his male friends to dominate. At Stanwell Park, where he surfs with his mates, and considers himself a local, he suggests that tolerance and graciousness do not inform the social relationships. Instead, when asked to reflect on how non-locals were treated at his local break, Derrick underscored how the surfing gaze operates to maintain the informal surfing social ranking or hierarchy on the basis of familiarity and an ongoing appraisal of ability and style:

Derrick: You get to know who surfs there often, and who doesn't. I guess it depends upon if the person can surf, or if the person is getting in the way, and annoying people. If they stay out of the way, and don't stop locals from getting waves, they are fine.

As Derrick intimates, *all* unfamiliar faces who do not 'stay out of the way' become a nuisance, either by not taking off on a wave deemed good to go, or by taking off on too many waves. The later is as likely as the former, given that groups of young aspiring surfers are unlikely to 'stay out of the way', given the inherent scarcity of large barrelling waves along the Wollongong coastline. Furthermore, deliberately not staying out of the way and not following general surfing rules is one way that rogue surfers often use to make claims of ownership over breaks and challenge the social rankings in the local surfing hierarchy.

With shortboard riders at each break interpellating subjectivities of a 'local' and a 'good' surfer, those surfers that seek to challenge the 'ownership' of a break and the social hierarchy can provoke verbal harassment and physical assault. For example Harry, a 20-year-old apprentice who surfs the Port Kembla reef break, speaks of how locals, the 'ruling elite', deploy aggressive tactics against rogue surfers when clarifying dropping in:

Harry: Locals get umm [pause]. They sorta like [pause], get very narky at people that, you know, that come from other beaches. [pause] It is like a spider in a web, and you've got another spider that comes in the web. [pause] They're very territorial. You know what I mean?

Cheryl: So basically people aren't very friendly?

Harry: Nah well, they're, they don't go out of their way to say 'Hello'. So, they're not that accommodating at all. There's a bit of tension really. No words are spoken but there's that tension like, umm, telepathically. 'If you drop in on me, I'll kill you. Just don't get in my way.' And, if he happens to get in my way, straight away, if he's not from around here [unfinished]. People are territorial with their own breaks, yeah.

Harry reminds us how a hegemonic masculine surfing gaze informs and mediates the social ranking at a break. Harry draws the metaphor of a spider's web to illustrate how the ruling elite asserts ownership over the waves. The break is a territory through which surfers attain a social status and sense of self; they are willing to express themselves violently to mount a defence. Surfing, as a defence of space, where the opportunity to hurt apparently becomes 'acceptable' to retain 'ownership' over a particular break and the social status of a local is another way the social relationships between shortboard surfers help to constitute the surf as a masculine social space.

Respondents provided first-hand experiences of the defensive strategies of the Point Boys, a surfing mateship group who claim ownership over the reef break at Sandon Point. Interestingly, while Carl actively promotes hegemonic masculinity at his local beach break at North Beach, in the context of the social relationships that constitute the gendered social spaces at Sandon Point, by his decision to no longer surf here he is complicit in how hegemonic masculinity is layered over this reef break.

Andrew: Sandon Point, so this is where you were talking about when you said you don't go up there because you don't like the locals?

Carl: Yep, it's really local. Basically, if you're not a Point Boy you get no waves. They will just keep blocking you out. People get punched out for dropping in. It's full on.

Andrew: Have you heard of any other things happening to non-locals?
Carl: Heaps of stuff. Your gear gets flogged [stolen]. You get your boards
             dinged [bashed].
Andrew: So have you been treated like this?
Carl: I've been intimidated. I've never been punched-out, but I've been
             intimidated . . . especially by the old heads, you know: 'Piss off,
             this is our break.'

Carl emphasises how the social relationships at Sandon Point are characterised by hegemonic surfing masculinities: aggressiveness, competitiveness and
violence. Consequently, Carl designates these extreme performances of surfing masculinities at Sandon Point as 'really local'. Rather than pursue equal
access for all surfers, Carl becomes complicit in the hegemonic masculinity
layered over this break by his decision not to surf here. Indeed, challenging
the social order at Sandon Point would undermine his own position at North
Wollongong, where he is part of a male group that occupies a powerful
position within the heteropatriarchal order. Carl's willingness to consent to
the norms of hegemonic surfing practices at Sandon Point illustrates a spatial
expression of Connell's (1995) concept of the patriarchal divide: the socio-
cultural advantages that white, heterosexual and able-bodied subordinated
men receive in the gender order over women and marginalised others.

Similarly, George illustrates the importance of the patriarchal divide and
the role of complicity in maintaining the hierarchy of gender positions that
emerge in relation to the dominant gendered norms of surfing. George is a
20-year-old male who has been surfing for six years with friends from school
at his local beach break at Stadies, Wollongong. Here, he is aware of how
he occupies a subordinate position in the social hierarchy through his lack
of performance capital. When asked if locals and non-locals were treated
differently at Stadies beach break, George responded:

George: Yeah, there's a bit of pecking order, yeah, definitely. Body
            boarding's easy. Anyone can do it. Whereas, surfing, to get good
            at it you've got to spend a lot of time in the water. Some guys,
            they'll paddle straight out to the peaks and like they just do it.
            They've got that confidence. Whereas, you know, I wouldn't do
            that. I'd just paddle out and just sit and get what I can, and not
            try to dominate or anything. Yeah, there's a couple of guys like,
            like one guy in particular with a bald head that you see, and he's
            a really good surfer. Yeah, he's like, he sorts of owns it when he's
            out there I guess.

George is very aware of how hegemonic masculinity of the shortboard
pro-surfer and big wave rider has established a social surfing hierarchy that
positions body boarders on the bottom rung and the confident, physically
strong and highly skilled male shortboard surfers at the top. George is not

actively defending hegemonic masculinity, given he often chooses to 'just sit and get what I can, and not try to dominate'. Instead, George is one of the many young male surfers who are complicit in maintaining hegemonic masculinity by not attempting to challenge the gender order. As a white, heterosexual and able-bodied male surfer he still attains social status and gain from the subordination by surfing masculinities of women and non-white, non-heterosexual and differently abled bodies.

Derrick demonstrates how surfing masculinities of Wollongong youth subculture marginalise non-heterosexual identities. When discussing the social relationships at Stanwell Park, Derrick layers a regime of compulsory heterosexuality over the social spaces of the surf break by subordinating members of the Surf Life Saving Association (SLSA) as 'wankers' and 'queer'.

Luke: At your local surfing break, what sort of relationship do you have other groups of people? Like, say, the surf live saving club members?

Derrick: Oh, they are wankers! I don't think I have met a single clubby that doesn't love watching his mate bend over with Speedos [swimming costume] on, if you know what I mean!

Luke: What about swimmers?

Derrick: They can stay in the flags with their queer clubbie mates . . . Surf club people hang at the surf club and various gay bars.

Derrick calls upon non-heterosexualities to subordinate the masculinities and femininities found within the social spaces of the surf break regulated by the SLSA. According to Derrick, same-sex desire is seemingly prevalent in the former bastion of military masculinity, the SLSA. Following Derrick's logic, the heterosexuality of men-who-surf is assured because they are not permitted to enter the ocean patrolled by the SLSA. Derrick was not alone in evoking homophobia to subordinate other people in the surf. As Evers (2006) acknowledges, homophobia is widespread amongst groups of Australian men-who-surf. Pronger (1990) has highlighted how myths of hegemonic masculinities oppress non-heterosexualities as means of both naturalising heterosexuality and vanquishing any possibility of slippage into homoeroticism from close male bonds. In surfing, the appreciative gaze of a manoeuvre must never be mistaken for either a lusting look or loving glance.

For women-who-surf, Claire, a 25-year-old female student with four years' surfing experience, illustrates some important implications of the heteropatriarchal divide in surfing. When asked if she sees many women surfers at her local breaks, Claire replies:

Claire: No, it's pretty rare. I don't see many chicks in the water . . . I think you have to be quite aggressive toward the surf. Like, just get out there a go hard. There are some females who will do that, but the majority won't. Say, if a guy was getting smashed a lot in the surf he would probably keep going out, but if a female was in the same situation, she would probably go in.

On the one hand, through her presence in the surf at Austinmer and Corrimal beach breaks, Claire acts a reminder that gender order along the Wollongong coast is never fixed. As a woman-who-surfs, she has the capacity to be an active agent in challenging the social relationships in the surf through embodying the practices and competencies so long denied to women. Claire's presence is an example of the challenge to the gender order in surfing discussed by Booth (2004), Ford and Brown (2006) and more generally in extreme sports by Wheaton (2004). On the other hand, rather than transforming the gender order, Claire could be positioned as complicit with social relationships of hegemonic masculinity through how she refers to women-who-surf as 'chicks', and evokes a female surfing masculinity through the necessity to be 'aggressive towards the surf' and 'go hard'. For Clair, aggression remains a desirable and naturalised attribute of bodies that surf. Claire evokes the idea that women-who-surf often feel estranged from surfing because they feel no need to embody a female masculinity. 'Going hard', under the normative male gaze of the heterosexual female body, those women-who-surf aggressively always risk their own heterosexuality being questioned (Booth 2001).

(Hetero)sexy waves

Analysis of the interviews suggests that the relationship between young women- and men-who-surf is strongly informed by the normative male gaze of the heterosexual female body. In Wollongong, young women-who-surf are highly aware of their minority and sexualised status at breaks. For example, Alice, reflecting on the increase generally of female surfers at Fairy Meadow, replied:

Alice: It's good not to be the only girl out there.
Jennifer: Why is that?
Alice: I don't' know. I guess sometimes it's just intimidating being the only girl out there. It is a bit of a boys' club.
Jennifer: Have you ever seen female surfers being hassled at your local break?
Alice: No, they are all hot!

As a woman-who-surfs, Alice is very aware of her minority status and how she becomes a sexualised object. She is complicit with the normative gaze through how she actively configures her body to conventional ideas of femininity constituted by surfing masculinities. As heterosexy, or 'hot', women, she and her female friends are 'protected' from harassment based upon their courage, skills or ability. Similarly Belinda, who often chooses to

surf in her bikini, is consciously aware of configuring her body to the normative heterosexed male. While transforming the performances of femininities
through her participation in surfing, Belinda is only reorganising rather than
challenging hegemonic masculinities. For 'hot' women, like Belinda, the
breaks are a heterosexually safe space, given that, she comments, 'as a girl,
they think you're pretty harmless.' In many ways, through conforming to the
male gaze of the normative heterosexual female body, Belinda closes off any
opportunities of challenging the gender order in the surf. Amongst women
who participated in this project, there was little evidence of resistance. For
example, Belinda imagines a future where sporting femininities and masculinities remain tightly prescribed by normative conventions:

Belinda: Yeah, maybe as more girls start getting into surfing, mixed surfing
           groups might happen more. But, that's like everything though.
           Like, boys will always play football, and girls play netball. Like,
           it's just that divide I think.

In the context of research, men-who-surf do not speak at ease about gender. Questions about gender were often met by silence, avoidance, one-word
answers or jokes. When asked to think about the increase in the number of
women-who-surf all male respondents spoke positively about this change:
'awesome', 'cool', 'great' and 'fantastic'. As Ford and Brown (2006: 83) suggest, 'on the surface many practitioners consider there is "no issue" with
gender in surfing.' Yet, amongst men-who-surf shortboards, there were few
that had regularly witnessed this change and no respondents who regularly
surfed with women. Given the pre-existing layering of structures of power
informed by hegemonic masculinities over the social spaces of Wollongong
breaks, the increase of women-who-surf is configured around this gender
order. Consequently, the justification of why an increased participation of
young women was positive in a male-dominated leisure activity was usually given in highly heterosexist terms surrounding the sexualisation of the
athletic female surfing body.

For example, when Luke asked Derrick what he thought about the increase in the number of female surfers at Stanwell Park, he replied:

Derrick: A few younger girls have started having a go at surfing and they are
           all doing it together. This means that there are sometimes three or
           four girls in the water at one time. I don't mind especially if they
           are good looking. They can be distracting to my mates though
           [laughter].

For Derrick, women's legitimacy in the water is based on female bodies
conforming to the sexual desires of the heterosexual male gaze. Similarly,
Mark a 28-year-old truck driver who has nine years' experience as a shortboard rider at Sandon Point, support for women-who-surf is constitution

of the sporting body as a highly desirable sexualised body. When speaking about the increased numbers of women-who-surf, he said:

Mark: I'm all for it. There should be more of them. And, it actually surprises me there isn't more doing it [surfing] now. I mean they can meet heaps of hunky blokes like myself that would be out there. And, it's fairly safe and cheap. At the end of the day it's still you versus the wave, so it don't matter what gender you are.

Mark claims that gender doesn't matter at Sandon Point. Yet, clearly his relationship with women-who-surf is a highly heterosexualised one. For Mark, a primary motivation for women-who-surf becomes an opportunity to meet 'hunky blokes'. Women who surf prized breaks are clearly scrutinised under a masculine heterosexual gaze that constitutes athletic bodies as sexually desirable.

Interestingly, Ken explains how for certain women-who-surf, those that conform to socially constructed norms of aesthetic beauty, a different set of surfing rules applies. Ken responded when asked if he had witnessed female surfers being hassled in the surf:

Ken: Seen quite a few blokes get hassled in but if anything the girls get looked after . . . If they stuff-up and bump someone just about nobody says anything if they can, or if it's a close call on who is going to get a wave, sometimes I will, and, some guys I know will, drop off the wave to let the girl grab it, especially if they are a hottie.

Although the presence of women points towards the fluidity in the social relationships between surfers, rather than making profound changes to hegemonic masculinities, social relationships are merely reorganised within the dominant gender relations. Women-who-surf, when constituted as heterosexually attractive, pose no threat to the dominant gender order. Although illustrating fluidity of the social relationships in surfing and broadening expression of sporting femininities, gender relations are reproduced within hegemonic surfing masculinities. Young men-who-surf actively maintain the uneven heterosexist gender relation as means to subordinate women, and maintain their own heterosexuality and masculinity.

Conclusion

Over a decade ago (Fiske 1989: 74) argued that 'The surfie's sexuality is one of blatant male chauvinism.' Apparently, little has changed amongst young people who surf Wollongong breaks by privileging big waves, mateship, aggressive manoeuvres, heterosexuality and athleticism as found in the most recent surfing movies, magazines and company slogans, such as No Fear's

'Wimps don't surf'. In the performance of a local surfing subjectivity, while often positioning themselves as non-conformist, young surfers reinforce the norms of hegemonic surfing masculinities, including heterosexism, through the social relationships that constitute surf breaks. Hence, at Wollongong surf breaks, despite the overall increase in the number of women surfing since 1989, there is therefore little evidence of gender equity in the relationships between men and women-who-surf. These results confirm Booth's (2004) conclusion of the absence of a gender revolution in surfing. Rather than the increased numbers of women surfing opening up possibilities for challenging the gender order, big wave riding for most young surfers acts as a catalyst for a new set of pressures to perform the self in conventional gendered manners of femininity and masculinity. Hence, while increasing numbers of young women have access to the surf, this process has been one of masculine accommodation. This has led to a new visibility of women-who-surf, particularly at beach breaks. Some women-who-surf have rejected the ideas that women must sit passively on the beach and have instead adopted performances of surfing masculinity through emulating aggressive surfing styles of pro-surfers or forming their own groups of female surfers, territorialising breaks as their own. Amongst most young, white, able-bodied, heterosexual men-who-surf, surfing is understood as emulating pro-surfers who exit barrelling waves and slash and rip waves with their shortboards. Although the big wave rider brings a different set of pressures to perform surfing masculinity from, say, the Australian surf lifesaver, the big wave rider represent for most male surfers a way of reinforcing, rather than resisting, the historical constructions of the Australian male surfing subject as 'chauvinistic'. Men-who-surf extend a welcome to women to the social spaces of the break, so long as the female surfing subject is constituted as 'sexy'. Similarly, the heteronormative male gaze operates to sustain the invisibility of non-heterosexual men-who-surf. The uneven sets of social relationships that comprise the social spaces of Wollongong surf breaks clearly demonstrate how space is gendered and sexed.

Space matters in understanding how the surfing subject is gendered and sexed. Historically, while there have been many different performances of surfing masculinities, the traits of surfing have always been 'naturalised' as masculine: heroic, technically competent and muscular (Shields 2004). In other words, the social spaces of the surf are historically constituted within the gender order of hegemonic masculinity that naturalises heterosexuality. Although big wave riding, the most prestigious expression of surfing amongst Wollongong youth surf subculture, challenges what defines a 'good' surfer, in terms of those surfers who have the skills to 'ride tubes' and 'slash lips', conventional expressions of masculinity go unchallenged. The heroic, muscular and technically competent are reiterated rather than confronted. Further, given the limited number of breaks that are conducive to performing big wave riding, the geography of heterosexuality, that is, in terms of what it means to be a gendered and sexed surfer, varies between breaks and the surfing conditions at a particular break. In terms of the spatial imperative of subjectivity, the sexed and gendered subjectivities of a young surfer are interpellated through the social interactions at a break, during particular surfing conditions. Crucially, where, when and with whom young men and women choose to surf is just one way they negotiate, police and constitute their sexed and gendered subjectivities through the social relationships that operate at a particular break. The way each surfer is interpellated with a gendered and sexual identity through the social relations of a break demonstrates not only the fluidity of surfing masculinities as noted by Evers (2004) but also the fragmented geographies of genders and sexualities. Consequently, a young male shortboard surfer who successfully exits the tube of a barrelling wave at a prized break, in the presence of a surfing mateship, during peak conditions will be labelled as masculine and naturalised as heterosexual. Conversely, a young male witnessed by a surfing mateship riding a bodyboard in the inshore whitewater is likely to be labelled both feminine and queer. In short, the spatial offers huge potential for understanding more fully how gender and sexuality operate in the process of inclusion in and exclusion from not only surfing but also all arenas of sport.

Acknowledgements

Thanks to all participants and a team of dedicated research assistants, in particular Erin McCarthy, Megan Reed and Grant Lowe.

9 Sport, well-being and gender

*Richard Bailey, Andrew Bloodworth
and Mike McNamee*

Youth sport and well-being

It is widely accepted that sport may contribute to the development of young people's well-being. Countless statements by advocates, academics and policymakers attest to this claim. The precise nature of the claim and the bases upon which they rest are couched in the language of 'human rights', or at least as an entitlement for all young people. One alternative mode of expression is to be found beyond the typical realms of politics and social policy in an older language of more fundamental arguments about human well-being, and the necessary conditions for human flourishing.

This philosophical nomenclature and its orbiting ideas do not find a ready home in recent international sports proclamations. Consider, by way of example, some recent claims in support of sports promotion:

- The 'Declaration of Athens', the outcome of the Fourth International Conference of Ministers and Senior Officials Responsible for Physical Education and Sport in 2004, affirmed that 'the development of physical education and sport is one of the most effective means of improving, *inter alia*, health, hygiene, the prevention of HIV/AIDS, and the overall well-being of individuals, in particular young people' (MINEPS IV 2004).
- The Finnish government's 'Sports Act', which came into force in 1998, and recognises and guarantees state subsidies of sport, states that 'The purpose of this Act is to promote recreational, competitive and top-level sports and associated civic activity, to promote the population's welfare and health and to support the growth and development of children and young people through sports' (cited in Kidd and Donnelly 2000: 145).
- A Canadian report on children's developmental needs stated that sport plays a 'key role' in helping children achieve 'optimal physical well-being'. It also reports that there is a 'general consensus' that 'participation in a well-balanced sport program stimulates physical growth and can be a good way to maintain optimum health', and 'can contribute to long term health and well-being' (Tipper and Avard 1999).

- The United Nations actually *defines* sport as 'all forms of physical activity that contribute to physical fitness, mental well-being and social interaction including play; recreation; organized, casual or competitive sport; and indigenous sports or games' (United Nations 2003: v).

In light of these claims, and notwithstanding their validity, the considerable evidence of inequitable access to sports participation is a cause of concern (Sabo *et al.* 2004). Well-being is an intrinsic feature of social justice (Powers and Faden 2006), and social justice, in turn, is generally understood to be concerned with those dimensions of well-being that are of moral import precisely because they matter to everyone. It follows, then, that if certain sections of society are deprived of opportunities to engage in sport, or are offered second-rate or partial provision, this should be viewed as a matter of societal interest and intervention, at least for those societies which claim to promote the well-being of all of their members. In fact, most recent accounts of social justice would seem to take the matter further, as they take as their most fundamental aim the neutralising of *luck*, or that for which individuals are not responsible (Hurley 2003; Roemer 1998). It could be argued, therefore, that any approach to the promotion of activities which aims at social justice and seeks to promote those activities (like sports) that enhance well-being should give greater priority to marginalised and disadvantaged groups in an attempt to counter the unjust advantages presented to privileged groups. In other words, the luck-neutralising approach to social justice would reflect an emphasis on equity rather than universalising instantiations of treatment such as equality of access or opportunity or other treatment:

> Whereas 'equality' means treating persons the same, 'equity' means giving all persons fair access to social resources, while recognizing that they may well have different needs and interests. Put in terms of a familiar sporting metaphor, if 'equality' means providing everyone with the same starting line, 'equity' means helping everyone to reach the most appropriate finish line.
>
> (Kidd and Donnelly 2000: 139)

Of course this rather raises the question of what 'appropriate finishing lines' actually amount to and who decides on the criteria for appropriateness. More generally we can also note that where and how one finishes in one contest can affect one's capacities in others. As Aristotle pointed out long ago, our potentials in different areas of human endeavour are not necessarily fixed, harmonious or uniformly valuable (Scheffler 1985).

There seems little doubt that the distribution of social resources around the world is typically neither equal nor equitable, and that the demand for the constituents of well-being is often (but not only) violated on grounds of sex. Martha Nussbaum (1999: 5) has highlighted the obstacles posed by various cultural and political practices to women's flourishing. She argues that:

many women all over the world find themselves treated unequally with respect to employment, bodily safety and integrity, basic nutrition and health care, education and political voice. In many cases these hardships are caused by their being women, and in many cases laws and institutions construct or perpetuate these inequalities.

(Nussbaum 1999: 5)

Consequently, women in such circumstances are deprived of the elements necessary to lead 'fully human' lives, a memorable phrase used extensively by Nussbaum (2000) and by MacKinnon (2006). In short, they suffer from unequal well-being, or, in Nussbaum's terms, unequal capabilities for being and doing the sorts of things that are worthy of human dignity (Nussbaum 2000).[1]

For those seeking to find the reproduction of inequalities, Western competitive sports often supply particularly fecund examples. Hall (2002) describes the long history within both everyday and, especially, academic discourses of assuming that athleticism among females was indicative of psychological and sexual deviation. She shows how even contemporary researchers often continue to presume a conflict between being a woman and being an athlete. Responses to gender inequality still tend to assume that the 'solutions' to the 'problem' are for women to change their behaviour in some way, such as learning new skills (to be more assertive, confident, competitive), or seeking to address social barriers to participation, such as child-care and time pressures, in order to be accepted within the world of sport (Talbot 2002). It is not surprising then that, despite the advances of feminism and economic expediency, structural and institutionalised practices within sports groups continue to exclude large numbers of women. Numerous studies have reported differential levels of physical activity between girls and boys (e.g. Trost *et al.* 2002), and reviews (e.g. Sallis and Owen 1999) have highlighted the importance of social and cultural factors, like family values, role models and peer groups, in mediating levels of activity. Interestingly, however, recent research has suggested that gender differences in overall physical activity are fully accounted for by differences in enrolment in organised sports groups (Vilhjalmsson and Kristjansdottir 2003).

Prudential value and well-being

Theories of well-being are essentially concerned with what is prudentially valuable: what is valuable to us as individual agents; what makes *our* lives go well (Griffin 1996). Griffin (1986) refers to 'well-being', but it is important to note that not all theories that concern prudence use this term. Sumner, for example, proposes a theory of *welfare*, defined as 'the condition of faring or doing well' (1996: 1), which he acknowledges is 'more or less the same as her well-being or interest' (ibid.). Nussbaum (2000) indicates her theory's primary concern with the level at which a person's capability becomes what

Marx called "truly human," that is, *worthy*, of a human being. Note that this idea contains, thus, a reference to an idea of human worth or dignity.

(Nussbaum 2000: 73)

We can add her notion of the 'fully human life' to Nussbaum's concern with worth, dignity and the truly human. All of the ways of understanding what is prudentially valuable can inform our understanding of sport, its value to us, and its contribution to our well-being. Thus, our reference to well-being should be understood not as representing a commitment to a particular theory, but as shorthand. These terms have not been stipulated to the extent that they refer to exclusive domains of prudential value; they are, and will continue to be, used interchangeably. The particular label a theory uses is, therefore, unlikely to shed a great deal of light on its main contentions. This requires the more detailed analysis to which we now turn.

What is this thing called well-being?

The concept of well-being continues to be the source of considerable debate (Griffin 1986; O'Neill 1998), and the points of contention and dispute have important implications for those who justify youth sport in terms of well-being, and for addressing differences in terms of access to sporting experiences. Most academic discussions of well-being centre on a distinction between 'subjective' and 'objective' accounts (Arneson 1999; O'Neill 1998; White 1986). Both views are influential, albeit in different fields, and both have their critics. At its heart, the subjective/objective divide centres on the different responses to the claim of agent sovereignty, of whether what is good for people depends on what they want or they think they want, or on what they need or it is thought they need.

Subjective theories of well-being predominantly take one of two forms: 'hedonistic' accounts are premised on the view that what would be best for someone is what would make his/her life happiest, or place greatest emphasis on the quality of personal experience; 'desire fulfilment' theories focus on those things that would allow an individual to fulfil or satisfy his/her desires. Objective theories, by contrast, are characterised by the belief that certain things are good for people, irrespective of whether or not they want to have them (Parfit 1984).

Hedonistic theories ultimately equate well-being with a certain quality of experience. Psychologists have been anxious to distance *subjective well-being*, a psychological theory of well-being, from hedonistic theories defined in this fashion (Diener *et al.* 1998). *Subjective well-being* is composed of a judgement of life satisfaction, alongside positive and negative affect (Diener and Suh 1999); the life satisfaction domain, in particular, should ensure a relation with what is 'important in life' (Diener *et al.* 1998: 35), not just short-term pleasures such as 'partying and entertainment' (ibid.). This is one of the primary concerns with hedonistic theories: their scope does not extend beyond the experiences themselves; there are all sorts of ways of ensuring pleasurable experiences, but would a life filled with such experiences necessarily constitute a life of well-being?

Awareness of the limitations of hedonistic theories is evident within mainstream psychology, yet exercise psychologists appear to have allowed affect, or pleasurable experience, elevated status as an indicator of well-being. Numerous textbooks discuss sport and other physical activities' contribution to individuals' positive psychological states (Biddle *et al.* 2000; Weinberg and Gould 2003), and this is reflected in the academic research literature (Fox 1999; McAuley *et al.* 2000). Moreover, positive feelings, like fun, are frequently cited by teachers and coaches as primary goals in introducing young people to sport (Garn and Cothran 2006; O'Reilly *et al.* 2001).

In his modern classic of political philosophy, *Anarchy, State and Utopia*, Robert Nozick (1974) highlighted the limitations of hedonistic views with an ingenious thought experiment. He described an imaginary experience machine that can give an individual a perfect simulation of the experiences associated with any type of life. Hooked up to this machine, the individual can lead any life she might choose, whilst floating in a tank. Most people would be repelled by the thought of being plugged into this machine, in place of actually living, even if real life was unable to match the quality of experience offered by the simulation. Although positive experiences matter, our sense of well-being extends to aspirations beyond such experiences.

A reflection on sports experiences provides other reasons to doubt the hedonistic account of well-being. The first relates to the sustainability of feelings linked to sports participation. Numerous studies have found that a positive mood following exercise can be short-lived (for example, Faulkner and Biddle 2004), possibly because the exerciser adapts, and the elevated feelings disappear. Some experiences, though, seem immune to this effect:

> The "flow" experiences (of being caught up in exercise of skills) reported by Csikszentmihalyi's subjects also can be related to sense of self, especially when there is room to be proud of the skills involved; and these satisfactions too can be largely exempt from the hedonic treadmill.
>
> (Kupperman 2003: 26)

Satisfactions related to our sense of self may be longer lasting, such as when engagement in sport requires the mastery of new skills. This point is interesting because it highlights the importance of the type of activity to be undertaken. It also, implicitly, cuts away the case for purely pleasurable experiences with its emphasis on meaningful activities and the learning of new skills. Pleasure or satisfaction in isolation it seems, is not enough to ensure enhanced well-being. We need to differentiate between different types of satisfaction, as Kupperman (2003) suggests, and we must pay attention to the activity with which the pleasure or satisfaction is associated (McNamee 1994). Indeed Kupperman states 'it looks as if the values of such a pleasure enhanced life would have a great deal to do, not merely with the pleasure, but also with the values of the activities that give the pleasure' (Kupperman 2006: 14).

The second difficulty with hedonistic theories concerns the association (or, worse, reduction) of sport with (or to) fun. Although it certainly seems to be the case that sport is enjoyable for some (perhaps most) players, some (perhaps most) of the time, it is not the case that all derive pleasure from engagement in sport. Many young people do not enjoy sport, and even those who initially derive enjoyment from it may gradually disengage as they find sources of pleasure elsewhere (Fuchs *et al.* 1988). Even those who have demonstrated a commitment to sport cannot expect a life of pleasure. There may be times when it is positively boring, such as when players are trying to automatise skills through repeated and sustained, and not necessarily motivating, practice (Ericsson *et al.* 1993). In fact, focusing completely on pleasure might deprive learners of sport's more significant long-term benefits, such as competence in the skills necessary for lifelong participation. Hochstetler captures what all experienced sportspersons know well: 'Part of understanding sport, then, is paying attention to the prose, the everyday, the arduous, the repetitive' (2003: 232).

None of this should be taken to mean that sport experiences ought not be positive and enjoyable, nor that teaching sessions should not be fun. It is merely that such feelings alone cannot provide an adequate basis for justifying the value of sport or explaining its contribution to well-being. A stronger case is needed, and perhaps this is provided by an alternative subjective account.

Desire fulfilment theories claim that life goes well when one's desires are satisfied. A difficulty with this sort of perspective is that it is easy to conceive of an instance in which an individual's desires might not bear at all on their well-being; indeed, they might be harmful to it. The political philosopher John Rawls (1971) famously imagined a person who, having reflected on alternatives, decides to spend as much time as possible counting blades of grass in city parks. If that seems implausible, consider, instead, someone glued to a television set, or to a computer game, or countless other activities that seem impossible to equate with a flourishing, fulfilling life.

Consider, too, the case of an individual whose desires lead to actions that are actually harmful to their well-being, such as those resulting in eating disorders or exercise dependence (Loumidis and Wells 2001). Those who mistakenly perceive their body shape and their exercise dependence clearly act in ways that they subjectively deem contributory to their well-being. The palpable fact that we recognise erroneous misperception or judgement suggests something more objective, more super-personal, than the mere satisfaction of desires. This immediately raises another problem with desire fulfilment theories of well-being, at least with regard to its scope. Even if we are inclined to accept an adult's judgement about their interests, we would be foolish to extend this to children. Consider John O'Neill's sketch of the most defensible presentation of this position (1998: 47):

> Well-being can be identified with the satisfaction of fully informed preferences. The position allows for error but still holds that whether something is good for a person depends ultimately on what they would want or value. What is good for us is still determined ultimately by our preferences.

As this quotation makes clear, the desire fulfilment approach adopts the standpoints of a mature adult, looking competently and impartially at his/ her or others' well-being. Can we really claim that children's preferences and desires are 'fully informed'? Most people would say not. Indeed, the whole rationale for compulsory schooling and generally adults' duty of care for young people is premised precisely on their inability to make such judgements (Noggle 2002).

There is a further difficulty with desire fulfilment theories of well-being, which is that desires are highly malleable. This phenomenon, sometimes called 'adaptive preference' (Nussbaum 1995), has attracted considerable attention from both feminists and those studying international development. Amartya Sen (1988) has shown how people's assessments of the quality of their lives are mediated by identities, norms and institutions. Women, in particular, often find their options constricted by notions of obligation and legitimacy, which affect the decisions they feel able to make. Thus it is that women's perceptions of themselves are largely constituted by the circumstances before them, and, as Julia Annas (1996) put it, in a society where women have fewer options, they settle for less. Thus the less one desires in life the less one is frustrated. The adaptive preference is not necessarily or even typically a conscious act, as norms and expectations become internalised. The privileged quickly become accustomed to their wealth and opportunity; the marginalised frequently adapt their expectations and desires to the lower level of life they know. They may not demand fundamental elements of well-being because they are unaware that they exist (Nussbaum 1995). So, many women in Sen's (1988) study of Indian women did not seem to know what it was to be healthy, and the Bangladeshi women that Chen (1983) reported on did not know what it meant to benefit from education. Relying on personal preference in judgements of well-being will, in contexts like these, simply reinforce dominant structures and stand in opposition to radical change (Nussbaum 1995).

We are led, therefore, towards a conception of well-being that is substantially objective, rather than solely subjective. To be clear, it is not suggested here that objective and subjective accounts are mutually exclusive. It is entirely possible to envisage some of 'mixed' theory, such as where well-being could be equated with deriving or desiring pleasure from objectively valuable

activities (Parfit 1984). Nor is it necessary to go through the various criticisms that have been levelled at objective accounts, which focus primarily on
the genesis of the elements on specific lists (White 1986). The main point
is simply that an account of well-being that is not grounded in objective,
non-personal measures is necessarily inadequate, and in discussing sport's
supposed contribution to human flourishing it is important to frame this
with reference to objective measures of well-being.

Youth sport's contribution to well-being

A plethora of objective lists of the elements of well-being have been published
(Gasper 2004). The philosopher Martha Nussbaum, as we have noted, does
not speak specifically of well-being, referring more to the fully or truly human life. Her 'capabilities approach' (Nussbaum 1999), however, represents
one of the best-known objective theories of the human good. According to
Nussbaum, whose work relates to that of the economist Amartya Sen (1998),
certain 'central capabilities' are essential for a fully human life of dignity and
value, including life; bodily health; bodily integrity; senses, imagination and
thought; emotions; practical reason; affiliation; other species; play; control
over one's environment.

Obviously, Nussbaum gives substance to these headings; the aim, here,
is simply to give some general sense of an objective theory. Other theorists
offer their lists, with different elements and foci, but there are also recurring
themes, related to things like physical and psychological health, education
and opportunities for social interaction (Gasper 2004; Saith 2001; Qizilbash
1998).

Although none of the cited theories include specific mention of 'sport',
there are numerous references to related concepts within descriptions of
well-being. For example, Robeyns talks about 'being able to be physically
healthy' (2006: 81) and 'being able to engage in leisure activities' (ibid.: 82).
Nussbaum explains well-being partly in terms of sport's conceptual cousins:
her 'play' capability is partially in terms of the need to 'enjoy recreational
activities' (1999: 85), and she elsewhere writes of people's need to 'move
from place to place with their own bodies' (ibid.: 77). Beyond these specific
mentions, it is worth examining the extent to which sport and other physical
activities might contribute to some of the most frequently appearing themes
within objective lists.[2]

Physical health

The physical health benefits of regular physical activity are well-established
(WHO 1995). Regular participation in such activities is associated with a
longer and better quality of life, reduced risks of a variety of diseases and
many psychological and emotional benefits. There is also a large body of literature showing that inactivity is one of the most significant causes of death,
disability and reduced quality of life in the developed world.

Physical activity may influence the physical health of young people in two ways. First, it can affect the causes of disease during childhood and youth. Evidence suggests a positive relationship between physical activity and a host of factors affecting their physical health, including diabetes, blood pressure and the ability to use fat for energy (Malina *et al.* 2004). Second, physical activity could reduce the risk of chronic diseases in later life. A number of 'adult' conditions, such as cancer, diabetes and coronary heart disease, have their origins in childhood, and can be aided, in part, by regular physical activity in the early years. Also, regular activity beginning in childhood helps to improve bone health, thus preventing osteoporosis, which predominantly affects females (Sabo *et al.* 2004).

Obesity deserves special mention. There seems to be a general trend towards increased childhood obesity in a large number of countries, and this increase seems to be particularly prevalent in girls from highly urbanised areas, some ethnic minorities and the disabled (Dietz and Gortmaker 1984). Obesity in childhood is known to have significant impact on both physical and mental health, and sport can be an important feature of a weight control programme for young people, increasing calorific expenditure and promoting fat reduction.

We would, however, urge some caution in the use of sports and exercise to counter obesity. Evans (2003) states that obesity ought not simply be viewed positivistically as a mere physical condition. Such concepts as 'obesity' and 'overweight', he argues, are better understood as a 'social arbitrary' (Evans 2003: 88), since the norms that they are predicated upon do not exist in nature but are, rather, chosen or constructed against arbitrary markers. The relationship between size and health is complex and uncertain (Gard and Wright 2005), and we must be careful, particularly with young people, in using sport and exercise as a response to the research on obesity and indeed the vast media interest that surrounds it.

Reproductive health

Adolescent pregnancy and sexual ill-health are major social problems across the globe (WHO 2004). Although there is a shortage of research in this area, early studies conducted in the US have found that adolescent girls who participate in sports tend to become sexually active later in life, have fewer partners, and, when sexually active, make greater use of contraception than non-sporting girls (Sabo *et al.* 1999). Projects are currently under way in the developing world that use sports participation as a strategy for empowering girls to avoid high-risk sexual behaviour (Reijer *et al.* 2002).

Mental health

In recent years, there has been evidence of disturbingly high rates of mental ill-health among adolescents and even younger children, ranging from low self-esteem, anxiety and depression to eating disorders, substance abuse and suicide (Sallis and Owen 1999). Adolescent girls are particularly vulnerable to anxiety and depressive disorders: by 15 years old, girls are twice as likely as boys to have experienced a major depressive episode; girls are also significantly more likely than boys to have seriously considered suicide (CDC 2002).

Research suggests two ways in which sporting and other physical activities can contribute to mental health in girls. First, there is fairly consistent evidence that regular activity can have a positive effect upon young people's psychological well-being (Biddle and Mutrie 2001). Second, research has indicated that physical activity can contribute to the reduction of problem levels of anxiety and depression. Evidence is beginning to be gathered for exercise as a treatment for clinical depression, with studies finding that physical activity is as effective a treatment as anti-depressants and psychotherapy. Similarly, a variety of non-clinical studies have found that higher levels of activity were related to lower rates of depression. A position statement of the International Society of Sport Psychology drew out numerous mental health benefits of physical activity from the research literature, including reduced state of anxiety, neuroticism and anxiety, mild to moderate depression, and various kinds of stress (Singer 1992).

Educational development

A range of evidence suggests that, for many young people, sports and physical activities are positive features of their academic aspirations and achievement. A number of studies have found improvements for many children in academic performance when time for sport is increased in their school day (Sallis *et al.* 1999). A report of three longitudinal studies emphasises that 'academic performance is maintained or even enhanced by an increase in a student's level of habitual physical activity, despite a reduction in curriculum or free time for the study of academic material' (Shephard 1997).

There is considerable evidence of a positive relationship between the participation of young people, especially girls, in sports and pro-educational values, although, at present, it is difficult to distinguish between correlation and causation. Studies from the United States (Sabo *et al.* 2004) report a host of relevant findings including: girls who participate in sports are more likely to achieve academic success than those who do not play sports; female high school athletes expressed a greater interest in graduating from both high school and college; female athletes from ethnic minority groups reported better school grades and greater involvement in extra-curricular activities than non-athletes, and in some cases are considerably less likely to drop out from school (Fejgin 1994). Other studies have suggested that sports participation can help undermine traditional gender stereotyping in terms of academic aptitude, by demonstrating an association between girls' engagement in sports and improved performance in science and mathematics (Hanson and Kraus 1999).

Social inclusion and affiliation

Combating social exclusion, or the factors that result in people being excluded from the normal exchanges, practices and rights of modern society, has become a focus of attention for governments and non-government organisations in recent years. Some writers have argued that sports not only reflect but can also contribute to young people's social exclusion in sports and wider society (Collins and Kay 2003). Certainly, the dominance of sports as culturally valued physical activities, and the close identification of sports with traditional and exclusive conceptions of masculinity, means that other groups can become pushed to the margins (Wellard 2002). Nevertheless, positive sports experiences do seem to have the potential to, at least, contribute to the process of inclusion by bringing individuals from a variety of social and economic backgrounds together in a shared interest in activities that are inherently valuable; offering a sense of belonging, to a team, a club or a programme; providing opportunities for the development of valued capabilities and competencies; and increasing 'community capital', by developing social networks, community cohesion and civic pride.

Studies of women's experiences of sports participation have suggested that they can contribute to a more generalised feeling of empowerment (Deem 1986). In many settings, adolescents may be encouraged to view their bodies as sexual and reproductive resources for men, rather than sources of strength for themselves (Brady and Kahn 2002). Sporting activities may help them develop a sense of ownership of their bodies and access the types of activity experiences traditionally enjoyed by boys (Thompson 1995). This may be because participation augments girls' self-esteem, or because being an athlete carries with it a strong public identity (Brady 1998). Some female athletes report having a stronger sense of identity and self-direction – what Margaret Talbot calls 'being herself through sport' (Talbot 1989). Whatever the reasons, increasing the numbers of girls participating in sports and physical activities does seem to open up routes through which they can acquire new community affiliations and begin to operate more openly and equally in community life. In doing so, girls' participation can challenge and change social norms about their roles and capabilities.

Taken together, evidence of this sort lends support to the frequent claims that sport can make a significant and distinctive contribution to the well-being of young people. Whether sport is seen as a necessary feature of well-being, in itself, or as one route to elements of well-being, it deserves to feature in discussions of the good life and the things that one can be and do, as part of a fulfilling and flourishing life.

Conclusion: objectivist well-being, agency and advocacy

> Sport is a training ground where boys learn what it means to be men . . . because sport is identified with men and masculinity, women in sport become trespassers on male territory and their access is limited or blocked entirely.
> (Griffin 1998: 16)

I have always been astonished ... that the established order, with its relations of domination, its rights and prerogatives, privileges and injustices, ultimately perpetuates itself so easily, apart from a few historical accidents, and
that the most intolerable conditions of existence can so often be perceived as
acceptable and even natural. And I have also seen masculine domination, and
the way it is imposed and suffered, as the prime example of this paradoxical
submission.

(Bourdieu 2001: 1–2)

Sport can make a significant and distinctive contribution to individual well-
being. Beyond its frequently cited physical health benefits and its characteri-
sation as a source of pleasure and enjoyment, appropriately presented sports
experience can play a role as sources and features of a fulfilling life. We have
questioned traditional associations of well-being with positive experiences
and the satisfaction of desires, in favour of a more objective, supra-personal
account. This account is based on a notion of capacities and capabilities
which are universal and essential, and focuses on what is common to all.
In Nussbaum's terms, 'it begins with the human being: with the capabilities
and needs that join all humans, across barriers of gender and class and race
and nation' (1995: 61). There is little doubt that sport has yet to cross these
barriers in many contexts.

Gender presents a particularly challenging barrier, as women and girls
continue to be excluded from what is still widely considered a male arena
(Birrell and Cole 1994; Scraton 1992). However, the solution to such exclusion cannot simply be to increase opportunities for girls to participate in
sport. There is a substantial body of evidence demonstrating that, even when
given seemingly equal access to facilities and activities, girls, as a group, participate less than boys, and from an early age (Bailey *et al.* 2004). Both boys
and girls continue to view sporting and physically active girls with suspicion,
perceiving them to be unfeminine (Vu *et al.* 2006).

This situation reflects a familiar dilemma for feminists. On the one hand,
they believe that gender, as a social construction, limits people's choices, in
part by shaping and deforming their preferences (Nussbaum 1995). On the
other hand, feminists argue that women, themselves, need to be the agents of
change and emancipation. But 'valuing women's agency inclines feminists to
value women's wishes and choices, and provide a political framework within
which women's real experiences and actual choices are taken seriously, even
though these choices may sometimes be the result of patriarchy' (Chambers
2005: 326).

Subjective theories of well-being offer neither cause nor method for
change since individuals' (mis)perceptions of the sense of pleasure or desires
in relation to sports are viewed as given or having primacy simply in virtue
of the fact that they are the subjects'. As Nussbaum (2000) has shown, one's
preferences are all too readily adaptive, and readily adjust, consciously or
otherwise, to social norms and opportunities. Objective theories of well-

being, however, offer support for those calling for change, not because of personal wishes, or local norms and values, but because they aspire for an account of well-being that is common to all human beings. Sporting activities, we contend, are plausible candidates for inclusion in such an account.

Notes

5 Being 'able' in a performative culture

1 The concept of 'performativity' is drawn from the work of Stephen Ball (2001, 2004, following Lyotard 1984) and is a little different from how it used in Judith Butler's work (Butler 1993). She uses the term to denote the way in which our (individual) subjectivities or identities are shaped, made and brought into play by and through particular discourses, and how these identities (for example of masculinity and femininity) constantly have to be 'made' and/or 'performed' on the cultural terrain. We, like Stephen Ball, use the term to highlight how performativity is embedded in 'culture'; a culture that 'employ judgements, comparisons and constant evaluations as means of control, attrition and change' and in which the manifest (surface/superficial) features of the performance of individuals or organisations are constantly used as measures of their productivity, or output, or displays of their 'quality'. Thus 'performance' comes to stand for, or represent the worth, quality, or value of an individual or organisation within a field of judgement (Ball 2004: 144). Butler concentrates on the ontological significances of 'performativity', while Ball emphasises its expression through the cultures and structures of schools. We illustrate how schools in the UK are now dominated by 'performative culture' and how this influences the way in which teachers and pupils think, not only about their work but their bodies. So, for example, in PE it is not enough for teachers to be educating the child to be healthy; one has to ensure that he or she can display 'health' in order to be defined as 'good' or successful. Being 'healthy' in a performative culture means being/displaying the right shape and size, usually defined as being thin, even though being thin may not be a good indicator of a person's health. In a performative culture producing the right size and shape becomes a 'performance indicator' of good teaching and of being a good pupil/student.

2 The child obesity PSA target was set in July 2004. The target is jointly owned by the Department of Health, the Department for Culture, Media and Sport, and the Department for Education and Skills, and is working towards the halting of the year-on-year rise of obesity in children under 11 by 2010.

6 Gender and secondary school National Curriculum physical education

1 The term 'sex' is used throughout this paper to refer to the variable relating to males and females. This term is different from the analytic concept of 'gender' which is used at times to refer to the socially constructed aspects of sex.

9 Sport, well-being and gender

1 We are aware, of course, that the forms of inequality are many and varied. We are not seeking to privilege gender, here. Rather, given the focus of this volume, we are concentrating on it in this instance.

2 The following section is based on data collected for Bailey *et al.* (2004).

References

Abra, J. (1987/8) The Dancer as Masochist. *Dance Research Journal*, 19: 33–39.

Abraham, S. (1996a) Eating and Weight Controlling Behaviours of Young Ballet Dancers. *Psychopathology*, 29: 218–222.

Abraham, S. (1996b) Characteristics of Eating Disorders among Young Ballet Dancers. *Psychopathology*, 29: 223–229.

Anderson, A.E. (1995) Eating Disorders in Males. In K.D. Brownell and C.G. Fairburn (eds), *Eating Disorders and Obesity: A Comprehensive Handbook*. New York: Guilford Press.

Anderson, A. and Williams, J.M. (1999) A Model of Stress and Athletic Injury: Prediction and Prevention. *Journal of Sport and Exercise Psychology*, 10: 294–306.

Annas, J. (1993) Women and the Quality of Life: Two Norms or One? In M. Nussbaum and A. Sen (eds), *The Quality of Life*. New York: Oxford University Press.

Aphramor, L. (2005) Is a Weight-Centred Health Framework Salutogenic? Some Thoughts on Unhinging Certain Dietary Ideologies. *Social Theory and Health*, 3(4): 315–340.

Armour, K. and Jones, R.L. (1998) Physical Education Teachers' Lives and Careers. In *PE, Sport and Educational Status*. London: Falmer Press.

Arneson, R.J. (1999) Human Flourishing versus Desire Satisfaction. *Social Philosophy and Policy*, 16(1): 113–143.

Australian Sports Commission (1999) *How to Include Women and Girls in Sport, Recreation and Physical Activity: Strategies and Good Practice*. Canberra: Australian Sports Commission.

Azzarito, L. and Solomon, M.A. (2005) A Reconceptualization of Physical Education: The Intersection of Gender/Race/Social Class. *Sport, Education and Society*, 10(1): 25–48.

Bailey, R.P. (2005) Evaluating the Relationship between Physical Education, Sport and Social Inclusion. *Educational Review*, 57(1): 71–90.

Bailey, R.P. and Dismore, H. (2005) *Sport in Education: The Place of Physical Education and Sport in Schools – Final Project Report*. Berlin: International Council for Sport Science and Physical Education.

Bailey, R.P., Wellard, I. and Dismore, H. (2004) *Girls' Participation in Physical Activities and Sports: Benefits, Patterns, Influences and Ways Forward*. Technical Report for the World Health Organization. Geneva: WHO.

Bakker, F.C. (1988) Personality Differences between Young Dancers and Non-Dancers. *Personality and Individual Differences*, 9: 121–131.

Bakker, F.C. (1991) Development of Personality in Dancers: A Longitudinal Study. *Personality and Individual Differences*, 12: 671–681.

Bale, J. (1993) *Sport, Space and the City*. London: Routledge.

Bale, J. (2003) *Sports Geography*. New York: Routledge.

Ball, S.J. (1990) Politics and Policy Making in Education. *Explorations in Policy Sociology*. London: Routledge.

Ball, S. (2001) Performativities and Fabrications in the Education Economy: Towards the Performative Society. In D. Gleeson and C. Husbands (eds), *The Performing School: Managing, Teaching and Learning in a Performance Culture*. London: Routledge Falmer.

Ball, S. (2004) Performativities and Fabrications in the Education Economy: Towards the Performative Society. In S. Ball (ed.), *The RoutledgeFalmer Reader in Sociology of Education*. London: RoutledgeFalmer.

BBC Radio 4 (2006) Interviews with Billy Schwer and Johnny Nelson. *Between Ourselves*, 15 August.

Beals, K.A. (2000) Subclinical Eating Disorders in Female Athletes. *Journal of Physical Education, Recreation and Dance*, 71: 23–29.

Beauvoir, S. de (1989) *The Second Sex*, trans. H. Parshley. London: Vintage Books.

Beck, U. and Beck-Gernsheim, E. (1995) *The Normal Chaos of Love*. Cambridge: Polity.

Bedward, J. and Williams, A. (2000) Girls' Experience of Physical Education. In A. Williams (ed.), *Primary School Physical Education*. New York: RoutledgeFalmer.

Bell, D. (1991) *Husserl*. London: Routledge.

Bell, D. and Valentine, G. (1995) Introduction – Orientations. In D. Bell and G. Valentine (eds), *Mapping Desire: Geographies of Sexualities*. London: Routledge.

Bendelow, G. (2000) *Pain and Gender*. London: Prentice Hall.

Benn, C. (1982) The Myth of Giftedness. *Forum*, 24: 50–53.

Bergum, V. (2004) Birthing Pain. *Phenomenology Online*. Available at: www.phenomenologyonline.com/ (accessed October 2006).

Bernstein, B. (2000) *Pedagogy, Symbolic Control and Identity: Theory, Research, Critique*. Oxford: Rowman & Littlefield Publishers.

Bernstein, B. (2001) From Pedagogies to Knowledges. In A. Morais, I. Neves, B. Davies and H. Daniels (eds), *Towards a Sociology of Pedagogy: The Contribution of Basil Bernstein to Research*. New York: Peter Lang.

Biddle, S. and Mutrie, N. (2001) *Psychology of Physical Activity: Determinants, Well-Being and Interventions*. London: Routledge.

Biddle, S., Fox, K. and Boucher, S. (2000) *Physical Activity and Psychological Well-Being*. London: Routledge.

Biddle, S.J.H., Gorely, T., Marshall, S.J., Murdley, I. and Cameron, N. (2004) Physical Activity and Sedentary Behaviours in Youth: Issues and Controversies. *Journal of the Royal Society for the Promotion of Health*, 124: 29–33.

Biddle, S.J.H., Coalter, F., O'Donovan, T., MacBeth, J., Nevill, M. and Whitehead, S. (2005) *Increasing Demand for Sport and Physical Activity by Girls*. Edinburgh: sportscotland.

Birrell, S. and Cole, C. (1994) *Women, Sport, and Culture*. Champaign, IL: Human Kinetics.

Bond, K. and Stinson, S. (2000/1) 'I Feel Like I'm Going to Take Off!' Young People's Experiences of the Superordinary in Dance. *Dance Research Journal*, 32(2): 52–87.

Bondi, L. (1998) Sexing the City. In R. Fincher and J. Jacobs (eds), *Cities of Difference*. New York: Guilford Press.

Booth, D. (1995) Ambiguities in Pleasure and Discipline: The Development of Competitive Surfing. *Journal of Sport History*, 22(3): 189–206.

Booth, D. (1999) Surfing: The Cultural and Technological Determinants. *Culture, Sport, Society*, 2(1): 35–55.

Booth, D. (2001) *Australian Beach Cultures: The History of Sun, Sand and Surf*. London: Frank Cass.

Booth, D. (2004) Surfing: From One (Cultural) Extreme to Another. In B. Wheaton (ed.), *Understanding Lifestyle Sports: Consumption, Identity and Difference*. London: Routledge.

Booth, D. (2005) Paradoxes of Material Culture: The Political Economy of Surfing. In J. Nauright and K.S. Shimmet (eds), *The Political Economy of Sport*. Basingstoke: Palgrave Macmillan.

Bordo, S. (1993) *Unbearable Weight: Feminism, Western Culture and the Body*. Berkeley, CA: University of California Press.

Bordo, S. (1997) *Twilight Zones: The Hidden Life of Cultural Images from Plato to O.J.* Berkeley, CA: University of California Press.

Bourdieu, P. (1977) *Outline of Theory of Practice*, trans. R. Nice. Cambridge: Cambridge University Press.

Bourdieu, P. (1986) The Forms of Capital. In J. Richardson (ed.), *Handbook of Theory and Research for the Sociology of Education*. New York: Greenwood Press.

Bourdieu, P. (1990a) *In Other Words: Towards a Reflexive Sociology*. Cambridge, Polity

Bourdieu, P. (1990b) *The Logic of Practice*. Cambridge: Polity.

Bourdieu, P. (1993) *Sociology in Question*, trans. by R. Nice. London: Sage.

Bourdieu, P. (2001) *Masculine Domination*. Cambridge: Polity Press.

Bourdieu, P and Wacquant, L. (1992) *An Invitation to Reflexive Sociology*. Cambridge: Polity Press.

Brady, M. (1998) Laying the Foundation for Girls' Healthy Futures: Can Sports Play a Role? *Studies in Family Planning*, 29(1): 79–82.

Brady, M. and Kahn, A. (2002) *Letting Girls Play: The Mathare Youth Sports Association's Football Program for Girls*. New York: Population Council.

Braidotti, R. (1994) *Nomadic Subjects: Embodiment and Sexual Difference in Contemporary Feminist Theory*. New York: Columbia University Press.

Bramham, P. (2003) Boys, Masculinities and PE. *Sport, Education and Society*, 8(1): 51–71.

Brettschneider, W.-D. and Naul, R. (2004) *Study on Young People's Lifestyles and Sedentariness and the Role of Sport in the Context of Education and as a Means of Restoring the Balance*. Paderborn: European Union.

Brinson, P. and Dick, F. (1996) *Fit to Dance? The Report of the National Inquiry into Dancers' Health and Injury*. London: Calouste Gulbenkian Foundation.

Brown, D. (2005) An Economy of Gendered Practices? Learning to Teach Physical Education from the Perspective of Pierre Bourdieu's Embodied Sociology. *Sport, Education and Society*, 10(1): 3–23.

Browne, K. (2005) Stages and Streets: Reading and (Mis)reading Female Masculinities. In B.A. Hoven and K. Horschelmann (eds), *Spaces of Masculinities*. New York: Routledge.

Buckroyd, J. (2000) *The Student Dancer: Emotional Aspects of the Teaching and Learning of Dance*. London: Dance Books.

Bull, C.J.C. (1997) Sense, Meaning and Perception in Three Dance Cultures. In J. Desmond (ed.), *Meaning in Motion: New Cultural Studies of Dance*. Durham, NC: Duke University Press.

Burrows, L. (2005) Do the 'Right' Thing: Chewing the Fat in Physical Education. *Journal of Physical Education New Zealand*, 38(1): 7–16.

Burrows, L. and Wright, J. (2004) The Discursive Production of Childhood, Identity and Health. In J. Evans, B. Davies and J. Wright (eds), *Body, Knowledge and Control: Studies in the Sociology of Physical Education and Health*. London: Routledge.

Burrows, L. and Wright, J. (2006) Prescribing Practices: Shaping Healthy Children in Schools. Paper presented at 'Children and Young People as Social Actors' symposium, University of Otago.

Burstyn, V. (1999) *The Rites of Men: Manhood, Politics and the Culture of Sport*. Toronto: University of Toronto Press.

Butler, J. (1990) *Gender Trouble*. New York: Routledge.

Butler, J. (1993) *Bodies that Matter: On the Discursive Limits of 'Sex'*. New York: Routledge.

Butler, J. (1994) Gender as Performance: An Interview with Judith Butler. *Radical Philosophy*, 67: 32–39

Butler, J. (1997) *Excitable Speech*. New York: Routledge.

Butler, J. (2006) Curriculum Constructions of Ability: Enhancing Learning through Teaching Games for Understanding (TGfU) as a Curriculum Model. *Sport, Education and Society*, 11(3): 243–258.

Campbell, H., Law, R. and Honeyfield, J. (1999) What it Means to be a Man: Hegemonic Masculinity and the Reinvention of Beer. In R. Law, H. Campbell and J. Dolan (eds), *Masculinities in Aotearoa/New Zealand*. Palmerston North: Dunmore Press.

Carmichael, K. (1988) The Creative Use of Pain in Society. In R. Teddington (ed.), *Towards a Whole Society*. London: Fellowship Press.

Carter, A. (1999) Staring Back, Mindfully: Reinstating the Dancer and the Dance in Feminist Ballet Historiography. In *Proceedings of Society of Dance History Scholars Twenty-Second Annual Conference*, University of New Mexico. Albuquerque, NM: Society of Dance History Scholars.

Carter, K. (2000) Consuming the Ballerina: Feet, Fetishism and the Pointe Shoe. *Australian Feminist Studies*, 15: 81–90.

Cashmore, E. (2005) *Making Sense of Sports*, fourth edition. London: Routledge.

Caudwell, J. (2003) Sporting Gender: Women's Footballing Bodies as Sites/Sights for the [Re]articulation of Sex, Gender and Desire. *Sociology of Sport Journal*, 20: 371–386.

Caudwell, J. (2006) *Sport, Sexualities and Queer Theory: Challenges and Controversies*. London: Routledge.

Centers for Disease Control and Prevention (CDC) (2002) Surveillance Summaries. *Morbidity and Morality Weekly Report*, 51: SS-4.

Chambers, C. (2005) Masculine Domination, Radical Feminism and Change. *Feminist Theory*, 6(3): 325–346.

Chen, M. (1983) *A Quiet Revolution*. Cambridge, MA: Schenkman.

Clarke, G. (2002) Making Space for the Tortoise – Educating Creative Individual Artists! In *Finding the Balance: Dance in Further and Higher Education in the 21st Century. Conference Proceedings*. CD-ROM. Liverpool John Moore's University, Liverpool, UK.

Cloke, P. (2005) Masculinity and Rurality. In B.A. Hoven and K. Horschelmann (eds), *Spaces of Masculinities*. New York: Routledge.

Coalter, F. (1999) Sport and Recreation in the United Kingdom: Flow with the Flow or Buck the Trends? *Managing Leisure*, 4(1): 24–39.

Coalter, F. (2004) Future Sports or Future Challenges to Sport? In Sport England (ed.), *Driving up Participation: The Challenge for Sport*. London: Sport England.

Cockburn, C. and Clarke, G. (2002) Everybody's Looking at You! Girls Negotiating the 'Femininity Deficit' they Incur in Physical Education. *Women Studies International Forum*, 25: 651–665.

Cohane, G.H. and Pope, H.G. (2001). Body Image in Boys: A Review of the Literature. *International Journal of Eating Disorders*, 29(4): 373–379.

Cohen, S. (2002) *Folk Devils and Moral Panics*, third edition. London: Routledge.

Cole, C.L. (1993) Resisting the Cannon: Feminist Cultural Studies, Sport and Technologies of the Body. *Journal of Sport and Social Issues*, 17: 77–97.

Collins, M. and Kay, T. (2003) *Sport and Social Exclusion*. London: Routledge

Colwell, S. (1999) Feminisms and Figurational Sociology: Contributions to Understandings of Sports, Physical Education and Sex/Gender. *European Physical Education Review*, 5(3): 219–240.

Connell, R.W. (1995) *Masculinities*. Cambridge: Polity.

Connell, R.W. (2000) *The Men and the Boys*. Cambridge: Polity.

Connell, R.W. (2005) Change among the Gatekeepers: Men, Masculinities and Gender Equality in the Global Arena. *Signs: Journal of Women in Culture and Society*, 30: 1801–1825.

Cornell, D. (1992) *The Philosophy of the Limit*. New York: Routledge.

Cothran, D. (2001) Curricula Change in Physical Education: Success Stories from the Front Line. *Sport, Education and Society*, 6(1): 67–79.

Cox, L., Coleman, L. and Roker, D. (2006) *Understanding Participation in Sport: What Determines Sports Participation among 15–19 Year Old Women?* London: Sport England.

Criste, A. (2002) ANA Journal Course. Update for Nurse Anesthetists. Gender and Pain. *ANNA Journal*, 70: 475–480.

Crum, B.J. (1983) Conventional Thought and Practice in Physical Education: Problems of Teaching and Implications for Change. *Quest*, 45: 336–356.

Csikszentmihalyi, M. (1990) *Flow: The Psychology of Optimal Experience*. New York: HarperCollins.

Curry, T.J. and Strauss, R.H. (1994) 'A Little Pain Never Hurt Anybody': A Photo Essay on the Normalisation of Sport Injuries. *Sociology of Sports Journal*, 11: 195–208.

Daily Mirror (2004) War on Obesity, 12 February: 11.

Davies, M. (1995) *Helping Children to Learn through a Movement Perspective*. London: Hodder and Stoughton.

Deem, R. (1986) *All Work and No Play? The Sociology of Women and Leisure*. Milton Keynes: Open University Press.

Department for Culture, Media and Sport (DCMS) (2000) *A Sporting Future for All*. London: DCMS.

Department for Education (DfE) and Welsh Office (WO) (1992) *Physical Education in the National Curriculum.* London: DfE.

Department for Education and Employment (DfEE) (1999) *Physical Education.* London: Qualifications and Curriculum Council.

Department for Education and Skills (DfES) (2004a) *Every Child Matters: Change for Children.* Available at: www.everychildmatters.gov.uk/ (accessed 23 January 2007).

Department for Education and Skills (DfES) (2004b) *The Children Act.* Available at: www.dfcs.gov.uk (accessed 23 January 2007).

Department for Education and Skills (DfES) (2006) *Physical Education, School Sport and Club Links.* Nottingham: DfES Publications.

Department for Education and Skills (DfES) (2007) *Personalised Learning.* Available at: www.everychildmatters.gov.uk/ete/personalisedlearning/ (accessed 19 March 2007).

Department for Education and Skills (DfES)/Department for Culture, Media and Sport (DCMS) (2003) *Learning through PE and Sport.* London: DfES/DCMS.

Department for Education and Skills (DfES)/Department for Culture, Media and Sport (DCMS) (2004) *High Quality PE and Sport for Young People.* London: DfES Publications.

Department for Education and Skills (DfES)/Department of Health (DH) (2005) *National Healthy School Status.* London: DH Publications Orderline.

Department of Health (2006) *Healthy Schools – Health and Education Going Hand-in-Hand.* Available at: www.dh.gov.uk/ (accessed 16 May 2006).

Diener, E. and Suh, E.M. (1999) National Differences in Subjective Well-Being. In D. Kahneman, E. Diener, N. Schwarz (eds), *Well-Being: The Foundations of Hedonic Psychology.* New York, Russell Sage Foundation.

Diener, E., Sapyta, J.J., and Suh, E. (1998) Subjective Well-Being is Essential to Well-Being. *Psychological Inquiry*, 9(1): 33–37.

Dietz, W. and Gortmaker, S. (1984) Factors within the Physical Environment Associated with Childhood Obesity. *American Journal of Clinical Nutrition*, 39: 619–624.

Dowling, R. (2000) Power, Ethics and Subjectivity in Qualitative Research. In I. Hay (ed.), *Qualitative Methods in Human Geography.* Melbourne: Oxford University Press.

Doyle, J. and Bryant Waugh, R.A. (2000) Epidemiology. In B. Lask and R. Bryant Waugh (eds), *Anorexia Nervosa and Related Eating Disorders in Childhood and Adolescence.* Hove: Psychology Press.

Duerden, R. and Fisher, N. (2002) Thinking Dancers: Finding a Balance in Training of Undergraduate Dancers. In *Finding the Balance: Dance in Further and Higher Education in the 21st Century. Conference Proceedings.* CD-ROM. Liverpool John Moore's University, Liverpool, UK.

Eating Disorders Association (2004) http://www.edauk.com/student_info.htm

Elias, N. and Dunning, E. (1986) *Quest for Excitement: Sport and Leisure in the Civilising Process.* Oxford: Basil Blackwell.

Encarnacion, M.L.G., Meyers, M.C., Ryan, N.D. and Pease, D.G. (2000) Pain Coping Styles of Ballet Performers. *Journal of Sport Behavior*, 23: 20–32.

Epstein, D. Hewitt, R. Leonard, D. Mauthner, M. and Watkins, C. (2003) Avoiding the Issue: Homophobia, School Policies and Identities in Secondary Schools. In C. Vincent (ed.), *Social Justice, Education and Identity.* London: RoutledgeFalmer.

Ericsson, K.A. Krampe, R.T., and Tesch-Romer, C. (1993) The Role of Deliberate Practice in the Acquisition of Expert Performance. *Psychological Review*, 100(3): 363–406.

European Youth Heart Study Symposium (EYHS) (2006) Summary Statement on Children, Physical Activity and Health. Fourth European Youth Heart Study Symposium, University of Southern Denmark.

Evans, J. (2003) Physical Education and Health: A Polemic or 'Let Them Eat Cake!' *European Physical Education Review*, 9(1): 87–101.

Evans, J. (2004) Making a Difference? Education and 'Ability' in Physical Education. *European Physical Education Review*, 10(1): 95–108.

Evans, J and Davies, B. (2004) The Embodiment of Consciousness: Bernstein, Health and Schooling. In J. Evans, B. Davies and J. Wright (eds), *Body Knowledge and Control: Studies in the Sociology of Physical Education and Health*. London: Routledge.

Evans, J. and Davies, B. (2004) Sociology, the Body and Health in a Risk Society. In J. Evans, B. Davies and J. Wright (eds), *Body, Knowledge and Control: Studies in the Sociology of Physical Education and Health*. London: Routledge.

Evans, J. and Penney, D. (2002) Introduction. In D. Penney (ed.), *Gender and Physical Education: Contemporary Issues and Future Directions*. London: Routledge.

Evans, J and Penney, D. (2008) Levels on the Playing Field: The Social Construction of Physical Ability in the Physical Education Curriculum. *Physical Education and Sport Pedagogy*, in press.

Evans, J., Davies, B. and Penney, D. (1996) Teachers, Teaching and the Social Construction of Gender Relations. *Sport, Education and Society*, 1(2): 165–184.

Evans, J., Rich, E. and Holroyd, R. (2004) Disordered Eating and Disordered Schooling: What Schools do to Middle Class Girls. *British Journal of Sociology of Education*, 25: 123–143.

Evans, J., Rich, E., Allwood, R. and Davies, B. (2008) Body Pedagogies, P/policy, Health and Gender. *British Educational Research Journal* (in press).

Evers, C. (2004) Men who Surf. *Cultural Studies Review*, 10(1): 27–41.

Evers, C. (2005) Becoming Man, Becoming Wave. Unpublished PhD dissertation, University of Sydney.

Evers, C. (2006) How to Surf. *Journal of Sport and Social Issues*, 30(3): 269–243.

Faulkner G., and Biddle S. (2004) Exercise and Depression: Considering Variability and Contextuality. *Journal of Sport and Exercise Psychology*, 26: 3–18.

Fawkner, H.J., McMurray, N.E. and Summers, R.J. (1999) Athletic Injury and Minor Life Events: A Prospective Study. *Journal of Science and Medicine in Sport*, 2: 117–124.

Feinberg, J. (1980/1992) The Child's Right to an Open Future. In *Freedom and Fulfilment: Philosophical Essays*. Princeton, NJ: Princeton University Press.

Fejgin, N. (1994) Participation in High School Competitive Sports: A Subversion of School Mission or Contribution to Academic Goals? *Sociology of Sport Journal*, 11: 211–230.

Fernandez-Balboa, J.-M. (1993) Socio-Cultural Characteristics of the Hidden Curriculum in Physical Education. *Quest*, 45: 230–254.

Fernandez-Balboa, J.-M. (1997) *Critical Postmodernism in Human Movement, Physical Education and Sport*. Albany: State University of New York Press.

Firestone, S. (1979) *The Dialectic of Sex: The Case for Feminist Revolution*. London: The Women's Press.

Fiske, J. (1989) *Reading the Popular.* London: Unwin Hyman.

Fletcher, S. (1984) *Women First: The Female Tradition in English Physical Education 1880–1980.* London: Athlone Press.

Fletcher, S. (1987) The Making and Breaking of a Female Tradition: Women's Physical Education in England 1880–1980. In J.A. Mangan and R.J. Park (eds), *From 'Fair Sex' to Feminism: Sport and the Socialization of Women in the Industrial and Post-Industrial Eras.* London: Frank Cass.

Flintoff, A. (2005) Indifferent, Hostile or Empowered? School Physical Education and Active Leisure Lifestyles for Girls and Young Women. In A. Flintoff, J. Long and K. Hylton (eds), *Youth, Sport and Active Leisure: Theory, Policy and Participation.* Eastbourne: Leisure Studies Association.

Flintoff, A. and Scraton, S. (2001) Stepping into Active Leisure? Young Women's Perceptions of Active Lifestyles and their Experiences of School Physical Education. *Sport, Education and Society*, 6(1): 5–22.

Flintoff, A. and Scraton, S. (2005) Gender and Physical Education. In K. Green and K. Hardman (eds), *Physical Education: Essential Issues.* London: Sage.

Flintoff, A. and Scraton, S. (2006) Girls and Physical Education. in D. Kirk, D. Macdonald and M. O'Sullivan (eds), *The Handbook of Physical Education.* London: Sage.

Ford, N. and Brown, D. (2006) *Surfing and Social Theory: Experience, Embodiment and Narrative of the Dream Glide.* Abingdon: Routledge.

Foster, S.L (1997) Dancing Bodies. In J.C. Desmond (ed.), *Meaning in Motion: New Cultural Studies of Dance.* Durham, NC: Duke University Press.

Foucault, M (1977) *Discipline and Punish: The Birth of a Prison.* Harmondsworth: Penguin.

Foucault, M. (1988) *The History of Sexuality: An Introduction*, trans. R. Hurley. Harmondsworth: Penguin.

Foucault, M. (1992) *The Use of Pleasure: The History of Sexuality, Vol. 2*, trans. Robert Hurley. London: Penguin.

Fox, K. (1999) The Influence of Physical Activity on Mental Well-Being. *Public Health Nutrition*, 2(3): 411–418.

Fraleigh, S. H. (1987) *Dance and the Lived Body: A Descriptive Aesthetics.* Pittsburgh, PA: University of Pittsburgh Press.

Frank, A. (1990) Bringing Bodies Back In: A Decade Review. *Theory, Culture and Society*, 7: 131–162.

Frosh, S. Phoenix, A. and Pattman, R. (2002) Young Masculinities. Aldershot, UK: Palgrave.

Frost, L. (2001) *Young Women and the Body: A Feminist Sociology.* London: Palgrave.

Fuchs, R., Powell, K., Semmer, N., Dwyer, J., Lippert, P. and Hoffmoester, H. (1988) Patterns of Physical Activity among German Adolescents: The Berlin Bremen Study. *Preventative Medicine*, 17: 746–763.

Furedi, F. (2002) *Culture of Fear.* London: Continuum.

Gaffney, A. (1993) Cognitive Developmental Aspects of Pain in School-Age Children. In N.L. Schechter, C.B. Berde and M. Yaster (eds.), *Pain in Infants, Children and Adolescents.* Baltimore, MD: Williams and Wilkins.

Gaffney, A. and Dunne, E.A. (1986) Developmental Aspects of Children's Definitions of Pain. *Pain*, 26: 105–117.

Gaffney, A. and Dunne, E.A. (1987) Children's Understanding of Causality of Pain. *Pain*, 29: 91–104.

Gard, M. (2004a) An Elephant in the Room and a Bridge Too Far, or Physical Education and the 'Obesity Epidemic'. In J. Evans, B. Davies and J. Wright (eds), *Body Knowledge and Control: Studies in the Sociology of Physical Education and Health*. London: Routledge.

Gard, M. (2004b) Desperately Seeking Certainty: Statistics, Physical Activity and Critical Enquiry. In J. Wright, D. Macdonald and L. Burrows (eds), *Critical Inquiry and Problem Solving in Physical Education*. London: Routledge.

Gard, M. and Meyenn, R. (2000) Boys, Bodies, Pleasure and Pain: Interrogating Contact Sports in Schools. *Sport, Education and Society*, 5: 19–34.

Gard, M. and Wright, J. (2001) Managing Uncertainty: Obesity Discourse and Physical Education in a Risk Society. *Studies in Philosophy and Education*, 20: 535–549.

Gard, M. and Wright, J. (2005) *The Obesity Epidemic: Science, Morality and Ideology*. London: Routledge.

Garn, A. and Cothran, D. (2006) The Fun Factor in Physical Education. *Journal of Teaching in Physical Education*, 25: 281–297.

Garner, D.M. and Garfinkel, P.E. (1980) Socio-Cultural Factors in the Development of Anorexia Nervosa. *Psychological Medicine*, 10: 647–656.

Garner, D.M., Garfinkel, P.E., Rockert, W. and Olmsted, M.P. (1987) A Prospective Study of Eating Disturbances in the Ballet. *Psychotherapy and Psychosomatics*, 48: 170–175.

Garrett, R. (2004a) Gendered Bodies and Physical Identities. In J. Evans, B. Davies and J. Wright (eds), *Body, Knowledge and Control: Studies in the Sociology of Physical Education and Health*. London: Routledge.

Garrett, R. (2004b) Negotiating a Physical Identity: Girls, Bodies and Physical Education. *Sport, Education and Society*, 9(2): 223–237.

Gasper, D. (2004) *Human Well-Being: Concepts and Conceptualizations*. Helsinki: United Nations University, World Institute for Development Economics Research.

Giddens, A. (1992) *The Transformations of Intimacy*. Cambridge: Polity.

Gilroy, S. (1989) The Embodiment of Power: Gender and Physical Activity. *Leisure Studies* 8: 163–172.

Goffman, E. (1972) *Encounters*. Harmondsworth: Penguin.

Goldberg, M. (1997) Homogenized Ballerinas. In J. Desmond (ed.), *Meaning in Motion: New Cultural Studies of Dance*. Durham, NC: Duke University Press

Gray, K.M and Kunkel, M.A. (2001) The Experience of Female Ballet Dancers: A Grounded Theory. *High Ability Studies*, 12: 7–25.

Green, J. (2001) Socially Constructed Bodies in American Dance Classrooms. *Research in Dance Education*, 2: 155–173.

Green, K. (1998) Philosophies, Ideologies and the Practice of Physical Education. *Sport, Education and Society*, 3: 125–143.

Green, K. (2000) Exploring the Everyday 'Philosophies' of Physical Education Teachers from a Sociological Perspective. *Sport, Education and Society*, 5(1): 109–129.

Green, K. (2002) Physical Education and 'the Couch Potato Society': Part One. *European Journal of Physical Education*, 7(2): 95–107.

Green, K. (2003) *Physical Education Teachers on Physical Education*. Chester: Chester Academic Press.

Green, K. and Scraton, S. (1998). Gender, Coeducation and Secondary Physical Education: A Brief Review. In K. Green and K. Hardman (eds) *Physical Education: A Reader*. Aachen: Meyer & Meyer.

Green, K., Smith, A. and Roberts, K. (2005) Young People and Lifelong Participation in Sport and Physical Activity: A Sociological Perspective on Contemporary Physical Education Programmes in England and Wales. *Leisure Studies*, 24(1): 27–43.

Gregson, N. and Crewe, L. (1998) Dusting Down Second Hand Rose: Gendered Identities and the World of Second-Hand Goods in the Space of the Car Boot Sale. *Gender, Place and Culture*, 5: 77–100.

Griffin, J. (1986) *Well-Being*. Oxford: Clarendon Press.

Griffin, J. (1996) *Value Judgement*. Oxford: Clarendon Press

Griffin, P. (1998) *Strong Women, Deep Closets: Lesbians and Homophobia in Sport*. Champaign, IL: Human Kinetics.

Grogan, S. (1999) *Body Image*. London: Routledge.

Hall, C.M. (2005) Shifting Spaces of Masculinity: From Carisbrook to the MCG. In B.A. Hoven and K. Horschelmann (eds), *Spaces of Masculinities*. New York: Routledge.

Hall, M.A. (1996) *Feminism and Sporting Bodies: Essays on Theory and Practice*. Champaign, IL: Human Kinetics.

Hall, M.A. (2002) The Discourse of Gender and Sport: From Femininity to Feminism. In S. Scraton and A. Flintoff (eds), *Gender and Sport: A Reader*. London: Routledge.

Hamera, J. (2005) All the (Dis)comforts of Home: Place, Gendered Self-Fashioning and Solidarity in a Ballet Studio. *Text and Performance Quarterly* 25: 93–112.

Hamilton, L.A., Brooks-Gunn, J., Warren, M.P and Hamilton, W.G. (1988) The Role of Selectivity in the Pathogenesis of Eating Problems in Ballet Dancers. *Medicine and Science in Sports and Exercise*, 20: 560–565.

Hamilton, L.H. and Hamilton, W.G. (1991) Classical Ballet: Balancing the Costs of Artistry and Athletism. *Medical Problems of Performing Artists*, 6: 39–44.

Hanson, S. and Kraus, R. (1999) Women in Male Domains: Sport and Science. *Sociology of Sport Journal*, 16: 91–110.

Harbeck, C. and Peterson, L. (1992) Elephants Dancing in My Head: A Developmental Approach to Children's Concepts of Specific Pains. *Child Development*, 9: 133–161.

Hargreaves, A. (2003) *Teaching in a Knowledge Society*. Maidenhead: Open University Press.

Hargreaves, D. (2004) *Learning for Life: The Foundations for Lifelong Learning*. Bristol: The Policy Press.

Hargreaves, J. (1986) *Sport, Power and Culture*. London: Polity

Hargreaves, J. (1994) *Sporting Females: Critical Issues in the History and Sociology of Women's Sports*. London: Routledge.

Hargreaves, J. (1996) Bruising Peg to Boxerobics: Gendered Boxing Images and Meanings. In D. Chandler (ed.), *Boxer: An Anthology of Writing on Boxing and Visual Culture*. London: Institute of International Visual Arts.

Hartig, K. and Dunn, K. (1998) Roadside Memorials: Interpreting New Deathscapes in Newcastle, New South Wales. *Australian Geographical Studies*, 36(1): 5–20

Hauser, T. (1991) *Muhammad Ali: His Life and Times*. New York: Simon Schuster

Hay, P.J. and lisahunter (2006). 'Please My Hay, What are My Poss(abilities)?': Legitimation of Ability through Physical Education Practices. *Sport, Education and Society*, 11 (3): 293–310.

Heikkala, J. (1993) Discipline and Excel: Techniques of the Self and Body and the Logic of Competing. *Sociology of Sport Journal*, 10: 397–412.

Henderson, M. (1999) Some Tales of Two Mags: Sports Magazines as Glossy Reservoirs of Male Fantasy. *Journal of Australian Studies*, 62: 64–75.

Henderson, M. (2001) A Shifting Line-Up: Men, Women and *Tracks* Surfing Magazine. *Continuum*, 15(3): 319–332.

HMSO (1989) *The Children Act*. Available at: www.opsi.gov.uk/acts (accessed 23 January 2007).

HMSO (1998) Chapter 42. *Human Rights Act*. Available at: www.opsi.gov.uk/acts (accessed 23 January 2007).

Hochstetler, D.R. (2003) Process and the Sport Experience. *Quest*, 55: 231–243.

Hoffmann, D.E and Tarzian, A.J. (2001) The Girl Who Cried Pain: A Bias against Women in the Treatment of Pain. *Journal of Law, Medicine and Ethics*, 29(1): 13–27.

Holstein, J.A. and Gubrium, J.F. (1997) Active Interviewing. In D. Silverman (ed.), *Qualitative Research*. London: Sage.

Howe, D. (2001) An Ethnography of Pain and Injury in Professional Rugby Union. *International Review for the Sociology of Sport*, 36(3): 289–303.

Howe, P.D. (2004) *Sport, Professionalism and Pain Ethnographies of Injury and Risk*. London: Routledge.

Hubbard, P. (2000) Desire/Disgust: Mapping the Moral Contours of Heterosexuality. *Progress in Human Geography*, 24(2): 191–217.

Hughson, J. and Inglis, D. (2002) Inside the Beautiful Game: Towards a Merleau-Pontarian Phenomenology of Soccer Play. *Journal of the Philosophy of Sport*, 29: 1–15.

Hunter, L. (2004) Bourdieu and the Social Space of the PE Class: Reproduction of Doxa through Practice. *Sport, Education and Society*, 9(2): 175–192.

Hurley, S. (2003) *Justice, Luck, and Knowledge*. Cambridge, MA: Harvard University Press.

International Association for the Study of Pain (1979) Pain Terms: A List with Definitions and Notes on Usage. *Pain*, 6: 240.

Jago and Bailey (2001) Ethics and Paediatric Science: Issues and Making a Submission to a Local Ethics and Research Committee. *Journal of Sports Science*, 19: 527–535.

Jagose, A. (1996) *Queer Theory*. Melbourne: Melbourne University Press.

Jefferson, T. (1998a) On Muscle, 'Hard Men', and 'Iron' Mike Tyson: Reflections on Desire, Anxiety and the Embodiment of Masculinity. *Body and Society*, 4: 77–98.

Jefferson, T. (1998b) From 'Little Fairy Boy' to 'the Compleat Destroyer': Subjectivity and Transformation in the Biography of Mike Tyson. In M. Mac an Ghaill (ed.), *Understanding Masculinities: Social Relations and Cultural Arenas*. Milton Keynes: Open University Press.

Jenkins, R. (1992) *Pierre Bourdieu*. London: Routledge.

Johnston, L. (1998) Reading the Sexed Bodies and Spaces of Gyms. In H. Nast and S. Pile (eds), *Places through the Body*. London: Routledge.

Johnston, L. (2005) Man:Woman. In P. Cloke and R. Johnston (eds), *Spaces of Geographical Thought: Deconstructing Human Geography's Binaries*. London: Sage.

Kakuchi, S. (2006) Japan: Education Bill Sets Patriotism over Individualism. Inter Press Service News Agency. Available at: www.ipsnews.net/ (accessed 30 May 2006).

Kidd, B. and Donnelly, P. (2000) Human Rights in Sports. *International Review for the Sociology of Sport*, 35(2): 131–148.

Kirk, D. (1992) *Defining Physical Education: The Social Construction of a School Subject in Postwar Britain*. London: The Falmer Press.

Kirk, D. (2002) Physical Education: A Gendered History. In D. Penney (ed.), *Gender and Physical Education: Contemporary and Future Directions*. New York: Routledge.

Kirk, D. (2005a) Physical Education, Youth Sport and Lifelong Participation: The Importance of Early Learning Experiences. *European Physical Education Review*, 11(3): 239–256.

Kirk, D. (2005b) Physical Culture, Lifelong Participation and Empowerment: Towards an Educational Rationale for Physical Education. In A. Flintoff, J. Long and K. Hylton (eds), *Youth, Sport and Active Leisure: Theory, Policy and Participation*, Eastbourne: Leisure Studies Association.

Kirk, D., Fitzgerald, H., Wang, J. and Biddle, S. (2000) *Towards Girl-Friendly Physical Education: The Nike/Youth Sport Trust 'Girls in Sport' Partnership Project – Final Report*. Loughborough, UK: Youth Sport Trust.

Koivula, N. (2001) Perceived Characteristics of Sports Categorized as Gender-Neutral, Feminine and Masculine. *Journal of Sport Behavior*, 24: 377–393.

Kotarba, J.A. (1983) *Chronic Pain: Its Social Dimensions*. London: Sage.

Krasnow, D. Kerr, G. and Mainwaring, L. (1994) Psychology of Dealing with the Injured Dancer. *Medical Problems of Performing Artists*, 9: 7–9.

Kupperman, J.J. (2003) Comfort, Hedonic Treadmills, and Public Policy. *Public Affairs Quarterly*, 17 (1): 17–28.

Kupperman, J.J. (2006) *Six Myths about the Good Life: Thinking about What Has Value*. Indianapolis, IN: Hackett.

Lafferty, Y. and McKay, J. (2005) 'Suffragettes in Satin Shorts?' Gender and Competitive Boxing. *Qualitative Sociology*, 27(3): 249–276.

Lave, J. and Wenger, E. (1992) *Situated Learning: Legitimate Peripheral Learning*. Cambridge: Cambridge University Press.

Lavoie, M. (2000) Economics and Sport. In J. Coakley and E. Dunning (eds), *Handbook of Sports Studies*. London: Sage.

Le Grange, D., Tibbs, J. and Noakes, T.D. (1994) Implications and Diagnosis of Anorexia Nervosa in a Ballet School. *International Journal of Eating Disorders*, 15: 369–376

Lemert, C. (2003) *Muhammad Ali: Trickster in the Culture of Irony*. Cambridge: Polity.

Levine, M. and Piran, N. (1999) Reflections, Conclusion, Future Direction. In N. Piran, M. Levine and C. Steiner-Adair (eds), *Preventing Eating Disorders: A Handbook of Intervention and Special Challenges*. Philadelphia, PA: Brunner/Mazel.

Liederbach, M. and Compagno, J.M. (2001) Psychological Aspects of Fatigue Related Injuries in Dancers. *Journal of Dance Medicine and Science*, 5: 116–120.

Lock, R. (2006) Heterosexual Femininity: The Painful Process of Subjectification. In J. Caudwell (ed.), *Sport, Sexualities and Queer Theory: Challenges and Controversies*. London: Routledge.

Locke, F.L. (1992) Changing Secondary School Physical Education. *Quest*, 44, 361–372.

Loland, S. (2006) Three Approaches to the Study of Pain in Sport. In S. Loland, B. Skirstad and I. Waddington (eds), *Pain and Injury in Sport: Social and Ethical Analysis*. London: Routledge.

Longhurst, R. (2000) Geography and Gender: Masculinities, Male Identity and Men. *Progress in Human Geography*, 24(3): 439–444.

Longhurst, R. (2005) 'Man Breasts': Spaces of Sexual Difference, Fluidity and Abjection. In B.A. Hoven and K. Horschelmann (eds), *Spaces of Masculinities*. New York: Routledge.

Loumidis, K. and Wells, A. (2001) Exercising for the Wrong Reasons: Relationships among Eating Disorder Beliefs, Dysfunctional Exercise Beliefs and Coping. *Clinical Psychology and Psychotherapy*, 8: 416–23.

Lundy, K. and Gillard, J. (2003) Tackling Obesity and Promoting Community Well Being: Labor's Plan for a Healthier and More Active Australia. Labor Party Policy Paper 014. Victoria: Labor Party.

Lyotard, J. F. (1984) *The Post Modern Condition: A Report on Knowledge*. Minneapolis, MN: University of Minnesota Press.

Mac an Ghaill, M. (1994) *The Making of Men: Masculinities, Sexualities and Schooling*. Buckingham: Open University Press.

Mac an Ghaill, M. (1996) *Understanding Masculinities*. Buckingham: Open University Press.

McAuley, E., Blissmer, B., Marquez, D.X., Jerome, G.J., Kramer, A.F., Katula, J. (2000) Social Relations, Physical Activity and Well-Being in Older Adults. *Preventive Medicine* 31: 608–17.

MacDonald, I. (2003) The Politics of Race and Sport Policy. In B. Houlihan (ed.), *Sport and Society*. London: Sage.

McDowell, L. (1997) *Capital Cultural: Gender at Work in the City*. Oxford: Blackwell.

McGloin, C. (2005) Surfing Nation(s) – Surfing Country(s). Unpublished PhD dissertation, University of Wollongong.

McKay, J., Messner, M. and Sabo, D. (2000) *Masculinities, Gender Relations and Sport*, London: Sage.

MacKinnon, K. (2006) *Are Women Human? And Other International Dialogues*. Cambridge, MA: Harvard University Press.

McNamee, M. J. (1994) Valuing Leisure Practices: Towards a Theoretical Framework. *Leisure Studies*, 13(4): 288–309.

MacPhail, A., Kirk, D. and Eley, D. (2003) Listening to Young People's Voices: Youth Sports Leaders' Advice on Facilitating Participation in Sport. *European Physical Education Review*, 9(1): 57–73.

Mainwaring, L.M., Krasnow, D. and Kerr, G. (2001) And the Dance Goes On: Psychological Impact of Injury. *Journal of Dance Medicine and Science*, 5: 105–115.

Malina, R., Bouchard, C. and Bar-Or, O. (2004) *Growth, Maturation and Physical Activity*. Champaign, IL: Human Kinetics.

Malson, H. (1998) *The Thin Woman in the Body: A Cultural Analysis of Reproduction*. Milton Keynes: Open University Press.

Marqusee, M. (2005[2000]) *Redemption Song*, London, Verso.

Martin, D.E. and Coe, P.N. (1991) *Training Distance Runners*. Leeds: Human Kinetics.

Massey, D. (1994) *Space, Place and Gender*. Cambridge: Polity Press.

Massey, D. (1998) Blurring the Binaries? High Tech in Cambridge. In R. Ainley (ed.), *New Frontiers of Spaces, Bodies and Gender*. London: Routledge.

Melzack, R. (1973) *The Puzzle of Pain*. New York: Basic Books.

Melzack, R. and Wall, P.D. (1996) *The Challenge of Pain*. London: Penguin Books.

Mennesson, C. (2000) 'Hard' Women and 'Soft' Women *International Review for the Sociology of Sport*, 35(1): 21–33.

Merleau-Ponty, M. (1962) *Phenomenology of Perception*. London: Routledge and Kegan Paul.

Messner, M. (1992) *Power at Play: Sports and the Problem of Masculinity*. Boston, MA: Beacon.

Messner, M. (2002) *Taking the Field: Women, Men and Sports*. Minneapolis, MN: University of Minnesota Press.

Messner, M. and Sabo, D.F. (eds), (1994) *Sex Violence and Power in Sports*. Freedom, CA: Crossing Press.

Miah, A. and Rich, E.J. (2006) Genetic Tests for Ability?: Talent Identification and the Value of an Open Future. *Sport, Education and Society*, 11(3): 259–273.

Miah, A., and Rich, E. (2007) *The Medicalisation of Cyberspace*. London: Routledge.

Miller, T. (2001) *Sportsex*. Philadelphia, PA: Temple University Press.

MINEPS IV (2004) Fourth International Conference of Ministers and Senior Officials Responsible for Physical Education and Sport – Declaration of Athens, Greece, 6–8 December.

Ministry of Education (2003) *Statement of Intent 2003–2008*. Available at: www.minedu.govt.nz/ (accessed 19 March 2007).

Monaghan, L. (2005) Discussion Piece: A Critical Take on the Obesity Debate. *Social Theory and Health*, 3(4): 302–314.

Morris, M. (2006) Working Smarter, Not Just Harder – Depth versus Diversity in Dance Training. Paper presented at Dance UK Conference 'In the Balance: Achieving Excellence through Effective and Healthy Dance Training', Elmhurst School, Birmingham, UK.

Mossop, J. (1997) Lewis Looks Forward to a Bout of Unification after McCall Fiasco. *Sunday Telegraph*, 9 February: S7.

Mulvey, L. (1975) Visual Pleasure and Narrative Cinema. *Screen*, 16(3): 6–18.

Nairn, K. (2002) Doing Feminist Fieldwork about Geography Fieldwork. In P. Moss (ed.), *Feminist Geography in Practice: Research and Methods*. Oxford: Blackwell.

National Assembly of Wales (2006) *Key Statistical Indicators at School Level, 2000–2005*. Cardiff: National Assembly for Wales.

Nazer, D. (2004) The Tragicomedy of the Surfers' Common. *Deakin Law Review*, 92(2): 655–713

Nelson, B. (2005) Underpinning Prosperity: Our Agenda in Education, Science and Training. Speech at the Sustaining Prosperity Conference, University of Melbourne, 31 March 2005.

Nemeth, R.L., von Baeyer, C.L. and Rocha, E.M. (2005) Young Gymnasts' Understanding of Sport-Related Pain: A Contribution to Prevention of Injury. *Child Care, Health and Development*, 31: 615–625.

Nixon, H.L. (1989) Reconsidering Obligatory Running and Anorexia Nervosa as Gender Related Problems of Identity and Role Adjustment. *Journal of Sport and Social Issues*, 13: 14–24.

Nixon, H.L. (1992) A Social Network Analysis of Influences on Athletes to Play with Pain and Injuries. *Journal of Sport and Social Issues*, 13: 14–24.

Nixon, H.L. (1993) Accepting the Risks of Pain and Injury in Sport: Mediated Cultural Influences on Playing Hurt. *Sociology of Sport Journal*, 10: 183–196.

Nixon, H.L. (1996) Explaining Pain and Injury Attitudes and Experiences in Sport in Terms of Gender, Race and Sports Status Factor. *Journal of Sport and Social Issues*, 20: 33–44.

Noggle, R. (2002) Special Agents: Children's Autonomy and Parental Authority. In D. Archard and C.M. MacLeod (eds), *The Moral and Political Status of Children*. Oxford: Oxford University Press.

Novella, T. (1994) Foot Care for Pointe Shoes – Ballet Dancers' Health. *Dance Magazine*, April. Available at: www.dancemagazine.com (accessed 23 January 2007).

Nozick, R. (1974) *Anarchy, State and Utopia*. New York: Basic Books.

Nussbaum, M. (1995) Human Capabilities, Female Human Beings. In M. Nussbaum and J. Glover (eds), *Women, Culture, and Development: A Study of Human Capabilities*. Oxford: Clarendon Press.

Nussbaum, M. (1999) *Sex and Social Justice*. Oxford: Oxford University Press.

Nussbaum, M. (2000) *Women and Human Development: The Capabilities Approach*. Cambridge: Cambridge University Press.

Nye, R.A. (2005) Locating Masculinity: Some Recent Work on Men. *Signs: Journal of Women in Culture and Society*, 30(31): 1937–1962.

O'Connor, D. (ed.) (2002) *Iron Mike: A Mike Tyson Reader*. New York: Thunder's Mouth Press.

O'Donovan, T. and Kay, T. (2005) Focus on 'Girls in Sport'. *British Journal of Teaching Physical Education*, 36(1): 29–31.

O'Donovan, T. and Kay, T. (2006) *Girls in Sport: Monitoring and Evaluation: Final Report*. Loughborough University: Institute of Youth Sport/Youth Sport Trust.

O'Neill, J. (1998) *Ecology, Policy and Politics: Human Well-Being and the Natural World*. London: Routledge.

O'Reilly, E., Tompkins, J. and Gallant, M. (2001) 'They Ought to Enjoy Physical Activity, You Know?': Struggling with Fun in Physical Education. *Sport, Education and Society*, 62: 211–221

Oates, J.C. (1987) *On Boxing*. London: Bloomsbury.

Office of the Deputy Prime Minister (ODPM) (2006) *Indices of Deprivation 2004 – Summary (Revised)*. London: ODPM.

Oliver, K.L. and Lalik, R. (2004) Critical Inquiry on the Body in Girls' Physical Education Classes: A Critical Poststructural Perspective. *Journal of Teaching in Physical Education*, 23(2): 162–195.

Paechter, C. (2003a) Power, Bodies and Identity: How Different Forms of Physical Education Construct Varying Masculinities and Femininities in Secondary Schools. *Sex Education*, 3(1): 47–59.

Paechter, C. (2003b) Masculinities, Femininities and Physical Education: Bodily Practices as Reified Markers of Community Membership. In C. Vincent (ed.), *Social Justice, Education and Identity*. London: RoutledgeFalmer.

Paechter, C. (2006) Masculine Femininities/Feminine Masculinities: Power, Identities and Gender. *Gender and Education*, 18 (3): 253–263.

Parfit, D. (1984) *Reasons and Persons*. Oxford: Clarendon Press.

Park, R.J. (1987) Biological Thought, Athletics and the Formation of a 'Man of Character' 1830–1900. In J.A. Mangan and James Walvin (eds), *Manliness and Morality: Middle-Class Masculinity in Britain and America 1800–1940*. Manchester: Manchester University Press

Parry, J. (2006) Shaping the Dancer. Paper presented at Dance UK Conference 'In the Balance: Achieving Excellence through Effective and Healthy Dance Training', Elmhurst School, Birmingham, UK.

Pearson, K. (1979) *Surfing Subcultures of Australia and New Zealand*. St Lucia, Qld: University of Queensland Press.

Penney, D. (2002a) Gendered Policies. In D. Penney (ed.), *Gender and Physical Education*. London: Routledge.

Penney, D. (2002b) Equality, Equity and Inclusion in Physical Education and School Sport. In A. Laker (ed.), *The Sociology of Sport and Physical Education*. London: Routledge.

Penney, D. (2006) Curriculum Construction and Change. In D. Kirk, D. Macdonald and M. O'Sullivan (eds), *The Handbook of Physical Education*. London: Sage.

Penney, D. and Chandler, T. (2000) Physical Education: What Future(s)? *Sport, Education and Society*, 5(1): 71–87.

Penney, D. and Evans, J. (1999) *Politics, Policy and Practice in Physical Education*. London: E & FN Spon.

Penney, D. and Evans, J. (2005) Policy, Power and Politics in Physical Education. In K. Green and K. Hardman (eds), *Physical Education: Essential Issues*. London: Sage.

Penney, D. and Harris, J. (1997) Extra-curricular Physical Education: More of the Same for the More Able. *Sport, Education and Society*, 2(1): 41–54.

Penney, D. and Hunter, L. (2006) (Dis)abling the (Health and) Physical in Education: Ability, Curriculum and Pedagogy. *Sport, Education and Society*, 11(3): 205–211.

Petrie, T.A. (1992) Psychosocial Antecedents of Athletic Injury: The Effects of Life Stress and Social Support on Female Collegiate Gymnasts. *Behavioural Medicine*, 18: 127–138.

Pfister, G. and Reeg, A. (2006) Fitness as 'Social Heritage': A Study of Elementary Pupils in Berlin. *European Physical Education Review*, 12(1): 5–30.

Piran, N. (2004) Teachers: On 'Being' (Rather than 'Doing') Prevention. *Eating Disorders*, 12: 1–9.

Plummer, K. (2001) *Documents of Life 2: An Invitation to Critical Humanism*. London: Sage.

Powers, M. and Faden, R. (2006) *Social Justice: The Moral Foundations of Public Health and Health Policy*. Oxford: Oxford University Press.

Preston-Whyte, R. (2002) Constructions of Surfing Spaces at Durban, South Africa. *Tourism Geographies*, 4(3): 307–328.

Pringle, R. (1999) The Pain of Sport: Socialization, Injury and Prevention. *Journal of Physical Education New Zealand*, 32: 14–16.

Probyn, E. (2000) Sporting Bodies: Dynamics of Shame and Pride. *Body and Society*, 6(1): 13–28.

Probyn, E. (2003) The Spatial Imperative of Subjectivity. In K. Anderson, M. Domosh, S. Pile and N. Thrift (eds), *Handbook of Cultural Geography*, London: Sage Publications.

Professional Association of Teachers (2000) *Tested to Destruction? A Survey of Examination Stress in Teenagers. PAT's Interim Commentary.* Derby UK: Professional Association of Teachers.

Pronger, B. (1990) *The Arena of Masculinity: Sports, Homosexuality and the Meaning of Sex.* New York: St. Martin's Press.

Pronger, B. (2002) *Body Fascism: Salvation in the Technology of Physical Fitness.* Toronto: University of Toronto Press.

Qizilbash, M. (1998) *Poverty: Concept and Measurement.* Islamabad: Sustainable Development Policy Institute.

Rawls, J. (1971) *A Theory of Justice.* Cambridge, MA: Harvard University Press.

Redman, P. (1996) 'Empowering Men to Disempower Themselves': Heterosexual Masculinities, HIV and the Contradictions of Anti-oppressive Education. In M. Mac an Ghaill (ed.), *Understanding Masculinities.* Buckingham: Open University Press.

Redman, P. (2000) 'Tarred with the Same Brush': 'Homophobia' and the Role of the Unconscious in School-based Cultures of Masculinity. *Sexualities*, 3: 483–499.

Reijer, P., Chalimba, M. and Ayazikwa, A. (2002) Malawi Goes to Scale with Anti-AIDS Clubs and Popular Media. *Evaluation and Program Planning*, 25(4): 357–363.

Rich, E., Holroyd, R. and Evans, J. (2004) 'Hungry to be Noticed': Young Women, Anorexia and Schooling. In J. Evans, B. Davies and J. Wright (eds), *Body Knowledge and Control.* London: Routledge.

Rinehart, R.E. and Sydnor, E. (2003) *To the Extreme: Alternative Sports, Inside and Out.* New York: State University of New York Press.

Roberts, K. (1996a) Young People, Schools, Sport and Government Policy. *Sport, Education and Society*, 1(1): 47–57.

Roberts, K. (1996b) Youth Cultures and Sport: The Success of School and Community Sport Provisions in Britain. *European Physical Education Review*, 2(1): 105–115.

Robinson, V., Hockey, J. and Meah, A. (2004) 'What I Used to Do . . . on my Mother's Settee': Spatial and Emotional Aspects of Heterosexuality in England. *Gender, Place and Culture*, 11(2): 417–435.

Roderick, M., Waddington, I. and Parker, G. (2000) Playing Hurt: Managing Injuries in English Professional Football. *International Review for the Sociology of Sport*, 35: 165–180.

Robeyns, I. (2006) Three Models of Education: Rights, Capabilities and Human Capital. *Theory and Research in Education*, 4(1): 69–84.

Roemer, J. (1998) *Equality of Opportunity.* Cambridge, MA: Harvard University Press.

Roessler, K.K. (2006) Sport and the Psychology of Pain. In S. Loland, B. Skirstad and I. Waddington (eds.), *Pain and Injury in Sport: Social and Ethical Analysis*, London: Routledge.

Rose, G. (1993) *Feminism in Geography: The Limits of Geographical Knowledge.* Cambridge: Polity Press.

Rose, G. (2001) *Visual Methodologies.* London: Sage.

Sabo, D., Miller, K., Farrell, M., Melnick, M. and Barnes, G. (1999) High School Athletic Participation, Sexual Behavior and Adolescent Pregnancy: A Regional Study. *Journal of Adolescent Health*, 25(3): 207–216.

Sabo, D., Miller, K., Melnick, M. and Heywood, L. (2004) *Her Life Depends on It: Sport, Physical Activity and the Health and Well-Being of American Girls*. East Meadow, NY: Women's Sports Foundation.

Saith, R. (2001) *Capabilities: The Concept and its Operationalisation*. Oxford: University of Oxford.

Sallis, J. and Owen, N. (1999) *Physical Activity and Behavioral Medicine*. Thousand Oaks, CA: Sage.

Sallis, J.F., McKenzie, T.L., Alcaraz, J.E., Kolody, B., Faucette, N. and Hovell, M.F. (1997) The Effects of a 2 year Physical Education Program (SPARK) on Physical Activity and Fitness in Elementary School Students. *American Journal of Public Health*, 87:1328–1334.

Sallis, J., McKenzie, J., Kolody, B., Lewis, M., Marshall, S. and Rosengard, P. (1999) Effects of Health-related Physical Education on Academic Achievement: Project SPARK. *Research Quarterly for Exercise and Sport*, 70: 127–134.

Sammons, J. (1988) *Beyond the Ring The Role of Boxing in American Society*. Chicago: University of Chicago Press.

Sartre, J.P. (1971) *Saint Genet: Actor and Martyr*. New York: New American Library.

Sauerbruch, F. and Wenke, H. (1936) *Wesen und Bedeutung des Schmerzes*. Berlin: Junker and Dunnhaupt.

Scambler, G. (2005) *Sport and Society: History, Power and Culture*. Milton Keynes: Open University Press.

Scheffler, I. (1985) *Of Human Potential*. London: Routledge.

Scheibel, Dean (1995) 'Making Waves' with Burke: Surf Nazi Culture and the Rhetoric of Localism. *Western Journal of Communication*, 59 (Fall): 256–257.

Schnitt, J.M. and Schnitt, D. (1986) Eating Disorders in Dancers. *Medical Problems of Performing Artists*, 1: 39–44.

Scraton, S. (1992) *Shaping up to Womanhood: Gender and Girls' Physical Education*. Buckingham: Open University Press.

Scraton, S. (1993) Equality, Coeducation and Physical Education in Secondary Schooling. In J. Evans (ed.), *Equality, Education and Physical Education*. London: The Falmer Press.

Segal, L. (1997) *Slow Motion: Changing Masculinities, Changing Men*. London: Virago.

Sen, A. (1988) Freedom of Choice: Concept and Content. *European Economic Review*, 32: 269–294.

Sen, A. (1998) *Freedom as Development*. New York: Knopf.

Shephard, R.J. (1997) Curricular Physical Activity and Academic Performance. *Pediatric Exercise Science*, 9: 113–126.

Shields, R. (2004) Surfing: Global Space or Dwelling in the Waves? In M.M. Sheller and J. Urry (eds), *Tourism Mobilities: Places to Stay, Place in Place*. London: Routledge.

Shilling, C. (1993) *The Body and Social Theory*. London: Sage.

Siedentop, D. and Tannehill, D. (2000) *Developing Teaching Skills in Physical Education*, fourth edition. Mountain View, CA: Mayfield.

Singer, R. (1992) Physical Activity and Psychological Benefits: A Position Statement of the International Society of Sport Psychology (ISSP). *The Sports Psychologist*, 6: 199–203.

Smith, A. (2006) Young People, Sport and Leisure: A Sociological Study of Youth Lifestyles. Unpublished PhD dissertation, University of Liverpool.

Smith, A. and Parr, M. (2007) Young People's Views on the Nature and Purposes of Physical Education: A Sociological Analysis. *Sport, Education and Society*, 12(1): 37–58.

Smith, A., Green, K. and Roberts, K. (2004) Sports Participation and the 'Obesity/Health Crisis': Reflections on the Case of Young People in England. *International Review for the Sociology of Sport*, 39: 457–464.

Smith, A., Thurston, M., Green, K. and Lamb, K. (2007) Young People's Participation in National Curriculum Physical Education: A Study of 15–16-Year-Olds in the North-West of England and North-East of Wales. *European Physical Education Review*, 13: 165–194.

Sobchack, V. (2004) *Carnal Thoughts: Embodiment and Moving Image Culture*. Berkeley, CA: University of California Press.

Sport England (2003) *Young People and Sport in England 1994–2002*. London: Sport England.

Sports Council for Wales (SCW) (2003) *Secondary Aged Children's Participation in Sport 2001*. Cardiff: SCW.

Stamford, B. (1987) No Pain, No Gain? *Physician and Sportmedicine*, 15: 244.

Stedman, L. (1997) From Gadget to Gonad Man: Surfers, Feminists and Postmodernisation. *Australian and New Zealand Journal of Sociology*, 33(1): 75–90.

Steiner-Adair, C. and Vorenburg, A. (1999) Resisting Weightism: Media Literacy for Elementary School Children. In N. Piran, M.P. Levine and C. Steiner-Adair (eds.), *Preventing Eating Disorders*. London: Brunner/Mazel.

Stinson, S.W., Blumenfield-Jones, D. and Van Dyke, J. (1990) Voices of Young Women Dance Students: An Interpretive Study of Meaning in Dance. *Dance Research Journal*, 22: 13–22.

Sugden, J. (1996) *Boxing and Society: An International Analysis*. Manchester: Manchester University Press.

Sumner, L.W. (1996) *Welfare Happiness & Ethics*. Oxford: Clarendon Press

Sundgot-Borgen, J., Skarderud, F. and Rodgers, S. (2003) Athletes and Dancers. In J. Treasure., Schmidt, H. and van Furth, E. (eds), *Handbook of Eating Disorders*. Indianapolis, IN: Wiley and Sons Publishing.

Tajet-Foxell, B. and Rose, F.D. (1995) Pain and Pain Tolerance in Professional Ballet Dancers. *British Journal of Sports Medicine*, 29: 31–34.

Talbot, M. (1989) Being Herself through Sport. In J. Long (ed.), *Leisure, Health and Well Being*. Eastbourne: Leisure Studies Association.

Talbot, M. (2002) Playing with Patriarchy: The Gendered Dynamics of Sports Organization. In S. Scraton and A. Flintoff (eds), *Gender and Sport: A Reader*. London: Routledge.

Tännsjo, T. and Tanburrini, C. (2000) *Values in Sport*. London: E and FN Spon.

teachernet (2006) *National Physical Education, School Sport and Club Links Strategy*. Available at: www.teachernet.gov.uk// (accessed 30 May 2006).

Theberge, N. (1987) Sport and Women's Empowerment. *Women's Studies International Forum*, 10: 387–393.

Theberge, N. (2003) 'No Fear Comes': Adolescent Girls, Ice Hockey, and the Embodiment of Gender. *Youth & Society*, 34(4): 497–516.

Thomas, H. (2003) *The Body, Dance and Cultural Theory*. Basingstoke: Palgrave Macmillan.

Thompson, S. (1995) *Going All the Way: Teenage Girls' Tales of Sex, Romance, and Pregnancy*. New York: Hill and Wang.

Tipper, J. and Avard, D. (1999) *Building Better Outcomes for Canada's Children*. Ottawa: Canadian Policy Research Network.

Trost, S., Pate, R., Sallis, J., Freedson, P., Taylor, A., Dowda, M and Sitard, J. (2002) Age and Gender Differences in Objectively Measured Physical Activity in Youth. *Medicine and Science in Sports and Exercise*, 34(2): 350–355.

Turner, B. (1984) *The Body and Society*. Oxford: Basil Blackwell.

Turner, B. (2002) Thinking Right(s) Sociologically. Plenary presentation at British Sociological Association Annual Conference 'Reshaping the Social', University of Leicester, March 2002.

Turner, B.S. (1992) *Regulated Bodies: Essays in Medical Sociology*. London: Routledge.

Turner, B.S. and Wainwright, S.P. (2003) Corps de Ballet: The Case of the Injured Ballet Dancer. *Sociology of Health and Illness*, 25: 269–288.

United Nations (1995) *Beijing Declaration*. Fourth World Conference on Women: Beijing.

United Nations (2003) *United Nations Inter-Agency Task Force on Sport for Development and Peace*. Paris: United Nations.

Vilhjalmsson, R. and Kristjansdottir, G. (2003) Gender Differences in Physical Activity in Older Children and Adolescents: The Central Role of Organized Sport. *Social Science and Medicine*, 56(2): 363–374.

Vu, M., Murrie, D., Gonzalez, V. and Jobe, J. (2006) Listening to Girls and Boys Talk about Girls' Physical Activity Behaviours. *Health Education & Behavior*, 33(1): 81–96.

Wacquant, L. (1995a) Pugs at Work: Bodily Capital and Bodily Labour among Professional Boxers. *Body and Society*, 1(1): 65–93.

Wacquant, L. (1995b) Why Men Desire Muscles (review article). *Body and Society*, 1: 163–179.

Wacquant, L. (2004) *Body and Soul: Notebooks of an Apprentice Boxer*. Oxford: Oxford University Press.

Waddington, I., Malcolm, D. and Cobb, J. (1998) Gender Stereotyping and Physical Education. *European Physical Education Review*, 4(1): 34–46.

Wainwright, S.P. and Turner, B.S. (2004) Epiphanies of Embodiment: Injury, Identity and the Balletic Body. *Qualitative Research*, 4: 311–337.

Waitt, G. (2003) Gay Games: Performing 'Community' out from the Closet of the Locker Room. *Social and Cultural Geography*, 4(2): 167–184.

Waitt, G. (2005) Doing Discourse Analysis. In I. Hay (ed.), *Qualitative Research Methods in Human Geography*, second edition. Melbourne: Oxford University Press.

Waitt, G. and Hartig, K. (2005) All at Sea: Rethinking Fisher's Identities in Australia. *Gender, Place and Culture*, 12(4): 403–418.

Wallhead, T. and Buckworth, J. (2004) The Role of Physical Education in the Promotion of Youth Physical Activity. *Quest*, 56(3): 285–301.

Walters , J. (2005) I'll Take on Men Says Woman Boxer. *The Observer*, 29 May: 22

Watson, L. (2003) *Lifelong Learning in Australia*. Canberra: Commonwealth of Australia.

Weinberg, R. and Gould, D. (2003) *Foundations of Sport & Exercise Psychology*, third edition. Champaign, IL: Human Kinetics.

Wellard, I. (2002) Men, Sport, Body Performance and the Maintenance of 'Exclusive Masculinity'. *Leisure Studies*, 21: 235–247.

Wellard, I. (2003) Game, Set and Match to Exclusive Masculinity: Men, Body Practices, Sport and the Making and Remaking of Hegemonic Masculinity. Unpublished PhD dissertation, Open University.

Wellard, I. (2006a) Able Bodies and Sport Participation: Social Constructions of Physical Ability for Gendered and Sexually Identified Bodies. *Sport, Education and Society*, 11(2): 105–119.

Wellard, I. (2006b) Exploring the Limits of Queer and Sport. In J. Caudwell (ed.), *Sport, Sexualities and Queer Theory: Challenges and Controversies*. London: Routledge.

Wellard, I. (2006c) Re-thinking Abilities. *Sport, Education and Society*, 11(3): 311–315.

Wellard, I., Pickard, A. and Bailey, R. (2007) 'A Shock of Electricity Just Sort of Goes through My Body': Physical Activity and Embodied Reflexive Practices in Young Female Ballet Dancers. *Gender and Education*, 19(1): 79–91.

Wenger, E. (1998) *Communities of Practice: Learning, Meaning and Identity*. Cambridge: Cambridge University Press.

West, L. (2004) The Trouble with Lifelong Learning. In D. Hayes (ed.), *Key Debates in Education*. London: RoutledgeFalmer.

Wheaton, B. (2004) *Understanding Lifestyle Sports, Consumption, Identity and Difference*. London: Routledge.

White, J. (1986) The Problem of Self-Interest: The Educator's Perspective. *Journal of Philosophy of Education*, 20(2): 163–175.

White, P.G., Young, K. and McTeer, W.G. (1995) Sport, Masculinity and the Injured Body. In D. Sabo and F. Gordon (eds), *Men's Health and Illness: Gender, Power and the Body*. London: Sage.

Whitehead, S.M. (2002) *Men and Masculinities*. Cambridge: Polity.

Wolf, N. (1990) *The Beauty Myth*. London: Chatto & Windus.

Woodward, K. (1997) Motherhood Myths and Meanings. In K. Woodward (ed.), *Identity and Difference*, London: Sage.

Woodward, K. (1998) It's a Man's Life!: Soldiers, Masculinity and the Countryside. *Gender, Place and Culture*, 5: 277–300.

Woodward, K. (2004) Rumbles in the Jungle: Boxing, Racialization and the Performance of Masculinity. *Leisure Studies*, 23(1): 1–13.

Woodward, K. (2006) *Boxing, Masculinity and Identity: The 'I' of the Tiger*. London, Routledge.

World Health Organization (WHO) (1995) Exercise for Health. *Bulletin of the World Health Organization*, 73(2): 135–136.

World Health Organization (WHO) (1998) Obesity – Preventing and Managing the Global Epidemic. *Report of a WHO Consultation on Obesity*. Geneva: World Health Organization.

World Health Organization (WHO) (2004) *Social Science Research Initiative on Adolescent Sexual and Reproductive Health: Synopsis of On-going Research*. Geneva: Department of Reproductive Health and Research, World Health Organization.

Wright, J. and Dewar, A. (1997) On Pleasure and Pain: Women Speak Out about Physical Activity. In G. Clarke and B. Humberstone (eds), *Researching Women and Sport*. London: Macmillan Press.

Wulff, H. (1998) *Ballet across Borders*. New York: Oxford University Press.

Yannakoulia, M., Sitara, M. and Matalas, A. (2002) Reported Eating Behaviour and Attitudes Improvement after a Nutrition Intervention Program in a Group of Young Female Dancers. *International Journal of Sport Nutrition and Exercise Metabolism*, 12: 24–32.

Young, I.M. (1990) *Throwing Like a Girl and Other Essays on Feminist Philosophy and Social Theory*. Bloomington, IN: Indiana University Press.

Young, I.M. (2005) *On Female Body Experience: Throwing Like a Girl and Other Essays*. Oxford: Oxford University Press

Young, K. (1993) Violence, Risk and Liability in Male Sports Culture. *Sociology of Sport Journal*, 10: 373–396.

Young, K., White, P. and McTeer, W. (1994) Body Talk: Male Athletes Reflect on Sport, Injury and Pain. *Sociology of Sport Journal*, 11(2): 175–194.

Zaman, H. (1998) Islam, Well-Being and Physical Activity: Perceptions of Muslim Young Women. In G. Clarke and B. Humberstone (eds), *Researching Women and Sport*. London: Macmillan.

Film texts

Blue Crush (2002) Directed by John Stockwell, Universal Studios.

Billabong Odyssey (2003) Directed by Phillip Boston, Arenaplex.

The Red Shoes (1948) Written, produced and directed by Michael Powell and Emeric Pressburger, Carlton International Media.

Step into Liquid (2003) Directed by Dana Brown, Top Secret Productions, Artisan Entertainment.

Index

eBooks – at www.eBookstore.tandf.co.uk

A library at your fingertips!

eBooks are electronic versions of printed books. You can store them on your PC/laptop or browse them online.

They have advantages for anyone needing rapid access to a wide variety of published, copyright information.

eBooks can help your research by enabling you to bookmark chapters, annotate text and use instant searches to find specific words or phrases. Several eBook files would fit on even a small laptop or PDA.

NEW: Save money by eSubscribing: cheap, online access to any eBook for as long as you need it.

Annual subscription packages

We now offer special low-cost bulk subscriptions to packages of eBooks in certain subject areas. These are available to libraries or to individuals.

For more information please contact webmaster.ebooks@tandf.co.uk

We're continually developing the eBook concept, so keep up to date by visiting the website.

www.eBookstore.tandf.co.uk